STRUGGLE AGAINST THE STATE

To Ranjula, and our children, Kabir and Simran

Struggle Against the State
Social Network and Protest Mobilization in India

ASHOK SWAIN
Uppsala University, Sweden

Routledge
Taylor & Francis Group

LONDON AND NEW YORK

First published 2010 by Ashgate Publishing

2 Park Square, Milton Park, Abingdon, Oxon OX14 4RN
711 Third Avenue, New York, NY 10017, USA

Routledge is an imprint of the Taylor & Francis Group, an informa business

First issued in paperback 2016

British Library Cataloguing in Publication Data
Swain, Ashok.
  Struggle against the state : social network and protest
  mobilization in India.
  1. Protest movements--India. 2. Communication in social
  action--India. 3. Pressure group members--Social
  networks--India. 4. Social structure--Political aspects--
  India.
  I. Title
  322.4'0954-dc22

Library of Congress Cataloging-in-Publication Data
Swain, Ashok.
  Struggle against the state : social network and protest mobilization in India / by Ashok
Swain.
      p. cm.
  Includes bibliographical references and index.
  ISBN 978-1-4094-0867-3 (hardback)
  1. Protest movements--India. 2. Social networks--India. 3. India--Politics and
government--1977- I. Title.

  JQ281.S93 2010
  322.40954--dc22

                                                                    2010009586

ISBN 978-1-4094-0867-3 (hbk)
ISBN 978-1-138-26835-7 (pbk)

Contents

Contents

List of Tables

Preface

The rise of social movements[1] in the West in the late 1960s and early 1970s triggered the scholarly debate on the origins and outcomes of this process. In fact, the formation of social movements is shaped by the kind of state they face. The state, unique among other social institutions, seeks to standardize its own set of rules to supersede other institutional hierarchies that exist within the family, clan, race, cast, tribe, community or the market. As Joel S. Migdal writes, 'Since the beginning of the contemporary state system in the fifteenth to seventeenth centuries change has moved towards accepting an axiom that the state organization should provide the predominant (if not exclusive) set of "rules of the game" in each society' (Migdal 1988: 14). The capacity to exert control over other social forces has been a defining feature of the state. The works of Karl Marx and Max Weber, which have been the foundation of two main traditions in modern social science, argue that the state as an institution monopolizes the legitimate use of violence and organized coercion in society (Grindle 1996).

Throughout history humans have dissented about the things they loathed; or else, as Sunstein argues, 'unchecked by dissent, conformity can produce disturbing, harmful and sometimes astonishing outcomes' (Sunstein 2003: 1). The rules which structure interactions between the state and other components of society are continuously being contested and often being restructured. States as well as societies vary in their abilities to restructure this interaction process and their struggle and accommodation produce a range of outcomes (Migdal 1994). The state may dominate social forces altogether and penetrate at all levels; it may completely fail to influence society and collapse, and it may indulge in incorporating each others concerns and demands.

Protest can be classed as an opposition to a particular government agency or just a regular parliamentary process. Moreover, due to their values and dependence on popular support, democratic elites more often respond favourably to the demands of various associations, which tend to enhance future protests.

---

1 Tarrow distinguishes between contentious episodes of collective action (riots and rebellion) and social movements. To him, contentious politics is a collective activity on the part of claimants or those who claim to represent them in adopting some sort of non-institutional forms of interaction with the state or their opponents. Social movements, on the other hand, are sustained challenges to elites from the disadvantaged population living under their jurisdiction or influence (Tarrow 1996).

Protest reflects the key aspect of this relationship between the state and society (Andrain and Apter 1995). The state is responsible for formulating and carrying out policies for a society however it may lack the resources to meet the demands and expectations of various competing social groups. Resource scarcity forces the state to prioritize the allocation and that may lead to anger among some groups in the society, which can take the shape of a protest movement. Protest arises from disagreement over limited issues, such as opposition to particular policies of a government, or antagonisms between groups competing for political influence. The character of the protest is that of a short duration, low degree of organization, and of limited goals (Gurr 1979). The type of political system sharply affects the nature of protest. Democracies are distinctive in having more extensive but less deadly protests than the autocracies (Zimmermann 1980; Gurr 1993). The structure and ethos of democratic regimes are such that they are adjusted to respond to limited challengers in a conciliatory way, which reinforces the utility of protest over rebellion. On the other hand, authoritarian regimes generally rely more on coercive control, which increases the relative utility of rebellion for challengers. Ronald A. Francisco's empirical evaluation of the relationship between coercion and protest in three coercive states (the German Democratic Republic, Czechoslovakia, and the Palestinian *Intifada*) found that protesters react violently to extremely harsh coercion (Francisco 1995).[2] Indian sociologist T.K. Oommen outlines three possible relations between the state and social protests. First, the authoritarian regimes most often oppress, or attempt to oppress all protest movements that challenge state authority. However, to deflect the attention of the opposition, state authority may encourage people to protest against a foreign enemy. Most of the non-democratic authoritarian regimes in the Middle East actively encourage popular protest against the USA and Israel while brutally suppressing any other form of popular action at home. Second, one-party systems oppress most of the protest movements but sponsor some to their advantage to sustain and strengthen state power. Chairman Mao's support for the 'Red Guard' movement is one example. Similarly President Mugabe's patronage for the 'farm raiders' is another. Third, a large number of protests in the society originates and flourishes in a democratic system but the state mostly takes actions only against those who pose an explicit threat to its very existence. Undoubtedly, a multi-party democracy provides a fertile setting, which permits a variety of protest movements to emerge and operate (Oommen 1991). Advocating on the same line, Eckstein and Gurr write, 'the risk of chronic low-level conflicts is one of the prices democrats should expect to pay for freedom from regimentation by the state' (Eckstein and Gurr 1975). Democracies provide no immediate obstacles to mobilizing and organizing people on certain issues as

---

2   However, by bringing in the role of international context and the importance of press freedoms and information flows, Kurt Schock, finds in a comparative study of the Philippines and Burma, the excessive repression of authority might able to curb the popular protest (Schock 1999).

liberty to do so is supposed to be guaranteed by law and tradition. Authorities in democracies usually refrain from using the full strength of their coercive power against popular mobilization and group formation due in part to the fact that the state as an actor is often not altogether or directly involved in the conflictual issues in democracies from the beginning. Even a peaceful protest by few thousand residents compelled US Navy in 2003 to cease their exercises and practice bombing of Puerto Rican island, Vieques (McCaffrey 2002). As the discussion suggests, there is a greater probability both of the occurrence of higher number of protests and of positive outcomes in the democratic system in comparison to the other political systems.

Todd and Taylor argue that in a democracy, social movements provide an essential channel through which ordinary citizens can participate in the decision making process and have a direct input to the political process (Todd and Taylor 2004). But, within democracies, we do not see a uniform pattern of popular protest movements. France hosts more protests annually than Germany does. Bangladeshis invade the streets much more than the people in Sri Lanka do. Answers to this difference may be found in their political cultures or by carefully auditing the performance of their democratic institutions. However, it is more puzzling when within the same democracy, people in some areas protest more successfully than other areas. It seems that some ordinary people, who are busy in their struggle for day-to-day survival, attain the degree of coordination and mutual awareness that they need to wage strategically effective protests, while others fail. We need to ask, why some groups sharing a grievance mobilize successfully while others do not in democracies? In recent years, democratization has spread to the South and with it increasing numbers of social movements. The origin and outcome of these movements are being explained with the help of theoretical frameworks developed to study social actions in the North. Here, the aim is to examine the relevance of these theories to evaluate the success and failure of protest mobilizations in developing countries.

Protest Movements: Origin and Mobilization

Research on social movements have evolved enormously over time (Goodwin and Jasper 2003) and therefore the term can denote different meanings to different people. Nancy Langton defines social movements as 'Collective behaviours engaged in by non-institutionalized groups oriented towards achieving specific goals, particularly the goal of extracting or resisting social change' (Langton 1987: 51). It is true that social movements come in different sizes and shapes. To some, the civil rights movement in the USA is a social movement while some others also put the German Nazi movement of the 1930s in the same category. To some, organized protest groups are social movements, while others favour any spontaneous largely unorganized group actions to be included in this category

(Zirakzadeh 1997).[3] Social movements, as Stephen R. Thomas describes, 'are unlikely to have any stable character, and they bear varying relations to other political and social institutions and practices' (Thomas 1996: 579).

The revival of interest in social mobilization process in 1960s and 1970s brought a new paradigm to the social movement literature.[4] While the American sociologists developed the Resource Mobilization theory in order to explain its outcome, Europeans in their effort to trace its origin, called it 'new social movement' (Tarrow 1989). Resource Mobilization theories reflected the American experience in 1960s, while the structural approach adopted by European sociologists got its inspiration in the intellectual and political life of nineteenth century Europe. These two schools differ in their premises, and in their assumptions about social change (D'Anieri, Ernst, and Kier 1990). Furthermore, the researchers from both sides of the Atlantic failed to find the agent that successfully activates this change. The writings of European scholars, which emphasized the structural causes of mobilization, resulting from the changes in advanced capitalism, could not explain the group mobilization universally (Offe 1985). The Resource Mobilization approach, by emphasizing the need of internal resources to mobilize groups, failed to explain the mobilization of the groups who are poor in terms of resources (Zald and McCarthy 1987).

The New Social Movement Approach

The structural paradigm approach or the New Social Movement (NSM) theory proposed by European scholars argues that the new movements are the result of increasing domination of the system over everyday life. It is not a unified body of thought. New social movement theory developed as a critique to the Resource Mobilization and Marxist approach, to explain collective action (Shefner 1995). Proponents of the NSM approach criticized orthodox Marxism for its economy centric views and its failure to recognize the fundamental shift that had taken place in post World War II Western capitalism (Somerville 1997). Drawing on the Marxist tradition and at the same time differing considerably from it, these social

---

3   Cyrus Ernesto Zirakzadeh studies Germany's Greens, Poland's Solidarity and Peru's Shining Path as cases of social movements.

4   Prior to this, Marxist historical–structural approach was used to explain the organizational level of the collective action. Marxist theory focused on class movements as the only meaningful or truly insurgent, movement type. A traditional collective behaviour approach evolved in 1950s, when in the United States there was a consensus in social science over the fundamental importance of democratic institutions. This perspective considered social movements as symptoms of system malfunction and it emphasized their spontaneity and lack of structure, especially in its early formative stage (Melucci 1984; Blumer 1969) Besides, Marxists and traditional collective behaviour approach, the rational choice theory also attempted to explain defiance of authority while focusing at the individual level.

scientists have explored the connections between contradictions, crises and social movements.

In the post-industrial society, Touraine argues that social movements replace the organization of labour as the focus of political action. It means that intellectuals, new professionals and students replace the working class as the agents of revolutionary change (Touraine 1971). Consumer capitalism and the welfare state create social regulation through mass culture and welfare intervention extending the state into the social and personal sphere. To Habermas, this form of colonization of the 'lifeworld' leads to a generalized 'legitimation' crisis and that provokes new forms of resistance outside the political channels of institutional politics. These resistances are as much against dominant rationalities as they are against institutional control (Habermas 1976). Claus Offe categorizes the social base of NSM into three fold: the new middle class, elements of the old middle class, and 'decommodified' groups outside the labour market (Offe 1985).

Castells criticizes the resource mobilization approach for its refusal to accept that the social movement has a reality of its own. And also, trying to incorporate it into the political process aimed primarily at the state (Castells 1983). NSM theorists value symbolic action in civil society or the cultural sphere as an important form of collective action alongside instrumental action in the state or political sphere (Cohen 1985; Melucci 1989). The European School[5] believes that the social movements are of the anti-institutional orientation and spontaneity is a positive feature of the formation of the movement. NSM theory puts importance on the processes that promote autonomy and self-determination of movement rather than striving for influence and power maximization (Habermas 1984–1987). The role of post-materialist values – not the conflicts over material resources – is the key to the social movement, some argue (Dalton and Keuchler 1990).

Counter-posing to the 'strategy' paradigm of the resource mobilization theory, the new social movement theory tries to subsume under what has been called 'identity' paradigm. This 'identity paradigm' is argued to be better suited to understand the new struggles, which are focused on everyday democratic life, communicative action and an autonomous definition of community identity rather than being only state or economy centred (Cohen 1985). The NSM theory also recognizes that a number of submerged, informal and temporary networks helps to organize collective action (Mueller 1994).

The NSM theory has raised debates and intellectual concerns in four areas, as Steven M. Buechler argues:

---

5 Prominent New Social Movement theorists are: Manuel Castells (Spain), Alain Touraine (France), Alberto Melucci (Italy), and Jürgen Habermas (Germany) (Buechler 1995).

The first concerns the meaning and validity of designating certain movements as 'new' and others (by implication) as 'old'. The second debate involves whether new social movements are primarily or exclusively a defensive, reactive response to larger social forces or whether they can exhibit a proactive and progressive nature as well. The third debate concerns the distinction between political and cultural movements and whether the more culturally oriented new social movements are inherently apolitical. The fourth involves the social base of the new social movements and whether this base can be defined in terms of social class. (Buechler 1995: 447)

Melucci argues that the resource mobilization approach is valuable in explaining *how* a movement is set up and manages its structure but it does not say anything about *why* the movement arises in the first place (Melucci 1984). In response to it, Hannigan has argued that the NSM theory provides the mirror image of this, focusing on *why* rather than *how* (Hannigan 1985). It is true that if one theory is focusing on 'how' and another is focusing on 'why' it will lead to a theoretical gap. As Klandermans and Tarrow argue, this gap stands in the way of a better understanding of 'how structural change is transformed into collective action' (Klandermans and Tarrow 1988: 9). However, the aim here is a more modest one. It is not to bridge this 'huge' theoretical gap; rather it is to provide a hypothesis to explain the variation in movement mobilization in developing democracies.

NSM theory, by focusing on origin, fails entirely to explain the outcome of the movement.[6] If we recognize that social movements are some form of struggle for political or social change, then we cannot just ignore the questions of success or failure. It is true that the NSM theory has provided an important tool to understand the macro-level social structure that raises contemporary activism. However, the strength of the theory has confined itself to be applied only 'to a limited number of movements in Western societies with mobilization biases towards white, middle-class participants pursuing politically or culturally progressive agendas' (Buechler 1995: 460).

NSM theory, being based on a very historic specificity, fails to provide us much help in understanding the social movements we witness in developing countries. Since developing countries have yet to industrialize they lack the conditions of a post-industrial state, which are necessary for the development of the type of social movements described by NSM theorists. Thus, to explain the success and failure of the protest movements in the non-industrialized countries, we need to find a theoretical tool other than the NSM approach.

---

6   NSM theory argues that success is unimportant since the establishment of community and constitution of a collective identity is a goal in itself.

The Resource Mobilization Approach

For the Resource Mobilization (RM) theorists, if the structural opportunities outweigh the structural constraints, people will tend to participate in the movement in order to change the political status quo. The proponents of this theory argue that grievance alone cannot lead to social movement. To them, in a society there is always a sufficient level of shared individual grievances. But, that does not always translate into protests. It is not the grievances they have, but how the actors develop strategies and interact with their environment in the pursuit of their own interests that matters (Canel 1997). Thus, the focus of the attention was diverted from stressing common grievances to mechanisms of mobilization and opportunities (McAdam and Scott 2005).

RM theory tries to explain how material resources and political opportunities affect social movements (McAdam 1982; Hannigan 1985; Pichardo 1988). It also examines how movements and their institutions are organized (Gerlach and Hine 1970; McCarthy and Zald 1977). The development and behaviour of social movements is seen as an inter-play between internal factors such as leadership, extent of available resources, group strength and degree of internal organization, and external factors such as degree of societal repression, extent of third party involvement and strength of pressure groups. There is a great deal of disagreement regarding the role of elites in the formation and development of social movements. The 'professional organizer' or 'circulation' model argues that the external actors can provide the leadership and resources for the movement. They also argue that the distinct incorporation mechanisms that match individual with groups needs are responsible for leadership recruitment (McCarthy and Zald 1973; Jenkins and Perrow 1977). Downplaying the role of elites, the 'political process' or 'progression' model on the other hand emphasizes the capacity of the community (Canel 1997; Pichardo 1988). According to this model, individuals gradually socialize into the movement and they assume increasingly greater responsibilities and finally take leadership positions (Gurr 1970; McAdam 1982; Tarrow 1998; Tilly 1978). The political process theory, in addition to political opportunities (attempts to specify factors external to social movements), also includes mobilizing structures and cultural framing processes (McAdam, McCarthy, and Zald 1996; Tarrow 1998). Though both NSM and RM approaches agree that individuals with greater resources are more likely to be actively recruited and progress with the social movement structure, they differ on the issue over the impact of the leadership status on the ordinary members' active involvement (Marullo 1998).

Overall, the RM approach shifted the focus of research away from the type of people who might engage in a movement toward the infrastructure required to sustain a movement. Money, membership and legitimacy are considered important resources for any social movement infrastructure (Jenkins 1983; Olson 1965). However, all resources do not have equal utility for a social movement (Weed

1989). The RM approach considers ideological and moral factors as secondary to material and organizational resources in affecting the results of the movements.[7] Protests over immoral issues may be able to force authorities to concede to the movements' demands if they mobilize the material and human resources from a large base of constituents and well-endowed, influential groups and elites (Weitzer 1991). If money is the most important resource, the movements in the South are at a disadvantage. However, as Freeman argues that people, rather than money, are the primary resources of a social movement (Freeman 1979).

RM theory argues that when the groups possess dense interpersonal networks, members are readily mobilized. Networks provide a base for collective incentives. The network, with its ties of trust and reciprocity, is a resource reservoir that a movement can use in recruiting support. Movements from below or in a particular section of the society may benefit from the support of other groups, and not merely from the support of better-situated individuals (Eckstein 1989). Despite widespread acceptance of the idea that 'network' plays a significant role in mobilization, only a few studies have made some progress toward understanding the significance of this factor.

Social Network and Protest Movements

Even though every movement has its own history and perpetuity, the timing of its collapse defines its quality. For a broader and successful movement, there is a need of larger and sustained popular mobilization. Social movements adopt three basic strategies to get their mission fulfilled: militancy, size and novelty (Rochon 1990). Researchers working in the classical tradition put emphasis on violence or militancy as the basic resource available to a social movement (Gurr 1970). Violence is a high-risk option as it can bring backlash from authority. Some success may come but at a high cost. However, in a democracy, the size of social movement matters more. DeNardo emphasizes the 'power of numbers' while admitting that violence can compensate when a movement lacks sufficient numbers (DeNardo 1985). If there is a massive support base for a social movement this may challenge the legitimacy and accountability of the authorities and their policy. Size of support can help the social movement to achieve its objectives in a democratic system as it can translate into electoral power. Social movements employ both orthodox tactics and unorthodox ones in attempting to achieve their goals (McCarthy, Smith, and Zald 1996). Tarrow argues that novel or unorthodox forms of protest are more important than the size of support or militant method used by social movements (Tarrow 1989). Novelty might give the social movements' initial

---

7 For examples, non-material resources are legitimacy, loyalty, authority, moral commitment, solidarity etc, and material resources are money, manpower and means of communication etc.

strategic advantage vis-à-vis the authorities, but in the long run movements need larger member support. By introducing new forms of protest, social movements may expect to get the attention and enlarge their support base.

Thus, understanding the process of deferential support base is important for comprehending the spread and growth of social movements. The diffusion of the movement is necessary in order to keep the protest alive when its initial spark begins to sputter. There is a need to transcend the 'volcanic' stage of collective action (Tarrow 1993). According to Tarrow, social movements emerge 'when new opportunities are at hand – such as a less repressive climate, splits within the elite, or the presence of influential allies or supporters' (Tarrow 1989: 51). Subsequently, protests spread through the diffusion of tactical innovations developed by initial protest groups to other groups. Tarrow emphasizes the role of the organizations (and the competition among them) to explain the changing repertoire of protest.

Is the diffusion of protests the work of social movement organizations, or is it spontaneous? Theories, emphasizing social–psychological attributes of the movements' participants, explain activities on the basis of (1) alienation, (2) relative deprivation, and (3) authoritarianism. However, these traditionally popular theories are increasingly being challenged on both theoretical and empirical grounds. The magnitude of theoretical and statistical association shown in the literature, between social–psychological factors and participation in social protests has been quite unconvincing (McCarthy and Zald 1977; Snow and Philips 1980).

Tarrow argues that people join movements in response to political opportunities, and subsequently through collective actions create new ones (Tarrow 1998). However, political opportunities draw people into collective action on the basis of social networks through which social relations are organized. More than three decades ago, Snow and his colleagues in their seminal article pointed to the importance of social networks to explain the variation in social movements mobilization (Snow, Zurcher, and Ekland-Olson 1980). By bringing sociological analysis into the resource mobilization approach,[8] they demonstrated that social ties were instrumental in drawing new member into the movements. The authors' examination of nine cases of movement participation revealed that in eight of the nine cases, most of recruits were mobilized through a friend or relative previously associated with it.[9] Clearly demonstrating the importance of pre-existing social

---

8 What Melucci has described was affected by 'political reductionism' (Melucci 1988).

9 The exception was Hare Krishna, which specifically recruited most of their members through channels other than social network. Most of the Hare Krishna devotees came into contact with the movement through public chanting session or encountering a devotee in the street.

networks in structuring movement recruitment, the authors brought attention to the 'micro-structural' bases of social movement.

Subsequent research has accepted the important role played by social networks or ties in the mobilization process of the movement (Briet, Klandermans, and Kroon 1987; Gould 1993; McAdam 1986). A movement drawing support from a dense social network is more likely to spread and be sustained. The weak ties among social networks are conducive for broader mobilization and large-scale collective action. Weak ties help to link members of different small groups with each other. As Granovetter argues, weak ties are necessary for individual opportunities and for their integration into communities (Granovetter 1973). Following the same line, for the formation of a broader and successful social movement, Tarrow puts emphasis on, 'networks of ties among different and interdependent social groups and localities' (Tarrow 1998: 59–60).

Since the 1990s, the concept of social network has gained popularity among the researchers of social movements. It has even been suggested that movements should be regarded as networks or as a 'network of networks' (Neidhardt and Rucht 1991). Despite widespread acceptance of the idea, there are very few studies on the significance and interaction of the networks or ties in a movement. Existing studies give a statistical count of the social ties and treat them as intermediate variables in the mobilization of social movements. Some like Diani are interested in the movement's networks (Diani 1995). Very few works address the issue of network multiplicity: multiple ties that comprise a person's social world. It is plausible that mobilization is simultaneously affected by more than one network. Roger Gould argues that the Republican revolt that shook Paris in the spring of 1871 was rooted in overlapping patterns of neighbourhood and National Guard solidarity (Gould 1991). Focusing on the presence or absence of specific ties neglects this network structure.

As Doug McAdam and Ronnelle Paulsen points out, individuals are invariably embedded in many associational networks or individual ties that may expose them to conflicting behavioural pressures (McAdam and Paulsen 1993). Looking into the recruitment to the 1964 Mississippi Freedom Summer project,[10] they have tried to determine which dimensions of social ties have the most causal potency and how the competing ties affect the decision to join the movement. Focusing on the micro or individual level, they found a very different role for social ties. Unlike the meso level, where the 'strength of weak ties' matters, at the micro level, the stronger the tie, the better the chance of recruitment. At the individual level, ties are less important as a source of information than as

---

10   This campaign brought hundreds of primarily white, northern college students to Mississippi in the summer of 1964 to help staff register black voters and dramatize the denials of civil rights throughout the south.

source of social influence. To McAdam and Paulsen, the ideal network structure of a social movement is the 'one in which dense networks of weak bridging ties linked numerous local groups bound together by means of strong interpersonal bond' (McAdam and Paulsen 1993: 640).

Robert Putnam, following Coleman's work (Coleman 1990), defines social capital as 'features of social organization, such as trust, norms, and networks, that can improve the efficiency of society by facilitating coordinated action.' (Putnam 1993: 167). Social capital promotes cooperation among people on common ventures and to take part in the political life of the community (Rodger 2000). As Krishna argues, 'Social capital represents a potential – a propensity for mutually beneficial collective action' (Krishna 2002: 163). However, for greater and better social capital, the attribute of existing ties among the people matters. In his book, which examines American evidence, Putnam writes that social networks are not always divided between 'bonding' and 'bridging' ties. For successful mobilization, an ideal groups structure should 'bond along some social dimensions and bridge across others' (Putnam 2000: 23). Bonding capital is the one which brings people together who are previously known to each other, whereas, bridging capital helps people and groups to come together who previously did not know each other (Gittell and Vidal 1998). Social capital supports the mobilization of a protest movement by building both bonds and bridges within the protesting community and providing bridges to outside support groups.

The network structure of a society is an evolving process and the impact of external actors and ideology can change the existing inter-personal relationship and with it, the mobilization dynamic of protest movements. The state may be successful in the implementation of its unsustainable policy decision through dominating and suppressive methods. These methods may, in the short term, constrain many conflict escalations however those who fail to successfully organize their protest today, may in future mobilize with much vigour to resist state action due to their dynamic social network structure. With the help of existing research on movement mobilization, this book asks why some groups sharing a grievance successfully mobilize within a democratic setup while others do not. Social network structure is the best possible explanation for the varied protesting abilities of different societies.

Protest Movements in India

Many developing countries pursue policies of rapid industrialization, unsustainable mining, and large-scale water and forest projects in order to achieve faster economic growth. All these developmental policies have lead to loss of source of living resulting in the displacement of the affected population. The resulting large-scale displacement or the threats of it force many to take up a fight against the state. Interestingly, some of these dissenting individuals are more successful in organizing their protests than others.

India is a rapidly growing economy, and at the same time, a country experiencing increasing number of protest movements. India's large indigenous population, who due to their restrictive social network structure were unable to mobilize successfully before have achieved significant progress in protesting abilities in recent years. The improved mobilization capability of indigenous groups coincides with their evolving social network structure thanks to the recent exposure to external actors like religious missionaries and radical left activists. With the help of surveys and field studies conducted in the country, this book studies the mobilization process against large industrial and other development projects. An in depth comparison is made between a traditionally protest rich region like Kerala in the South with Orissa in the East, which has a very poor past record in it. These two regions help elucidate how the network structure of a society, based on both bonding as well as bridging ties, is key to this variation. Furthermore, we can appreciate that the structure is not static but dynamic as it is likely to be influenced by external actors and ideologies.

Structure of the Book

The introductory chapter provides an overview of protest mobilization in developing regions where mobilization against policies resulting in displacement are most likely to take place. It is quite surprising that researchers studying protest movements in the developing regions have almost overlooked the impact of social network.

Despite the high mortality rate of democracies in the developing world, India has been able to maintain and strengthen its democratic structure for more than six decades. However, India is at present going through a phase of increased social mobilization. Indians have learned to assert their rights and are trying to emerge as the chief actors through the participatory process. Using options available to them within a democratic framework, they are mobilizing towards protecting their legitimate rights and interests. Chapter 2 analyzes the growing number of protest movements against various government policies in Indian democracy. This emerging phenomenon contributes to democratic "disorder" and creates apprehension about the state's effectiveness as the agent of development.

The state of Kerala is famous for its spectacular achievement in social development sector. With collective action, the state has implemented progressive social policies by overcoming the handicap of having a poor economy. But, why is Kerala so successful with organizing and mobilizing protest movements compared to other states in India? Chapter 3, with the help of case studies and surveys, argues that in Kerala, flexible coordination has been achieved through network of smaller groups and associations, which has achieved collective efficiency for the popular action.

In spite of larger number of grievances against the government and its policies, in the state of Orissa, people did not protest as often as their coastal counterparts. Even when they did protest they were unable to expand and sustain it for a decisive result. Case studies and surveys in Chapter 4 help claim that protests here have primarily failed to gather the momentum due to the failure of different groups joining the mobilization process. Strong communal ties prevented the coming together for a common cause. It not only restricted associational life, but also curbed the popular mobilization. Chapter 5 shows that the willingness and capability of Oriyas to protest have considerably improved recently mainly due to inroads of external actors, such as left wing radicals (Maoists) as well as Hindu and Christian missionaries into the region.

The concluding chapter argues that despite recent economic growth, India continues to face serious development crisis. Macro economic success has not been able to address serious poverty in the country and at the same time has widened economic inequality between poor and rich. This has resulted in dissatisfaction and anger particularly among the poor and indigenous population of the country. It is argued that new economic and political development will not only increase the number of dissenting citizens but will also progressively expose them to outside influences. These influences may transform the existing social network structure of the growing disadvantageous groups resulting in increased number of protest mobilization in various parts of the country.

Acknowledgements

The research questions in this book have engaged me for more than 15 years. There are many people who have been so important over the life span of this book project that I would like to acknowledge on this page. I am sure I may not remember all the names but here are many of those who helped make this book possible. The idea for this book originated in 1995 when I became part of an international research project titled "Democracy and Social Capital in Segmented Societies: A Comparative Analysis of India and South Africa" or which we used to call 'Agora' Project. Funded by the Swedish International Development Cooperation Agency (Sida), we formed a close partnership between Uppsala University, Sweden, Jawaharlal Nehru University, New Delhi, Utkal University, Orissa and University of Witwatersrand, Johannesburg. Hans Blomkvist, Per Nordlund and Per Strand of the Department of Government of Uppsala University, Aswini K. Ray, Dwaipayan Bhattacharyya, Niraja Gopal Jayal, Bishnu Mohapatra, and Sudha Pai of the Centre for Political Studies of Jawaharlal Nehru University, Amareswar Mishra, Madhusmita Mishra, Smita Nayak, Srinabas Pathi, and Brahmananda Satapathy of Department of Political Science of Utkal University and Tom Lodge of Department of Political Studies, University of Witwatersrand were the other principal collaborators on this project. Help to conduct personal interviews of 3,200 randomly chosen individuals in 31 districts of India in 1997–1998, would not have been possible without the valuable help of Anand Mavlankar of the Maharaja Sayajirao University of Baroda and V. Santhakumar of Centre for Development Studies, Trivandrum. The book has gained immensely from this long and rich collaboration. The Agora project came to an end in 2001 however the Swedish International Development Cooperation Agency (Sida) continues to generously support my research in this area. Quite simply, without Sida's financial support, this book project would not have been possible.

This book has resulted from cumulated research results that I have published in journal, edited books and working papers since 1996. Earlier versions of some of the arguments were also presented in seminars and workshops at Gothenburg University, Lund University, University of Oslo, University of Copenhagen, Jawaharlal Nehru University, New Delhi, Maharaja Sayajirao University, Baroda, American Studies Research Centre, Hyderabad, University of Science, Malaysia, Penang, University of Witwatersrand, Johannesburg, University of Chicago and the UN Research Institute for Social Development, Geneva. Parts of this book were also presented in various seminars and workshops which Agora Project had organized in and around Uppsala, and also in various parts of India and South Africa. I profited a great deal from the valuable comments and suggestions offered by the participants at these meetings. My sincere thanks in this regard to Pradeep K. Chhiber, Ken Conca, Peter Evans, Axel Hadenius, Anirudh Krishna, James Manor, Subrat K. Mitra, Pamela G. Price, Robert D. Putnam, Lloyd I. Rudolph, Susanne H. Rudolph, Harsh Sethi, Larry Swatuk, Ashutosh Varshney, Peter Wallensteen, Sten Widmalm, Michael Woolcock, and Yogendra Yadav.

Without the help of Florian Krampe it would have been impossible for me to finalize this book manuscript. I am extremely grateful to him for providing superb research assistance and in particular his help with the survey data and background information. I am also grateful to Ariel Martinez who went well beyond of his task of language refining to produce a number of improvements in both style and substance. Special thanks are also due to Bikram Mahunt for his support to conduct the survey in the inland part of Orissa back in 2007.

I wish to extend my thanks to Sanjoy Patnaik, Rashmi Ranjan Das, Debasis Panigrahi, Rupa Narayan Das, Soumyajit Patnaik, Subrat Das, Ambika Nanda, Subrat Sundar Ray, Binayak Mishra, and Sibashish Misra who have offered me the personal support and friendship essential for my long and repeated research trips to India. I wish to also thank my colleagues at the Department of Peace and Conflict Research, Uppsala University and the Uppsala Centre for Sustainable Development.

I am grateful to the anonymous readers for Ashgate Publishing. Warm thanks to Natalja Mortensen, the Commissioning Editor, who offered valuable help and advice at many stages of this project.

My final thanks go to my family for their ceaseless encouragement; my mother, sisters, parents-in-law and brothers-in-law have provided many years of support. My wife, Ranjula deserves much credit, for being there even during the most difficult of times, for which I extend a heartfelt thank you. The book is lovingly dedicated to her and to our children, Kabir and Simran.

Chapter 1

Introduction: Development and Displacement: Struggle for Survival

The post-Cold War period has witnessed a remarkable transformation in the Global South's political and social fabrics. The rule of the political game has changed. Authoritarianism is paving the way for democracy. The South is increasingly witnessing free elections, parliamentary politics, independent judiciary and social autonomy. It is no more (with few exceptions) that the official party is the only channel of popular mobilization to influence the political institution or mass mobilization is achieved even before the establishment of these institutions (Kamrava 1993). In this time of greater political participation, the government's inability or failure to 'deliver goods' creates a legitimacy crisis for the ruling elites, thereby helping to mobilize the people. The rising number of social movements is increasingly branded as 'new social movements in the South'.

Both Resource Mobilization (RM) and New Social Movement (NSM) theories consider social movements as inherently political phenomena, but at the same time, underestimated their political origin by failing to examine the interests and structures of the state. This has brought problems of comparability. As Jenkins rhetorically asks: 'Does protest potential, for example, have the same meaning in the Netherlands that is does in the slums of Mexico City? Or does participation in ethnic riots have the same determinants in Los Angeles as in Kinshasa or Nairobi?' (Jenkins 1995: 33–34). The emphasis on political process is also argued by Tarrow and according to this approach, economic and political changes take place independent of protesters' own efforts and that open up space for the movement (Tarrow 1998).

NSM theory is being commonly used to explain the movements in Latin America or Asia (Shah 1990; Slater 1985; Wignaraja 1993; Singh 2001). As Peet and Watts put it: 'Recent social movements theory has therefore moved away from what are frequently found to be restrictions of classical (Marxist) theories. But also the geographic focus of research has tended to shift towards new social movement in the Third World, particularly Latin America' (Peet and Watts 1996: 33). The limited theoretical frameworks available argue that the movements in the South are emerging out of peculiar contradictions within transitioning societies and cultures. Growing weakness of the state and the particular division of labour due to intervention of foreign capital are blamed for the rise in the number of popular mobilizations. Citizens in the South are identifying common interests that overcome the traditional division over class, interest, or clientism and evolving alterative identities such as community, ethnicity, gender or green (Karl 1990; Levine 1988).

Adopting the NSM theory to explain the rise of social movements in the South is a methodologically flawed approach. Even Alain Touraine has himself cautioned against this type of application (see Calderon, Piscitelli, and Reyna 1992). However, as we have mentioned earlier, our aim here is not to explain why the protest movements are there but how some protest movements in developing countries are more successful in mobilizing and sustaining support than the others. As forms of political struggle, protests sometimes succeed and sometimes fail. Sometimes they are able to get concessions from the state; sometimes they are ignored or suppressed. Of course, to determine the success and failure of a movement is not easy. There are some research works, which have tried to focus on the success or failure of the movement on the basis of their stated goals (Gamson 1975; Piven and Cloward 1979). As Giugni points out, this approach has many flaws: (1) it assumes social movement is a homogenous entity with a single goal; (2) it does not take into account the subjective side of the assessment, i.e., the perception of the participants, (3) consequences are not always intended (Giugni 1999). The outcomes of the social movements are not only shaped by the strength of the mobilized support, but it can also be affected by independent actions of authorities, third party intervention, environmental changes and non-movement politics (Tilly 1999). Thus, we are not looking at the success or failure of the movements on the basis of achieving a stated goal or not, rather the emphasis here is whether the movement has been able to spread and sustain itself from the initial stage of its eruption. The aim is to suggest a synthesis of meso-and micro-level processes in social movement activism. Resource mobilization framework operate almost solely on the meso-level of analysis, while some work have investigated the micro-level processes (Buechler 1993). But, that does not give us a clear 'mandate' to accept the RM approach as it is and apply it to explain the success and failures of social movement mobilization in the South. It has to incorporate the following two variables, which are significantly important enough to influence the outcome of the movements.

The RM approach emphasizes the critical role of resources, but forgets about the state. Jenkins provides three reasons to bring back the state into the study of social movements: (1) Social movements are political by nature; (2) the state is the one which provides the environment in which movements operate, and that environment can provide opportunities as well as obstacles for the mobilization; (3) all modern states provide some system to address social interests (Jenkins 1995: 16–17). The transformation of states and societies is a reciprocal process. The success and failure of a social movement depends on both the capacities and character of the state as well as the roles of a variety of social forces. Thus, while studying the mobilization of movements, particularly in the South, we cannot ignore the 'mutually conditioning interactions that occur between segments of state and society' (Kohli and Shue 1994: 321).

RM approach has been developed in North American context. Adopting this approach as such to explain the mobilizational strength and weakness of social movements in segmented societies of the South is sure to receive criticism on methodological grounds. The goals of the social movements are to large extent shaped and influenced by the state and its institutions. That is even the case among social movements in the industrialized democracies, in spite of their governments' generalized tendency towards openness (Frechet and Worndl 1993). The extent to which human rights are respected in a state that affects the possibilities for mobilization (Wiltfang and McAdam 1991), even states tax laws affect groups' mobilizing potential as it can help or hinder fundraising (McCarthy and Zald 1973). In the South, even if states are deemed democracies, they often continue to dominate private and public domains. Translating widely shared grievances into independent collective action requires much stronger mobilization efforts both at micro and meso levels than is necessarily the case in the democracies in the North.

There have been some proposals and attempts to study the mobilization of the social movements in the South with the help of techniques developed by the RM approach (Boudreau 1996; Jenkins and Schock 1992; Schock 1999; Zuo and Benford 1995). However, selecting cases from the South needs to be carefully made to avoid the problem of selection bias. Most of the studies in social movements are based on single and successful cases. Comparing cases within one state or a particular type of states, might able to keep the 'state' factor constant and provide a setting for in-depth investigation of social settings and its impact on micro and meso levels of mobilization.

Most of the research on social movements assumes that social movements are confined to a particular state boundary (McCarthy 1997). Studies of social movements need to address the external aspect of protests in an increasingly globalized society. While governments, particularly in the South are being forced to adjust to changing global forces, local movements are emerging to demand issues that governments ignore. Some of these local groups have regional and transnational connections and support (Barker 1999).

Smith, Pagnucco and Chatfield write:

> Social movements may be said to be transnational when they involve conscious efforts to build transnational cooperation around shared goals that include social change. Increasingly, many states are being challenged by movements, some of them operating across national borders in more than one country. Through regular communication, organizations and activists are able to share technical and strategic information, coordinate parallel activities, or even to mount truly transnational collective actions. Like national social movements, transnational ones incorporate a range of political actors, including individuals, church groups, professional associations, and other social groups. Movements are

distinguished by the actors and resources they mobilize and in the extent to which they communicate, consult, coordinate, and cooperate in the international arena. (Smith, Pagnucco, and Chatfield 1997: 59–60).

Globalization has provided social movements with novel and important opportunities and resources through international linkages, which helps to influence both state and non state actors (Guidry, Kennedy, and Zald 2000). Access to outside media has created a favourable situation for smaller, localized and resource poor protest groups and has provided them an amplified voice (Peterson 2001). The development of affordable communication networks and travel opportunities have provided a fertile setting for protest movements to emerge to spread beyond the area of its origin (Cohen and Rai 2000). These developments have facilitated, as Sikkink calls it 'issue networks' (Sikkink 1993). Such a network connects people of common interest in advancing a particular value and helps them to communicate and coordinate. Large social movement organizations mobilize external resources in domestic and localized struggles. These organizations gather information on local conditions through their contacts and when needed they bring it to the attention of their outside networks of supporters (Alger 1997). In order to response to a situation within a particular area, they create an emergency response network in a larger territory and mobilize pressure from the outside. They also work as cultural agents to shape personal identity and the broader 'moral-intellectual universe' (Gamson 1998). As Paul Wapner elaborates:

> *Amnesty International* for example, both pressures states and other actors to respect human rights and attempts to influence the way people through out the world fundamentally conceptualize human beings and the moral status of regimes within which many people live. Likewise, *Sisterhood is Global* seeks legislative change throughout the world on behalf of women but also works to change the way people in all walks of life think about and act toward women. (Wapner 2001: 1)

There are many attempts to provide outside support to locally based protest movements. The transnational public sphere exports organization structures, protest tactics, financial resources and even personnel. Taking the cause from local to external terrain might also alter the focus of the movements to suit the ideas and interest of outside actors (Sethi 2001). The external actors and ideologies can also influence the interactions within a society, which can alter the mobilization strength of the affected the people. According to Smith (2005), in spite of ideological and organizational tensions between Northern and Southern groups, protest groups in the South are more favourable to maintain ties with groups outside their region compare to their Northern counterparts. Moreover, they also give importance to become part of a transnational network as it helps them with resources and legitimacy.

As discussed earlier, developing democracies in the South have been exposed to growing number popular protests in recent years. That has affected the implementation of various development policies and goals set up by state authorities. The globalization process has further increased the role and influence of external actors and ideas in these internal opposition activities. Partly thanks to the increasing external involvement, the issues of protest, which was very local and limited in nature, have been expanded and the protesters are mobilizing in the name of larger environmental concerns and resource sustainability (Doherty and Doyle 2008).

Development and Sustainability in the South

The World Commission on Environment and Development defines sustainable development as 'development that meets the needs of the present without compromising the ability of future generations to meet their own needs' (World Commission on Environment Development 1987). To achieve sustainable development, the Report of the Commission expects that the world needs to redefine strategies that will enable nation-states to move from the present, often destructive, process of growth and development toward a new model that integrates environmental considerations into their economic decision-making. The integration of economic and environmental factors in the legal and policy sectors of countries also has to be backed at the international level. The Report of the Commission prescribes a more responsible use of environmental resources, a significant reduction in arms expenditure, the abolition of poverty, and multilateral efforts to address environmental issues. As many commentators agree, the Commissions' Report was able in moving environmental concerns from the periphery to the centre of the policy agenda. How to set man-environment equation in balance so as to secure sustainable development has become a major concern of nation-states and international organizations in recent years.

As early as the 1970s, the Club of Rome's Project on the 'Predicament of Mankind' had emphasized the need for a controlled and systematic transition from growth to a sustainable state of global equilibrium in order to address the 'world problematique'. Being invited by an Italian economic consultant, Dr Aurelio Peccei, a group of intellectuals met in Rome in 1968 and their discussion of the human condition led to the establishment of the Club of Rome to undertake the first serious modelling study of global future. The group's first report was published in 1972. The project envisioned many trade-offs in the process of growth, arising from the availability or scarcity of global natural resources.

The conclusions of the Club of Rome's Project were:

1. If the present growth trends in world population, industrialisation, pollution, food production, and resource depletion continue unchanged, the limits to growth on this planet will be reached sometime within the next one hundred years. The most probable result will be a rather sudden and uncontrollable decline in both population and industrial capacity.

2. It is possible to alter these growth trends and to establish a condition of ecological and economic stability that is sustainable far into the future. The state of global equilibrium could be designed so that the basic material needs of each person on earth are satisfied and each person has an equal opportunity to realise their individual human potential.

3. If the world's people decide to strive for this second outcome rather than the first, the sooner they begin to working to attain it, the greater their chances of success. (Meadows et al. 1972: 23–24)

Not surprisingly, among the developing countries, the idea of limited growth aroused not only intellectual scepticism but also political suspicion. The gap between developed and developing countries of the world is enormous and continues to widen. The huge disparity in development between North and South has reflected in their needs and agendas while addressing global environmental issues. While the North focuses its attention on environmental issues that threaten ecological stability, the South puts emphasis on immediate needs for economic growth to raise the standard of living.

The concept of sustainable development was developed by the Brundtland Commission to meet the concerns of developing countries. The Brundtland Report was notable for recognising that poverty and underdevelopment were important causes of environmental degradation. It implicitly rejected the 1970s idea of environmental limits to growth. By accepting the desirability of growth, it focussed on how development should be achieved. The Report made the point that developing countries must increase their wealth, because poverty is a major cause of environmental destruction. Environmental degradation was seen to be inimical to continued development. On the other hand, economic growth could assist to make available resources for environmental protection. The Brundtland Commission emphasized that the concept of 'sustainable development' itself contains within it two key concepts:

The concept of 'needs', in particular, the essential needs of the world's Poor, to which overriding priority should be given; and

The idea of limitations imposed by the state of technology and social organization on the environment's ability to meet present and future needs. (World Commission on Environment Development 1987: 43)

Since the release of the Brundtland Commission report in 1987, the concept of 'sustainable development' has been promoted by the international organizations to support and strengthen the future development of all nations. However, it is true that in the last years the definition of sustainable development has been subject to a number of modifications according different point of views. Clear disagreement still persists over the exact meaning of the term, though primarily it refers to the capability of renewable natural resources and ecosystems over time, and the preservation of human living standards and economic growth. The dramatic growth in the new economies, especially in China and India has forced the world to think about the management of economic development. Growing threat of climate change has further raised the support for sustainable development. Despite the proliferation of sustainable development strategies at the international level, there is considerable apprehension about the influence of the philosophy over the way state economies are organized. Developing economies are not only engaged in large scale natural resource exploitation to meet the increasing demand, many of the development projects are directly displacing large number of people by capturing the place of source of living.

Development Strategy and Population Displacement

One non-governmental agency engaged in refugee issues estimates that there are already 163 million displaced people worldwide, and it predicts that 'a further 1 billion people will be forced from their homes between now and 2050' (Christian Aid 2007). The majority of the on going displacement is not caused by conflicts or wars, rather 2/3 of the global displacement are induced directly and indirectly by development activities undertaken in different parts of the world. The situation is extremely serious in the South, as some of the major countries in the region are facing rapid population increase, and also they are in a rush to achieve faster economic growth.

Development Induced Displacement

Every year, the world population increases by 79 million, roughly the equivalent of another Germany. In the last 50 years, due to medical advances and increased agricultural productivity, the world has experienced rapid population growth. Michael S. Teitelbaum has described this world demographic trends as 'revolutionary', because though the human species emerged perhaps 150,000 years ago, most of its growth has been in the last five decades (Teitelbaum 1991). The world population took tens of thousands years to reach one billion around 1800, over a century to achieve the second billion mark somewhere in the beginning of twentieth century, about 33 years to the third billion around 1960, only 14 years to the fourth, 13 years to the fifth billion, and 12 years to the sixth billion in the year 1999. In 2009, according to the estimates by the United Nations Population

Division, the world's population has crossed 6.8 billion. Globally, the actual annual growth rate of the human population has begun to decline slightly, however, the world population is projected to reach ten billion around the year 2050. While population growth has stagnated in most of the industrialized world due to low fertility rates and even declined in Southern Africa because of the high number of HIV related deaths, it is still remains extremely high in the developing countries of Asia, the Middle East, Latin America and parts of Africa (Nielsen 2006).

Some researchers have found population growth pressure to have a significant impact on the likelihood of a state becoming involved in interstate military conflicts (Tir and Diehl 1998). It remains unclear if population growth directly affects the decision making of the state to go to war or not, but it undoubtedly generates scarcity of resources in a developing economy. Feeding a rapidly expanding world population may be technologically feasible, but at the same time it is likely to lead to widespread devastation of renewable resources (Bray 1994). In spite of tall claims by agricultural scientists, it is true that approximately 1 billion people in the developing world are still chronically undernourished, and 40,000 die every day of hunger and hunger related diseases. The availability of fresh water has also fallen short of meeting its increased demand. Some 1.1 billion people in developing countries lack access to clean water and nearly 2.6 billion do not have adequate sanitation facilities.

Availability of natural resources is increasingly falling short of meeting human needs. The growing population number and increased economic activities have already threatened the natural resource base in many parts of the world on which human beings are dependent for survival. As global population and consumption rise, unsustainable practices and policies are being followed by a large number of countries, which seriously threatens the well being of people and the planet. The Report by the UN Commission on Global Governance has made an effort to warn about the looming global crisis. Citing an increase in population levels and economic growth as a source of additional pressure on natural resources and the environment, the Commission pleads for the better management of demographic and economic change to protect the interests of future generations. As the Report of the Commission on Global Governance describes:

> Evidence has accumulated of widespread ecological degradation resulting from human activity: soils losing fertility or being eroded, overgrazed grasslands, desertification, dwindling fisheries, disappearing species, shrinking forests, polluted air and water. These have been joined by the newer problems of climate change and ozone depletion. Together they threaten to make the earth less habitable and life more hazardous. (Carlsson et al. 1995: 29)

The world has already lost a huge chunk of its fertile land due to rapid urbanization and increasing industrialization. Since the Second World War, an area of about

1.2 billion hectares – nearly the size of China and India together – has already endured modest to severe soil degradation because of human activity. Over three-fourths of this degradation is taking place in the developing countries. As a result of the massive soil degradation, yields and total harvests of crucial food crops are declining. It is also estimated that by 2010 unchecked soil erosion will have caused a 19 to 29 per cent decline in food production from rain fed cropland as compared to 1985 levels. The loss of cropland due to soil degradation leads to further clearing of forests and destruction of green cover.

The growth of global food production is slowing while the growth in demand due to population growth and a rising living standard continues to be strong. The heydays of the Green Revolution era are over: since 1985, there has been far less annual increase in food-grain production. Despite regular claims about vast opportunities for expanding the earth's cultivable land, the possibility to do so is in fact very limited, and with high economic and political cost. Reduced growth in agricultural production has already resulted in the loss of livelihood for millions of people. In the ongoing struggle of raising food production to meet the needs of the growing population and improving the quality of the diet, many developing countries are being forced to undertake highly controversial land and water development projects.

Industrialization and mining In the nineteenth century industrialization introduced a radical transformation to the economic and social sectors in the European societies (Marx 1990). The change from a rural, feudalist society towards an urban, industrial one brought massive shifts of population – voluntarily migrating to urban areas and also forced displacement to access resources or build industries. Today it is the same systemic shift that causes substantial displacement of populations, particular in the South.

Under the new liberal economic agenda, countries in the South in their post-independence period have taken over common property resources, such as forest and grazing land, to create space for new industrial and mining projects (Kothari 1995). Peasant, pastoral and tribal communities are being forcibly displaced in the name of national progress, causing significant changes to their socio-cultural environment. Thanks to the on-going industrial revolution projects in the South, these 'development-induced displacement and resettlement' involve an estimated 15 million people annually (Christian Aid 2007). The indigenous people are worst affected in this displacement process as their way of living is usually closely related to their own environment. Having less social and economic status in these societies, the displacement of these communities from their home base to new regions often brings disastrous results.

According to the US Committee for Refugees, in Sudan four million people have been displaced and approximately two million people have died due to the civil conflict between North and South (U.S. Committee for Refugees 2001). Beyond the effects of war, Southern Sudan has also witnessed massive population displacement due to the exploitation of its oil fields by multinational companies. International companies from Britain, Canada, China and Sweden have drilled for oil in the region since the 1970s, and have supported the warring parties to garner their support for the exploitation of the oil fields. The exploitation of oil resources has directly and indirectly displaced large numbers of people in Sudan.

The list of the large industrial projects, which have forced the people to displace from their homes is quite long in India. Industrialization in the tribal dominated Indian state of Chhattisgarh has displaced many people in recent years (Dhagamwar, De, and Verma 2003). Besides industries, various large projects in defence and science sectors have also forces people to move. In 1969, when the Indian Space Research Organization constructed the Sriharikota High Altitude project, nearly 2,085 people, mainly tribal communities, were displaced from the Sriharikota Island to the Indian mainland. Although rehabilitation was offered by the state on the mainland, the majority of people rejected the new homes and were unable to reintegrate into society (Reddy 1995).

One of the biggest causes of development-induced displacement is mining projects. Notwithstanding the devastating environmental affects of mining activities, excavation projects are considered to be an important factor for a country's development as it creates wealth and jobs simultaneously. Gold mining and diamonds are considered the backbone of economic development in South Africa as well as Russia. However, while global numbers have not been assessed yet, several cases illustrate the severely adverse effects of these mining activities leading to the large-scale displacement of populations from their native places. In India alone 2.55 million people were displaced from 1950 to 1990, to create space for new mining projects (Downing 2002).

A recent study of mining projects in Ghana reveals that these mines would employ a very small number of people to their workforce, while at the same time displacing several thousands of people. Adverse effects of the dislocation of several communities also include severe employment losses in the displaced communities (Owusu-Koranteng 2008) and with it their status and relevance. It illustrates the vicious chain of events that mining projects create for local communities as well as the fraudulent approach of transnational companies involved in the exploitation of these resources.

In some cases mining-induced displacement has led to violent conflicts in many societies. Some of them are on going in the Democratic Republic of Congo, Ghana, Nigeria, Peru, and Sierra Leone – just to name a few. However, the most cited conflict of this type is the one in Papua New Guinea. In April 1988 Francis Ona, who was still then working at the Bougainville Copper Limited (BCL), founded the New

Panguna Landowners Association, and demanded approximately 10 billion USD in compensation for the impact of the mine, considering it to be a just payment for the land for future generations. Furthermore, they demanded with support from the Bougainville provincial government, a 50 per cent share in BCL profits, consultation on all new projects and localization of BCL ownership within five years (Alleey 2002). After the demands were rejected, the first acts of sabotage were undertaken in November 1988 against BCL and the Bougainville Revolutionary Army (BRA) was (re)-founded. Already active in the 1960s and 70s the BRA had demanded secession from PNG and an independent Bougainville. After a ceasefire and negotiations in May 1989, Ona declared that the BRA not only demanded compensation for the mined land but also full independence for Bougainville, which was unacceptable for the PNG regime. The conflict became one of the bloodiest in South-East Asia resulting in more than 15,000 casualties within nine years.

Building Dams and Displacing People

There is a serious attempt in many parts of the world to increase the supply of water to meet the growing demand with the help of dams, canals and groundwater withdrawal. But, the price paid for these water resource development projects has been very high. Besides the economic and environmental costs of these schemes, the human cost is also staggering. Due to massive water projects, many people have already been forced to move away from their homes. The poor rural people have been the major victims. Due to inferior political and economic clout, they have become the early and easy targets (Swain 2000b). Massive projects are being planned and built to store water to provide irrigation and electricity for people in distant locations and to supply water to the cities, but at the same time they displace substantial populations and threaten their livelihoods. The dam projects submerge vast areas of land and forest and displace their inhabitants. There are millions of people who have already lost their homes and livelihoods due to these projects.

Parakrama Bahu, the Great, twelfth century king of present Sri Lanka gave a challenge to his water engineers: 'Let not even a small quantity of water obtained by rain go to the sea, without benefitting man.' The water engineers in the last two centuries seem to have picked up that challenge all over the world. The first recorded dam was constructed in Egypt some 5,000 years ago.

In the twentieth century, there was a tremendous increase in the construction of dams to meet the growing water demand. By 1949, there were nearly 5000 dams worldwide, out of which three-quarters were in industrialized countries. In 50 years, by the end of the century, there were over 45,000 large dams in more than 140 countries. In the last century, the world has spent more than two trillion dollars in constructing these large dams. Augmenting water storages and retaining floodwater for future use became an essential element of water resource management. The requirement of hydro-energy and commercial fishing has also contributed to human intervention in water. Dam building, which has already become out of fashion in North America and Western Europe, is still considered the panacea for water shortage problems in many developing countries. During the 1990s, the world was spending between 32 to 46 billion dollars annually on large dam construction, four-fifths of it by developing countries. In Europe and North America, the construction of large dams peaked in the 1970s but now these regions are witnessing the decommissioning of the dams. However, approximately 1,700 large dams are presently under construction in other parts of the world. India with a 40 per cent share of the total number of large dams leads the list, followed by China, Turkey and South Korea (cf. World Commission on Dams 2000). Moreover, these newly built dams and their reservoirs are becoming larger.

In 1992, 60 per cent of the dams being constructed were more than 30 meters high, compared with only 21 per cent of existing dams in 1986. The construction of dams higher than 100 metres has also increased considerably. This new tendency is due to the increasing scarcity of water and the reduced availability of suitable dam sites. In the world today, there are more than 100 'super dams' with a height of more than 150 metres. Lake Mead, behind the Hoover Dam was the largest dam reservoir in the world in 1936, with 38 billion cubic metres of water. By the 1970s, it was dwarfed by a series of dam reservoirs in developing countries: the Kariba dam in Southern Africa with 160 billion cubic metres, Aswan's Lake Nasser with 157 billion cubic metres and Ghana's Akosombo with 148 billion cubic metres. Nearly 500,000 square kilometres of land area is covered by dam reservoirs worldwide, with the capacity of storing 6,000 cubic kilometres of water (Pearce 1992).

One of the largest dams in the world is the Itaipu dam on the Parana River, which forms the border between Paraguay and Brazil (Pearce 1992). However, China's Three Gorges Dam project (Sanxia) is presently the largest dam in the world, based on reservoir volume. This dam and associated construction sites are the biggest public-works projects in China since the Great Wall. Standing 185 metres tall on the Yangtze River, just downstream from the scenic Three Gorges, it creates 632 square kilometres of reservoir with a total storage capacity of nearly 40 billion cubic metres. This huge project helps to increase the discharge flow of the river in the dry seasons to meet the increasing need for water. Besides inundating vast areas of farmland, the project has adversely affected the aquatic life of the river. Moreover, the dam and its reservoir have caused direct displacement of more than a million people.[1] China tops the list of dam-building nations. It is the site of 22,000 large dams, which is almost half the world's total number. Before the Communist revolution, China had only 22 of these dams.

---

1   The official figure is that 1.3 million people have been resettled, which is the largest population displacement in the history of dam building. Researchers suggest that the displacement number can be as high as 1.9 million. (Zich 1997; Heggelund 1993).

Construction and operation of large dams and their reservoirs have led to many significant, social, human and environmental impacts. Besides triggering earthquakes, they build up soil salinity, change groundwater levels and create water logging. Dams extract a high human toll as well. The dam projects submerge vast areas of land and forest and displace their inhabitants. There are millions of people who have lost their homes and livelihoods due to these projects. According to the World Commission on Dams, the construction of large dams has forced the displacement of 40–80 million people worldwide. The construction of 300 large dams on an average each year has displaced four million people annually between 1986 and 1993. In the late 1980s, China has officially admitted to have 10.2 million people as 'reservoir resettlers.' In India, one author estimates that the number of dam-related displaced people between 1951 and 1990 is 14 million (Fernandes 1993). Several movements have arisen in India recently to protest against these displacements. The dam-displaced people are gradually becoming organized and have taken their struggle to the streets (Swain 1997). A number of big dam projects were undertaken in India after independence in 1947 to meet the increasing demand for irrigation water. In spite of popular protests, dam building and its consequent population displacement are still taking place on a large scale in India.

Due to increasing water scarcity, there are very few rivers left in the world, which run freely towards the sea. While the slow flowing Amazon has been saved from dam construction until now, the Brazilian Government in its 'Plan 2010' envisages 80 dams on its tributaries in order to meet future demand for water. Another important river basin of South America, the Rio de la Plata, is threatened with a series of dam constructions, which will displace many people. A number of large dams have been built in Africa during its post-colonial period, to meet demands for increased energy and food production. Water scarcity in the Middle East has also led to the construction of a series of dams along the Euphrates–Tigris river basin. After China, Turkey is the next on the list of the countries engaged in building a large number of big dams (higher than ten meters) in the 1990s. These dams, particularly on the Euphrates-Tigris River, besides creating conflicts with downstream Syria and Iraq, have also displaced a large number of people from the submerged areas.

In the twentieth century, significant advances in the design and construction of dams were achieved. Factors of safety have been refined, human errors reduced, and design criteria have found international consensus (Veltrop 1993). But, the three most detrimental effects of big dams are still haunting policy makers and engineers: (1) displacement and resettlement of the population, (2) salination and water logging and (3) health issues resulting from water-related diseases. The range of such social and environmental effects is gradually becoming apparent. The dams are being built to store water to provide irrigation and electricity for people in distant locations and to supply water to the cities, but at the same time these dams displace substantial populations and threaten their livelihoods.

Protecting Environment and Displacing People

In October 2008 Achim Steiner, UN Under-Secretary General and Executive Director, United Nations Environment Programme (UNEP) wrote in the foreword of the forced migration review that by 2080 climate change and environmental degradation will cause millions of people to migrate from their homes (Couldrey and Herson 2008). Climate change is a growing global problem caused by the build up of greenhouse gases, particularly carbon dioxide and methane, in the Earth's atmosphere. In 2007, the Intergovernmental Panel on Climate Change brought to the fore evidence which clearly shows that human activity is 'very likely' to be causing climate change, as well as predicted rises in average temperature and sea level (IPCC WGI 2007). The world is warming faster now than at any time in the last 10,000 years. The predicted dramatic sea level rise caused by this climatic change may take away the living space and source of livelihood of millions of people in the near future. The Inter-governmental Panel on Climate Change (IPCC) has predicted that sea levels could rise an average rate of six centimetres per decade over the next century. A rise of this magnitude will no doubt threaten densely populated low-lying countries. Among the other impacts could be an increase in tropical cyclones. Increased cyclones would also enhance the risk of coastal flooding. Climate change can also potentially alter the usual rainfall and snowfall pattern, which may lead to more flooding, drought and soil erosion in tropical and arid regions of the world. With fewer resources in their hands, many developing countries stand to suffer disproportionately more as compared to the developed countries from a rapid climate change, due to the 'green house' effect. The production of ordinary rice varieties goes down alarmingly at temperatures just a few degrees higher than those presently existing in most of the rice producing areas.

High evapotransportation is expected as well. The humid tropical areas, which suffer from excessive rainfall already, might get more, resulting in further soil erosion and crop losses. At the same time, semi-arid areas might become even drier making the agricultural production even more difficult. The increasing threat of climate change has pushed countries to start planning large flood control projects, which threaten to displace many more people in the near future. In his first official response on this important issue, UN Secretary General Ban Ki-moon warned that changes in the environment, such as droughts and extreme flooding, were likely to become major drivers of violent conflicts as well as humanitarian disasters, and that climate change thus poses as much of a danger to the world as war (BBC News, 2 March 2007). The impacts of climate change are likely to be severe in countries where people are highly dependent on natural resources for their livelihoods.

While carbon emission is regarded as the main cause of the green house effect there is still debate on how to regulate carbon emissions globally. Attempts of finding agreements that regulate a reduction of emissions receive strong opposition by newly industrialized countries. Those countries make the case that reducing carbon emissions would have a significant negative effect on their economy by placing them at a competitive disadvantage. Failure of the developed countries, particularly the United States in agreeing to reduce their own emissions in an appropriate manner widens the North South divide further. The Copenhagen Climate Conference in December 2009 failed to get a global agreement on how to arrest the climate change. It is true that there is no global consensus on regarding measures to be taken to regulate carbon emission, but for some years now developed countries and international NGOs are supporting and promoting the creation of protected forest areas in the tropical and sub-tropical parts of the world. The following section will discuss how these forest protection measures are forcing people to move out from their traditional place of living.

Protecting forest without forest people   Population growth and the loss of croplands have led to the current levels of rapid tropical deforestation. People in developing countries, primarily in need of farmland or fuel for heating and cooking, are cutting down trees at a rate much faster than the forests can regenerate. During the last decades the tropical forest has receded like the temperate forest shrank during the nineteenth century (Mather and Chapman 1995). The Food and Agriculture Organization of the United Nations (FAO) estimates that each year about 13 million hectares of the world's forests are lost due to deforestation (FAO 2005). These days, three countries, Brazil, Indonesia and Malaysia account for half of the world's tropical rain forest loss. Forests provide livelihood to many people, those who are dependant on its resources directly and indirectly.

Historically, deforestation has contributed to the expansion of arable land. As Roper and Roberts argue, due the right mix of social needs, economic opportunities, and environmental conditions, it can be a rational conversion from one type of land use to a more productive one (Roper and Roberts 1999). Without deforestation, it would have been impossible to provide food and shelter to the world's rapidly increasing population. However, the scale of forest clearing in recent years is not only unsustainable but has brought multiple societal and environmental problems, and while some may consider this a local or regional problem, its consequences can be global.

Thus, deforestation threatens the existence of these indigenous peoples in many parts of the world. The cutting of the forests jeopardizes the way of life and survival of the indigenous communities. Among them are Kyuquot of the Amazonia, the Saami of Lapland and Kyuquot of Vancouver Island's temperate rainforest. According to Global Future Foundation:

There have been more extinctions of tribal peoples in this century than any other, with Brazil losing 87 tribes between 1900 and 1950. Even in the rare cases when forest dwellers are compensated for this loss, the changes visited upon their cultures by the inexorable expansion of industrial culture are devastating. (Future 500 2009).

In many regions, traditional land rights of forest people are not recognized by law or honoured by the authority. When the forests disappear, these people loose their access to plants and animals, the source of their survival. Many forest-based customary occupations are eroded due to deforestation. Logging affects the collection of non-timber forest products. Many timber trees are themselves sources of many non-timber products. Logging also destroys the trees, which are not commercially valuable as timber. The loss of these services upsets local communities and brings economic vulnerability to local population.

International environmental groups and international development and conservation agencies are promoting the establishment of protected areas. Sizeable amounts of foreign aid have also been provided for this effort. More recently tropical forests have come to be seen as a crucial link between the issues of biological diversity and climate change. In spite of the fact that the carbon binding capacity of old growth forests in temperate areas is often higher than that of tropical rain forests due to the larger storage capacity of understory vegetation and soils (Miller, Reid, and Barber 1991; Trexler 1991), in the climate negotiations industrialized countries are putting pressure on tropical countries to set aside larger areas of their forest for preservation. The forest-rich developing countries are opposed to the idea that they should refrain from utilizing their own resources. The forest-rich developing countries argue that they should receive compensation for refraining from utilizing their own forest resources. Thus, the creation of newly protected forest areas in many developing countries has become one of the most controversial and challenging issues.

Conflict over creation of protected areas is not limited to discourse between developing and industrialized countries however. In several developing regions, trans-frontier conservation areas are also being used as haven for insurgents and poachers, which have led to conflicts between neighbouring countries. Moreover, the establishment of protected areas in many cases has become a source of conflict between local people and the state, particularly in the South.

Protected areas play an important role in maintaining ecological systems, safeguarding forest cover, and providing refuge for biological diversity. Protected areas have generally gained support when they are perceived as promoting local resource management. As Borrie and others argue, 'The income derived from the protected area, and the attachments people form with the area, often becomes an important component of the local community' (Borrie, McCool and Stankey 1998).

However, if the management of the protected area affects disproportionately the local population and/or is perceived to be guided by external interest, it can lead to resentment and conflict.

Unfortunately, most protected areas are insufficiently or ineffectively managed. Rarely can a protected area be maintained well in a "hands-off" fashion. The economic, institutional and human resources needed for effective management are in short supply. Economic benefits generated by protected areas are rarely channelled into protected area management or local community development. In many countries tourism plays a major role in the establishment of protected areas. Though there is always the danger of damage from improperly managed tourism; tourism in a national park or any other protected area can be useful as a self-financing mechanism and therefore as a tool of conservation. Due to various factors, however, the benefits of the tourism sector often do not reach the people who have been traditionally dependent on the now 'protected' forest. Urban-based tourist interests benefit only a few. Moreover, the switch from agriculture to tourism as the source of livelihood makes forest-based communities vulnerable to economic swings in the tourism industry, which are beyond their control. A small group of elites are perceived to reap the benefits of the forest and wildlife conservation, while the poorest elements of society, farmers, agricultural workers and landless labourers, bear the costs in terms of restricted access to various forest resources. In addition, wild animals in the protected areas damage crops, attack livestock and harass nearby villagers, thereby enhancing their frustration.

A core issue in protected area management revolves around meeting the demands of resident populations that utilize resources within or adjacent to designate protected areas. Frequently, local demands for resource use conflict with other goals to conserve resources. When an area is protected, people living near or within it generally must restrict their use of its resources. According to Ghimire and Pimbert, 'most national parks legislation alienates protected areas to the state, thereby annulling, limiting or restricting local rights of tenure and use' (Ghimire and Pimbert 1997: 109). Local people suffer from serious restrictions to their customary livelihood activities, and tend to perceive that society at large reaps the benefits of protected areas at their expense. Though many people are dependent on forest resources, two groups that get hit hardest are women and tribal communities. Often they are prohibited from herding, hunting, fishing, and gathering food, wood and fodder in the protected areas. In several cases, open conflict has erupted between hunters, gatherers, loggers, miners, fishermen, or tourism operators and protected area staff or environmental advocates. Conflicts become severe when traditional forest users are not consulted and customary rights are disregarded. Indigenous inhabitants in the protected forest areas are dependent on shifting cultivation for food and on the forest as a source of firewood, construction material, medicinal plants and other necessities. Exclusion of these peoples from the decision-making process and the resulting restrictions imposed on their livelihood can result in physical conflicts between the forest authority and local people. Failure to recognize community interests at the local level fuels increased land and resource-based conflicts between the managing authorities of protected areas and the local community.

In some cases, when a protected area is established, people have to be relocated. In India alone, protected areas threaten to displace 600,000 tribal people. Mostly, these people are left to fend for them to find an alternative means of survival. When the state undertakes the responsibility for resettlement, it is often not properly carried out. In many cases, when monetary compensation is allocated for poor and uneducated displaced people, corrupt officials misappropriate a large proportion of the monies. Whatever money does reach the displaced persons is often quickly spent. The best the state can provide to the displaced people is to resettle them in a new place. The transfer of the people to a different socio-economic environment with the provision of land unsuitable for their traditional agricultural activities brings frustration and anger among the people towards the state in general and the protected area authorities in particular. In recent years, worldwide, experience with involuntary settlement has shown that most displaced people are left excessively aggrieved, and, in some other cases, certain groups end up poorer and more marginalized than others (Colson 1971; Cernea and Scott 1993; The World Bank 1998).

Protected area status increases state control over the forest while simultaneously decreasing community control. Though protected area initiatives make regular references to involvement of local communities, generally local people are only used as a labour pool for the maintenance and protection of protected areas. There are efforts by various NGOs and donor agencies to effect a transfer of rights over local resources to local actors, but when this happens it is only partial in nature and primarily designed as a temporary measure to diffuse conflict between the state and local communities. In general, the forest communities, those who traditionally consider the forest as common property, are excluded access to these protected area resources. The limited loggings that may be allowed usually take place under license or permit. Generally one observes that people care best for that which they own. Indigenous populations dependent on biodiversity of rich forests to sustain their livelihood may target these forests for unsustainable uses if they perceive they are losing their customary custodianship. Thus, not only have protected areas become the source of conflict, but also they have failed in their mandate to conserve the forest and wildlife. If the brutal state power is indeed able to enforce conservation within the protected forest areas, then the protected area often becomes an island of conservation amidst the massive destruction of nature that surrounds it (Ghimire 1994a, 1994b).

Developmental Refugees

Throughout history, people have been forced to leave home because the land on which they lived could no longer support them. Deforestation, desertification, and drought have had a significant impact on these population movements in the past (Refugees 1986). One could even reasonably argue that mankind's entire history has been a history of migration. As Louise Levathes writes, 'The genes of modern populations carry the encoded history of human's remote past and their early wandering around the globe' (Levathes 1993). However, what is more recent and more alarming is the potential for mass migration caused by irreversible destruction of the environment (Martin 1992). Increasing numbers of people in the developing regions leave their homes because life has become insupportable there. They are moving within and across international borders and from the rural areas to cities in large numbers.

Migration is a highly extensive and multifaceted term that comprises all types of voluntary as well as forced movements of a population. Whereas a number of demographic, economic, socio-cultural, and psychological factors determine the nature, pattern, and direction of voluntary human migration, forced migrants migrate to other areas to escape civil war, political and ethnic persecution, famine, and other environmental catastrophes.

Much of the existing literature on voluntary migration emphasizes the economic motives of the migrants. According to the proponents of this approach, migrants move to take advantage of better economic prospects in terms of employment and income. The neo-classical economic framework, 'the equilibrium model of migration', conceptualizes population movement as the geographical mobility of workers who are responding to imbalances in the spatial distribution of land, labour, capital, and natural resources (Wood 1982). The push (supply)-pull (demand) theory is the more general conceptual umbrella for this equilibrium model. Unlike this neo-classical equilibrium theory, which is based on a 'microeconomics' approach professed mainly by the North American research community, the historical-structural school on the study of migration is derived from various approaches adopted by the social scientists in Africa and Latin America. This historical-structural school consists of various macro-economic approaches: 'dependency theory', 'internal colonialism', 'centre-periphery' approach, and 'global accumulation' framework.

Whereas the explanation regarding 'voluntary' migration is dominated by the economic approach, the causes of 'forced' migration are usually attributed to political factors. Leon Gordenker's widely discussed model on forced migration clearly uses the domination of politics to explain this phenomenon. His model categorises the reasons for the forced movements into four types: The first one is international war; the second, internal disturbances; the third, deliberate changes within the social structure because of political transformation; and the final one involves international political tension (Gordenker 1989). Researchers who give only the political explanations for a forced migration do not differentiate between forced migrants and the highly defined term 'refugee'. Their interpretation of forced migration seems to have been moulded by the legal definition and the universal treatment of 'refugees'.

The legal definition of the term 'refugee' was imposed by the 1951 United Nations Convention on Refugees, together with the 1967 Protocol, which extended the Convention by excluding restrictions on time and geography.[2] As it is defined:

> The term 'refugee' shall apply to any person who...owing to a well-founded fear of being persecuted for reasons of race, religion, nationality, membership of a particular social group or political opinion, is outside the country of his nationality and is unable or, owing to such fear, is unwilling to avail himself of the protection of that country; or who, not having a nationality and being outside the country of his former habitual residence as a result of such events, is unable or, owing to such fear, is unwilling to return to it. (Gordenker 1988: 199)

This legal limitation to the term 'refugee' makes it inadequate for absorbing types of forced migration other than those stemming from persecution. In spite of efforts by the Organization of African Unity (OAU) and the Central American countries to make the term 'refugee' more inclusive,[3] the definition provided by the 1951 Convention is still ruling the common psyche and governmental policies. This definition is furthermore limited to trans-border migrants, which prohibits the inclusion of internally forced migrants in its terminology.

The contemporary significance of development and environment induced forced migration has led a number of researchers to attempt to conceptualize this phenomenon. Among the terms such as 'developmental refugees', 'environmental refugees', 'ecological refugees' and 'resource refugees' frequently used to describe this type of human migration. While economic migrants are voluntary migrants, these developmental refugees belong to the forced migration category. In the case of economic migrants, both push and pull factors may play equally significant

---

2   The 1951 Convention was limited to Europe and to persons whose status was determined by events preceding 1 January 1951.

3   African countries in the 1969 Organization of African Unity (OAU) Convention Governing the Specific Aspects of refugee Problems in Africa recognized, in addition to fear of individual persecution as a reason for fleeing one's country and being unwilling to return to it, reasons of 'external aggression, occupation, foreign domination or events seriously disturbing public order.' A similar definition was thought necessary by the Central American countries, which agreed in 1984 to the nonbinding Cartagena Declaration.

roles in their decision to migrate from their own land, but for the developmental refugees, the push factor completely overwhelms the pull factor. There may be some role for the pull factor in the selection of the area to which they migrate, but it does not contribute in any way to the decision to leave the homeland, as there is no other choice.

Development induced migration can cause more than one type of conflict at the same time in a developing society. Incompatibilities induced or elicited by the development stimulated migration, may create or activate a number of opposing actors in developing societies. The displaced population may engage in 'we versus they' conflict in their host locations. In some cases, people might take up the struggle against the state even before being physically displaced.

However, the displacement process varies from case to case, and a displaced population generally mobilizes itself formally or informally to either oppose the project or to receive better rehabilitation support. A democratic system provides possibilities and opportunities for the affected people to mobilize and organize protests. Some protests become successful and some fail to make serious impact. Some able to spread and sustain and some die before even properly taking off. India provides us a good case study as the country has a functioning democracy for more than six decades, and has experienced numerous of protests of various types. In some of the regions, displaced people have been more successful in mobilizing them than their counterparts in other parts. In some parts of the country, state has been facing sustained popular opposition against these projects, while in other areas it was able to carry out its policies without much problem. The areas, which were traditionally free from protest have started experiencing this phenomenon, posing severe challenges for the state to undertake its planned development an industrial projects. The careful study of the differing and developing strength and success of these protests in Indian democracy provides an excellent opportunity to locate the impact of social network structure on movement mobilization.

Chapter 2

India, its Development, Population Displacements and Protests

Considering the short lifespan of most of democracies in the developing world, the persistence and continuity of India's democracy has often evoked surprise as well as admiration. India has been able to maintain its democratic structure since independence[1] in spite of its multi-ethnic, multi-religious and multi-linguistic society. This 'Indian wonder' has recently passed through a period of transition. Crisis became the cliché used by political scientists and political economists to describe the state of Indian democracy in the 1980s and 1990s (Bardhan 1984; Kohli 1990; Kothari 1989a; Kothari 1989b, Rudolph and Rudolph 1987). These two decades were particularly turbulent for India: violent secessionist movements, assassination of two Gandhis and growing religious fundamentalism. The contradictions between the high level of political violence and sustainment of a democratic political system had encouraged Myron Weiner to describe the phenomenon as 'the Indian Paradox' (Weiner 1989).

In spite of various democratic institutions gaining strength and respectability and rapid economic growth in the last several years, communal and sectarian violence still claims thousands of lives every year in India. The inability of elected authorities to carryout socio-economic developmental policies due to the increasing organized popular opposition has produced serious concerns for the health and strength of the democratic structure. The weakening of domination of the major political party, the Congress Party, is often cited as the root of this crisis.

In recent years Indian society has also encountered a large number of protest movements:[2] anti-caste movements, the women's movement, farmers' movement, civil rights movement, and environmental movements. As Rajni Kothari had once described, India is involved in a 'democratic churning' process (Kothari 1989a). Larger and larger numbers of people are increasingly resisting an 'exploitative' state structure or a development model that they presume excludes them. The democratic awakening seems to have led to the increased self-assertion and political participation of these silent groups. Most of them are not aiming to

---

1   India obtained independence from British Rule in 1947. Many do not consider Indira Gandhi's two years of Emergency Rule (1975–1977) as period of democracy in India.

2   These movements are different in their aim and ideology from the classical form of social movements, i.e., working class movement and anti-colonial movements.

capture the national parliament in New Delhi or initiate a total revolution. Yet, they have already become an opposition power to state authority.

As a part of these new organized protests in India, movements against large projects have increased in frequency and intensity. These movements are more widespread and involve larger numbers of people from different sections of the society. This popular opposition is directed against some developmental policies adopted by the state thereby becoming a primary hindrance for the government's policy implementation. Most of these movements revolve around competing claims over renewable natural resources as well as the struggle for the rights of victims of environmental destruction. For centuries, resources like land, forests and water were controlled and used collectively by the communities. With the introduction of new technology after India's encounter with colonial rule, a different framework was established for the use of these natural resources. Colonial domination brought a systematic transformation of these resources into commodities for generating profits and growth of revenues. This paved the way for disagreement with the original user of the resource base.

Anti-Mining and Anti-Industrialization Movements in India

After independence, Indian leadership went on to pursue economic development through modern industry and agriculture. India was the first country in the non-communist world to begin its post-independence development strategy with comprehensive centralized planning. The Congress Party under the leadership of Jawaharlal Nehru publicly followed Mahatma Gandhi, respected him, used his rhetoric, but ignored his ideals (Omvedt 1989). Instead of following the Gandhian philosophy based on decentralized village society and rejection of modern technology, post-independent India dedicated herself to heavy industry, the public sector and national planning. Gandhi was concerned with the social environment and promoting the 'community', but these elements were largely absent in Nehru's approach (Roy and Tisdell 1992). Nehru believed that industrialization would promote economic interdependence and that would tie the country together (Parekh 1991). He adopted a central planning approach in order to distribute the economic growth among the regions.

Under the theme of 'national needs' independent India introduced several developmental projects that aimed at building large industries and exploiting mining areas all over the country; this policy led to the internal displacement of thousands of poor people. It took some time for the displaced population to realize their freedom to participate in an independent democratic state. Gradually, they participated politically to oppose government policies, which they felt excluded them from the benefits. Having experienced the exploitative colonial rule for centuries, they stood up against the exploitative national policies and also multinational companies. They began by refusing to carry the burden without gaining from it.

In recent years, Indian economy has opened itself up to foreign investment. Several multinational companies who have been engaged in various industrial and mining activities in many parts of the country have provoked strong local protests. Some of these protests are against establishing Special Economic Zones (SPZ) in Maharashtra and Karnataka, strip-mining projects in Jharkhand, an Aluminium plant in Uttarakhand and several mines and steel plants in Orissa. The government supports these projects in the name of development and employment generation in the region, however these 'industrial' projects would displace about 850,000 people (Pugh 2008). The people who are going to be displaced are opposing these projects to protect their home and source of livelihood.

The State of Maharashtra, in a joint venture with Reliance Company is establishing a Special Economic Zone (SEZ) on 35,000 acres of primarily rice fields. This SEZ is outlined by the India Business Directory as the most strategically placed SEZ in the country (India Business Directory 2009). However, this project might displace more than 250,000 people (Pugh 2008). The Visthapan Virodhi Jan Vikas Andolan (People's Movement against Displacement and for Development) is opposing the project to be established.

Since 1994, the people of Kashipur in the northern province of Uttarakhand, are resisting (and so far have prevented) the establishment of bauxite mine and aluminium plant – by a Canadian multinational ALCAN – on their land. The success of the local resistance against the project is remarkable, and it has also managed to receive substantial international support. A Canada based solidarity group supports the residents of Kashipur in their struggle to preserve power over the development of their land and resources and gives the struggle an international character (Alcan't in India Solidarity Campaign 2009). Another Aluminium plant farther South in Orissa is planed by the Indian subsidiary of the UK-based mining giant Vedanta Resources. Their plan of building a new aluminium refinery at Niyamgiri Mountain faces resistance by the local tribe, the Dongira Kondh, for whom the Mountain is 'both home and sacred temple' (Jakesika 2009).

Not far from the Niyamgiri Mountain, the Pohang Steel Company (POSCO), the worlds second largest steel maker, plans to build a new steel plant of 12 million tonne per annum capacity in Orissa. This massive industrial project faces strong opposition by the local communities. The impact of the new plant for the local communities is the seizure of their land and the displacement of 471 families living in seven villages in the Jagatsinghpur district. The founding of the Posco Kshatigrashth Sangharsh Samiti (PKSS) and Posco Pratirodh Sangram Samiti (PPSS) oppose the building of the steel plant and a nearby special port facility at Paradip (Asher 2007).

'Forest' Movements

After establishing the Forest Department in 1864, the British regime took control of India's large forest areas. The 67.83 million hectares of forest, which constitutes 20.64 per cent of India's geographical area, is the second largest form of land use in India till today (WWF India 2009). After destroying the forests in their own country, the colonial rulers embarked upon exploiting Indian forest resources to meet the need of timber for shipbuilding and railway tracks (Gadgil and Guha 1993).[3] Almost everywhere and throughout the colonial period, the take-over of the forest was bitterly resisted by the local population (Gadgil and Guha 1994). Besides the exploitation of forest resources, British rulers also tried to dictate the form of land use for producing raw materials needed for the industrial revolution back home. The setting up of an indigo plantation in eastern India to feed the dye industry and the introduction of a cotton plantation in the west and south of India to feed the textile industry led to the Indigo movement and the Deccan movement for land rights, respectively. However, all these protest movements meant to preserve the rights for land and forest use were usually regarded as a part of a grand national movement or anti-colonial movement. This excluded them from receiving the label of an environmental movement.

With the collapse of the colonial structure, the conflict over natural resources was expected to diminish. However, the resource use policies in independent India (the National Forest Policy of 1952) continued along with the old colonial pattern of the 1894 Forest Policy. This reinforced the right of the state to exclusive control over forest protection, production and management (Gadgil and Guha 1993). The concept of 'reserved forests' was justified in the name of 'national needs'. Maintaining a 'sustained supply of wood for industry' was considered an essential duty of the country (Arora 1994). The rapid expansion of forest-based industries exasperated the situation further. The needs of the commercial–industrial sector now replaced the strategic needs of the colonial power to guide the forest policy in independent India. Powerful corrupt alliances between the bureaucrats, politicians and businessmen emerged in all states and they involved themselves in the large-scale destruction of tree-cover (Bandyopadhyay et al. 1985). As Madsen argues, the sins of commission (exploiting the forest resources) as well as the sins of omission (inability to protect the forest) by the Forest Department resulted in massive deforestation in India (Madsen 1995b). Protest movements in different parts of the country came as a response to the threat of the survival base and as a demand for the conservation of natural renewable resources (Shiva and Bandyopadhyay 1986).

3　Madsen, however argues that the 'fissured lands' which characterize much of India today are not a product of British colonialism but due to centuries old practices of clearing for cultivation and unregulated grazing (Madsen 1995a).

The *Chipko* (Hug the Trees) movement is undoubtedly the most well known of environmental movements in modern India. It emerged in 1973 as a movement of the hill people in the northern state of Uttar Pradesh to save the forest resources from exploitation by outside contractors (Guha 1991). They effectively stopped commercial felling in the nearby forest by threatening to 'hug the trees'. The success of this movement led to a wave of popular protests against commercial logging in the Himalayan region. Due to its novel technique and Gandhian philosophy, the movement acquired quick fame and also inspired the *Appiko* movement in the southern part of India. These movements actively resisted illegal felling of Indian forests and at the same time worked to replant forestlands with multi-purpose broad-leafed tree species. Movements focused on the protection of forests to ensure their survival have also emerged in the tribal belts of the country, particularly in central India. The popular response in the Jharkhand and Bastar areas of central India were against the government's policy to convert the mixed natural forests into a plantation of commercial tree species. The Indian government's reforestation program aimed at planting commercial trees like eucalyptus and teak, which provide only timber and profits for industries and rich farmers, thereby disenfranchising the local people who prefer forests with mixed trees whose leaf, roots, bark, fruit and nuts may be as useful to them as the timber itself (Omvedt 1984).

Each of these protest movements had different demands in different phases but the most common theme was that control of forest ownership and management must revert from the state to communal hands and the local communities should be actively involved in the reforestation programs. Opposition to the Draft Forest Bill of 1982 brought these protests together to form networks at various levels. The proposed Bill aimed to further strengthen the power of the Forest Department, but was successfully resisted by the different forest-based environmental movements all over the country. The Government was therefore forced to reconsider its decision and did not bring the Bill to Parliament for ratification. The protest movements were also successful enough to compel the Government to cancel its commercial reforestation policy in the existing forest areas.

An upsurge in popular protests has brought significant changes in government policy. When Rajiv Gandhi launched the National Wastelands Development Board in 1985, he not only favoured the people's participation but emphasized that only through a people's movement could the catastrophic destruction of forests be arrested and reversed (Mehta 1993). The protest movements were ably assisted by a large number of NGOs in their efforts: the directory of environmental NGOs in India published by the Environmental Service Group of WWF–India in 1989 listed 879 large and small NGOs spread throughout the country who's number grew to over 2,342 environmental NGOs by 2008 (WWF India 2008). Half of those NGOs were involved with forest related issues. This apart, several donor NGOs were also quite actively involved in supporting the endeavour of the local organizations. The success of this collaborative struggle was clearly reflected in the Government of India's National Forest Policy of 1988 and the Circular on Joint Forest Management of 1990. While revising its National Forest Policy in 1988, India for the first time declared that forests were not to be commercially exploited for industries but must contribute to the soil conservation, environmental protection and meet the survival needs of the local population. The revised policy also emphasized the role of the local people's participation in the protection and development of the forests (Arora 1994). In June 1990 the Centre issued guidelines to state governments on involving village communities and voluntary agencies to aid in the regeneration of degraded forestlands on a usufruct sharing basis (Publication Division – Ministry of Information and Broadcasting – Government of India 1996).

In recent years, the forest-based popular protests have successfully asserted the peoples right to manage forests and brought a significant change in the existing forest policy to facilitate that. The Scheduled Tribes (Recognition of Forest Rights) Bill of 2005 has also become a law, which provides mining rights in addition to food-fuel and fodder rights to forest communities. After achieving a somewhat decent success to its demands in the forest sector, the focus of the protest movements in India have now been directed against the building of big dams. The change of focus can also be attributed to the decline of popular interest in a single issue, which is a common characteristic in democratic politics. The new issue has gathered a massive support base for protest movements in India. As the *Second Citizen's Report* of the Centre for Science and Environment claims, the large dams are the most controversial issue in the present-day India (Agarwal and Narain 1985).

Controlling the Big Rivers

India's water requirements have increased manifold in its post-independence period. The massive population growth in the last fifty years has put tremendous pressure on this finite natural resource. Comprising 15 per cent of the world's population, India possesses only 2.4 per cent of the land surface of the world (Sardana, Sangwan, and Grover 1987). In order to meet the country's food demands with limited land resources, highly intensive water agriculture has been undertaken in recent years. Moreover, as the population grows, the average amount of fresh water available to each person declines. The annual per capita fresh water availability in India was 5,277 cubic meters in 1955. In 1990 it came down to 2,464 and is projected to decline to 1,496 by the year 2025 (Engelman and LeRoy 1993).

Besides water scarcity, the country also suffers heavily from the uneven distribution of water resources among various regions. The environment of India is characteristically monsoonal. The rainy season extends four months only, from June to September. About 80 per cent of the annual river run-off passes through in these four monsoon months. The amount of rainfall also varies greatly from the desert areas of Rajasthan to the hills of the Northeast. Jaisalmer of Rajasthan received a paltry 4.6 millimetres of annual rainfall in 2002 (India Water portal 2009), while Cherapunji in Meghalaya gets not less than 11 meters. Floods and droughts also occur regularly from excesses and paucity of rainfall. In addition to the large regional variation in the rainfall, the monsoon character of the river run-off in India has led to human interference with the hydrological cycle for many centuries. For example, in 2500 BC the township of the Indus Civilization emerged in semi-arid North Western India due to flood-channel irrigation for crops along the rivers. The shallow storage across minor river in the peninsular India and excavated ponds in the eastern part of the country have been the traditional methods to improve the supply of water (Johnson 1979). However, the policy of extensive agriculture in the post independence period has brought significant change to these indigenous irrigation systems.

In its post-independence period, the exploitation of the river water has been the focus of Indian planning to meet the country's increasing water demand. The construction of large dams and diversion canals to transport huge quantities of river water from one region to another has been one of the major engineering achievements in the last 50 years. Immediately after independence, the Indian government launched a grand scheme of large-scale river water projects (Swain 1996a). In 1948, 160 large water projects were being considered, investigated or executed, and two years later, 29 per cent of the First Five Year Plan (1951–1955) budget was allocated for that purpose (Hansen 1966). To keep pace with the swelling population, large-scale irrigation schemes were further undertaken to increase agricultural production. Before the Eighth Five Years Plan, 600 billion rupees were spent for various major and medium irrigation projects (Gulati, Svendsen, and Choudhury 1994). In the Eighth Plan also, irrigation development continued to dominate planners' strategy for agricultural growth. More than 220 billion rupees were earmarked for major and medium irrigation schemes (Dhawan 1993). The Ninth, Tenth and Eleventh Five year Plans also followed the same trend.

Physiographic factors favour the successful development of irrigation projects in the Indo-Gangetic Plain. The Himalayan Rivers carry substantial amount of water perennially. Though the discharge is maximum during the rainy season, the melting of Himalayan snows provides a significant flow throughout the dry-season. However, these perennial rivers have not been able to meet the water demand of the 'Green Revolution' in the Indo-Gangetic region. Massive use of water for irrigation purposes has also led to severe water scarcity and struggle among various users to acquire the increasingly scarce water of these perennial rivers. The pattern of water availability and use is different in the southern part of the country. The rivers of peninsular India are usually rain-fed and tend to dry up during summer. Moreover, the majority of the Deccan plateau receives marginal rainfall and is therefore heavily dependent upon their river storages for irrigation

(Roy 1991). Thus, barring the water-abundant regions in eastern India and the long coastal strip below the Western Ghats mountains, the rest of the country is becoming water strapped in the face of increasing demand (Dhawan 1988).

All of the major Indian River basins are inter-state in character. About 77.67 per cent of India's geographical area falls within the inter-state river basins (Chitale 1992). The Indian part of the Indus basin includes five states: Kashmir, Punjab, Himachal Pradesh, Haryana and Rajasthan. The Ganges basin spreads through Himachal Pradesh, Haryana, Delhi, Uttar Pradesh, Rajasthan, Madhya Pradesh, Bihar and West Bengal. The Mahanadi runs through Madhya Pradesh, Maharashtra, Bihar and Orissa. The Godavari basin covers Maharashtra, Madhya Pradesh, Orissa, Karnataka and Andhra Pradesh. The Cauvery runs through Karnataka, Kerala and Tamil Nadu. Other major rivers like the Brahmaputra, Sabarmati, Mahi, Tapi Narmada, Damodar and Pennar are also inter-state rivers (Ramana 1992).

When multiple states are jointly dependent on the same river system problems of reconciling their interests arise. The increasing scarcity of water paves the way for inter-state disputes over the river water. These water sharing conflicts are spawned when upstream states through their water projects affect the quantity and quality of the water flow in the basin and curtail the scope of downstream water use. Besides the usual upstream-downstream conflicts, the inter-basin river water transfers also disturb the riparian rights and lead to inter-state disputes (Shiva 1991). These river disputes are most likely to be more intense and more prolonged whenever water scarcity is acute vis-à-vis the demand.

Dispute over Sharing the River Water

The sharing of inter-state rivers has already led to a number of bitter disputes between different states in India. Some of these disputes have directly or indirectly resulted in violence. Many of these disputes which arose in the post-1950s after the implementation of massive water development projects and reorganization of state boundaries continue to simmer, and the conflicting parties have yet to arrive at any long-term understanding on water sharing. Coinciding with the intensification of the on-going conflicts, a number of new disputes have started emerging in the face of growing water scarcity in the country.

Dispute in the Indus Basin

The 1947 partition line established between India and Pakistan cuts across the Indus and its five tributaries; the upper waters of the rivers are in India, but they all flow into Pakistan. The Indus Water Treaty of 1960 allocated the waters of the three eastern rivers – Ravi, Beas and the Sutlej – to India, while the waters of the western rivers – Indus, Jhelum and Chenab – were for the use of Pakistan.

The Indus Water Treaty brought a water sharing agreement between two arch rivals, India and Pakistan, but the dispute among Indian states still continues over the waters of Ravi, Beas and Sutlej (Corell and Swain 1995). In 1955, the Centre allocated the waters of the Ravi, Beas and Sutlej, between three states: Rajasthan got 8.00 MAF (million acre feet), Punjab (Punjab and Haryana) got 7.2 MAF and Kashmir got 0.65 MAF. For the proper utilization of these rivers, a major multi-purpose surface water project was conceived. The project consists of two units, the Beas dam at Pong and the Beas-Sutlej link. Besides the sharing of the cost of these projects, the dispute also came up over control of the link canal.

After the partition of the state of Punjab in 1966, a conflict surfaced over the respective shares in water. While Haryana demanded 4.8 MAF out of a total 7.2, Punjab claimed total control of the waters. After failing to solve the water sharing issue bilaterally, Haryana requested the Central Government to intervene and allocate the shares. In the time of 'Emergency', the Central Government issued an executive order on 24 March 1976, in which 3.5 MAF of water was allocated to Haryana, 0.2 MAF for Delhi and the balance, not exceeding at any time 3.5 MAF, to Punjab.

This decision of the Central Government invited opposition from Punjab. After coming to power in Punjab in 1977, Akali Dal demanded that the water sharing between Punjab, Haryana and Rajasthan be adjudicated by the Supreme Court (Gupta 1985). The Akali Dal went to the Supreme Court against the Central Government's order of 1976, which was challenged by the State of Haryana as well. After returning to power in 1980, Indira Gandhi started negotiating the issue among the states of Punjab, Haryana and Rajasthan, who had all returned back to Congressional rule. The executive order of 1976 was replaced by an accord on the 31st of December 1981, signed by the Chief Ministers of Punjab, Haryana and Rajasthan. In the new agreement, the Ravi-Beas-Sutlej water was calculated to 17.17 MAF against the earlier 15.85 MAF on the basis of a revised report. This 17.17 MAF was allocated between different states as follows; Punjab: 4.22 MAF, Haryana: 3.50 MAF, Rajasthan: 8.60 MAF, Delhi Water Supply: 0.20 MAF, and Jammu and Kashmir: 0.65 MAF.

Even though the 1981 Accord raised the quota of the state of Punjab from 3.5 MAF to 4.22 MAF, it also asked Punjab to construct the 6,500 cusecs (cubic feet per second) Sutlej Yamuna Link (SYL) Canal in its territory by 31 December 1983 at the latest, to deliver Haryana's share of the water. Akali Dal immediately started campaigning to prevent the construction of the SYL. Rajeev Gandhi while signing the accord with Sant Longwal in July 1985, agreed that the claims of Punjab and Haryana regarding the shares of the water, would be referred for adjudication to a judicial tribunal (*The Times of India*, 28 July 1985). The Centre decided to appoint the Eradi Tribunal to deal with the water dispute, but because of the protest from Haryana and Rajasthan, it did not include riparian principles in its terms of reference. A major faction of the Akali Dal launched a movement against any verdict by the Eradi Tribunal (*The Indian Express*, 5 February 1987). The tribunal in its report increased the water availability by another 1.11 MAF and fixed the quantum of water for each state (Punjab 5 MAF, Haryana 3.83, Rajasthan 8.6, Jammu and Kashmir 0.65 and Delhi 0.2 MAF). This verdict was not acceptable for both Haryana and Punjab and they have filed their representation before the tribunal on which no final decision has been taken (Singh 1997). In 1997, the Chief Minister of Punjab wrote to the Centre to scrap the Eradi Tribunal, which immediately received opposition from the state of Haryana (Banyal 1997).

The construction of the SYL canal has failed to reach its completion due to opposition in Punjab. Various separatist groups in Punjab regularly carried out killings of the migrant non-Sikh labourers till the early 1990s, which created problems that delayed the construction. Punjab has stopped work on its portion of the canal since 1990 after the militants opposed to the water transfer killed an engineer and his deputy (*The Times of India* 1997). With the return of certain normalcy in Punjab since 1993, the Chief Ministers of both Punjab and Haryana met regularly under the auspices of Congress ruled by the Centre to find a solution, unfortunately without any success. The return of the Akali Government in Punjab in 1996 ruled out any water agreement with Haryana. In their election campaign, Akali's had pledged to fill the SYL canal and not to spare a drop of water for any other state (*The Times of India*, 6 November 1997). The Chief Minister of Punjab also declared that Haryana and Rajasthan have no rights to the river waters, as these two states are not the riparian of the Indus river system (*The Indian Express*, 13 March 1997). In spite of Supreme Court intervention, Punjab refused to complete the SYL canal; and in 2004, it unilaterally abrogated all previous accords with its neighbouring state by passing an act in state assembly, which has virtually ended any hope of the resumption of canal construction in near future. After this development, the Haryana government started construction of a new Hansi-Butana canal to unilaterally withdraw water from the Sutlej-Beas rivers. This 109 kilometres long canal is already ready to use, but its operation has been stalled by the court proceedings initiated by Punjab.

Punjab, the breadbasket of India, is facing severe water scarcity. The state receives an average of 570 mm of rainfall during a year. This inadequate rainfall is also ill distributed in time and space. Eighty per cent of this rainfall occurs during four months from June to September. In the foothills, it exceeds 1000 mm but measures hardly 250 mm in the western part of the state (The Indian Express, 1 July 1993). Most of the water resources in the state are used for agricultural purposes. Eighty three per cent of all arable land of Punjab is already being cultivated and it is practically not possible to bring more area under tilling. The total demand for irrigation water is 43.55 MAF. The cropping intensity of Punjab is about 189 per cent (2004–05) and 95 per cent of the total area is under irrigation which is the highest in the country (Singh 1993; Envis Centre Punjab 2005). Canal water irrigates 38 per cent land of command area while the rest is dependent upon ground water. The groundwater table is receding at an alarming rate because of over-exploitation of water resources to meet the agricultural demand.

In the face of increasing water scarcity, Punjab is adamant about retaining all the Indian share of waters from the Indus basin. The water transfer to Haryana and Rajasthan is increasingly becoming difficult for Punjab to accept when its own farmers are in need of irrigation water. However, Haryana and Rajasthan maintain that their demand for water transfer is based on having a large chunk of arid area with a much lower intensity of irrigation compared to Punjab. Haryana also argues for its right over the water as the successor state of reorganized Punjab, and claims to be part of the Indus basin (Chaudhry 1997). The increasing scarcity of water has made it possible for the politicians in Punjab to highly ethnicize the issue. Centre is reluctant to intervene in fear of alienating Sikhs further. The inaction of the Central Government has exasperated the state of Haryana and it has put pressures by occasionally stopping the water supply to the national capital, New Delhi from the river Yamuna.

At the same time, the 1960 Indus Water Treaty with Pakistan restricts the further development of Indus water by India. There have been several disputes over few projects on the Western Rivers between India and Pakistan (Swain 2009). One of them is the issue of Tulbul Navigation Project/Wular Barrage being constructed by India on the Jhelum River to make the river navigable during the lean season. Pakistan is opposed to this project on the ground that it has storage utility. Similarly, Pakistan has shown her reservation to India's construction of Kishenganga hydropower project on Neelam-Jhelum River and Baglihar hydroelectric dam on Chenab River. The recent dispute was over the construction of Baglihar dam. While India insisted that the dam, built on the Chenab River, is meant to generate hydropower only, Pakistan claimed that the project violates the Indus Waters Treaty of 1960 and would divert Pakistan's rightful share of water. An attempt at arbitration requested by Pakistan failed to find a mutually satisfactory agreement. The tensions around the barrage continue in the background while the Indian Government is emphasizing its commitment to enhance the power development in Jammu and Kashmir (Hill 2009). Moreover, India is also worried of increasing Chinese support to Pakistan for large-scale water development projects in the Pakistani controlled Kashmir.

Yamuna River Dispute

The Yamuna is the largest tributary of the Ganges and its total catchment area is 345,848 sq. kilometres in five states, viz., Uttar Pradesh, Himachal Pradesh,

Madhya Pradesh, Haryana, Rajasthan and Delhi. Though Uttar Pradesh, Haryana and Delhi contributes only 21.5, 6.1 and 0.4 per cent of the total catchment area respectively, these states are the major users of this river system (Datta 1992). The increasing water demands of these states have brought them into dispute over sharing the river water. The 'Green Revolution' movement in Haryana and Uttar Pradesh is demanding larger amounts of water, while the urban water requirement has been multiplied in Delhi due to massive population growth. Nearly 30 per cent of Delhi's water supply comes from the Yamuna River.

The present claims of all Yamuna river basin states aggregates to about 26 million acre feet (MAF) while available waters in the river are only between 10 and 11 MAF (*The Times of India*, 17 January 1994). Nearly 90 per cent of these waters are already fully used. Back in 1954, an agreement of water sharing had been reached between Uttar Pradesh and undivided Punjab. According to that agreement, Uttar Pradesh is controlling the Eastern Yamuna Canal and Haryana controls the Western Yamuna Canal. However, from the beginning of 1970s, the problem of water sharing surfaced again. Delhi in order to meet its water supply requirements demanded a revision of traditional water sharing and asked for its own share. Instead of being a buyer of the Yamuna water, Delhi wanted to be a partner in the water sharing.

The ever-growing thirst of the national capital was decided by the powerful Congress Party, which forced the neighbouring states into meeting the city's shortfall. However, in 1988 the non-Congress Chief Minister of Haryana, Devi Lal stopped the water supply to New Delhi for almost a week. The Lok Dal Party leader insisted that local farmers be given priority to the need of the capital (Singh 1994). In December 1989, a draft agreement over water sharing was reached between officials of Delhi and other basin states, but it could not be ratified by the sates concerned. To reach the agreement over Yamuna water sharing, the Chief Ministers of five basin states met no less than eight times between 1990 and 1994. These meetings failed to arrive at any consensus mainly because of refusal of Haryana and Uttar Pradesh to share water with Delhi due to pressure from the powerful farmers lobby (*The Indian Express*, 8 May 1994).

In the summer of 1994, Delhi faced severe water scarcity and most parts of Delhi could not get water for several days. It prompted the Centre to act and at the initiative of the Union Water Minister, all the basin states signed a Memorandum of Understanding (MoU) on 12 May 1994. As per this MoU, Haryana has been allocated 5.73 billion cubic meters (bcm), Uttar Pradesh 4.032 bcm, Delhi 0.724 bcm, Rajasthan 1.119 bcm and Himachal Pradesh 0.378 bcm of Yamuna water annually (*The Indian Express* 1994). With the absence of the Chief Minister of Uttar Pradesh during the official signing of the MoU doubts were raised about the future of the agreement. He had sent his consent for the agreement through fax only. In the beginning of June 1994, Haryana started disputing Delhi's claim on its share of the Yamuna water (*The Indian Express* 25 June 1994). Opposition parties accused the Haryana Chief Minister of selling Haryana's interest and causing water scarcity in the state and that immediately made the Accord a non-starter (*The Indian Express* 25 June 1994).

With the change of the BJP supported government in Haryana, the water-sharing dispute with BJP ruled Delhi subsided for a short while. The Upper Yamuna River Board has come up as per the 1994 agreement to manage the sharing of the river water. However, Delhi is fast heading for severe water crisis. Most parts of the Outer Delhi areas are getting water supply only for two hours during the day Due to massive urban population growth in and around Delhi, an increasing amount of water will need to be diverted from the agricultural sector of neighbouring states to the urban population of Delhi. Haryana has begun complaining that Delhi is withdrawing Yamuna water in excess of its prescribed share. It is not only the quantity of water, but also the quality of water, which has also become the subject of controversy. The discharge of industrial wastes and large-scale use of pesticides by farmers from the Haryana side, have raised the level of pollution in the waters flowing to Delhi. The Delhi High Court, acting on public petition in 1997, seized the matter and had taken the Haryana Government to task (*Deccan Herald* 12 July 1997).

Acting upon another public interest lawsuit of 1992, the Indian Supreme Court passed an order for Haryana on 10 May 2000 to release 125 cusecs of water to Delhi on daily basis. The Supreme Court intervention has brought some respite to Delhi's water agony. However, in the middle of 2007 once again tensions started building up over the Western Yamuna Canal. While the Haryana Irrigation Department wanted to close the canal for several days after the monsoon season, the Upper Yamuna River Board ordered that the channel remain open. The Haryana Irrigation Department argued that the channel needs to be closed for repairs and de-silting. However, the main problem in the dispute is that the Delhi Jal (Water) Board did not release the money it had promised for repairs of the channel. The Delhi Jal Board withheld the money with the reason that Haryana should 'first release 125 cusecs of water for the Nangloi Plant from the supply that is being released from the Bhakra Beas Management Board' (Ramachandran 2007). Growing water scarcity undoubtedly extends the politically volatile Yamuna water-sharing issue for years to come.

The Cauvery River Dispute

The sharing of the Cauvery River has been a strenuous issue between two water starved southern states, Karnataka and Tamil Nadu. In the pre-independence period, there were agreements between the then Mysore and Madras over its water sharing. The riparian dispute started after India's post-independence rush for the construction of big dams. By 1950, a number of large dam projects were planned in Tamil Nadu. Mysore (Karnataka) objected to Madras (Tamil Nadu) taking up these irrigation projects, which violated the 1924 agreement. The pre-independence arrangement which had a 50-year lifespan expired in 1974, and since then numerous unsuccessful efforts have been undertaken to arrive at an acceptable solution of bilateral water sharing. Tamil Nadu wants the continuation of 1924 agreement, while Karnataka asks for the reallocation of water to meet the changing needs.

Acting on a petition filed by the Tamil Nadu Farmers Society, the Supreme Court of India directed the Indian government to organize the Cauvery Waters Disputes Tribunal in 1990. The Tribunal passed an order in June 1991 giving interim relief to Tamil Nadu, where Karnataka was told to release water on a weekly basis from June to May. One month later, the Governor of Karnataka issued an ordinance virtually rejecting the interim relief. However, the Supreme Court supported the jurisdiction of the tribunal and upheld its order of interim relief. Violence erupted in Karnataka, which spread and intensified resulting in arson and eviction of people from their homes, especially Tamils living in slum areas. At the end of December, the violence had spread to Tamil Nadu, where Kannadiga homes were attacked and Kannadiga landowners were driven out.

Since then a number of political initiatives have evolved around the Cauvery issue without any solution to the problem. The issue has been further aggravated recently, after Karnataka's rejection of the Centre's draft scheme for the Cauvery River Authority to monitor implementation of the 1991 award. While the scheme, devised at the directive of the Supreme Court, has been stalled, matters have been complicated further by Karnataka's closure of the Kabini reservoir (*The Indian Express* 22 March 1997).

The total utilization of the Cauvery waters is 671 tmc-ft (thousand million cubic feet), of which Tamil Nadu uses 489 tmc-ft, Karnataka 177 tmc-ft and Kerala 5 tmc-ft (Ramana 1992 Ref 9). Nearly 75 per cent of the catchment areas of the Cauvery basin lie within Karnataka, which provides 53.8 per cent of the total yield, but traditionally its utilization is small. For 50 years after the Mettur dam was completed in 1934, Tamil Nadu farmers used more than 75 per cent of the river water. Due to an increasing population, better techniques and a growing industry, Karnataka has in the last two decades rapidly begun to develop its irrigation system fed by the Cauvery River. A series of dams have since begun construction on several Cauvery tributaries. All these initiatives have heavily reduced the quantum of water available for Tamil Nadu farmers, who have been the traditional users of the river water (Mitra, Warrier, and Shankar 1993).

The conflict over the Cauvery River has escalated sharply in the last decade. Both Karnataka and Tamil Nadu are determined to appropriate more water for themselves. The dispute has become complicated because the river is almost fully utilized. The disagreement is not about the utilization of hitherto untapped waters, but about the redistribution of waters that are already being utilized (Guhan 1993). Politicians in both states are using the Cauvery issue to further their political interests. Tamil Nadu demands the intervention of the Centre to get their share of water from Karnataka. Any action by Karnataka to reduce the flow of the river provides ammunition to Tamil politicians to criticize Delhi. Centre bashing is the surest way to become a cult figure in Tamil Nadu (Swamy and Rai 1993). Karnataka is also eager to add political colour to the disagreement over water sharing. According to an admission by its own Chief Minister, 'The State's stand on the Cauvery water dispute had always been politically recalcitrant instead of practical and pragmatic' (*Deccan Herald* 12 July 1997).

Meanwhile the water sharing negotiation of Cauvery has been complicated further by the emergence of new actors. Kerala, an upper riparian state that contributes water to both Tamil Nadu and Karnataka and Pondicherry, the lowest riparian with little demand, are both hardening their stance on the sharing of river water (Iyer 2002). Kerala has submitted before the Cauvery Tribunal that it wants to increase its share to 99.8 TMC of Cauvery water from the presently allocated 5 TMC, claiming that it contributes 147 TMC to the river (*Deccan Herald*, 17 July 1996). Upset over his State being sidelined from the Centre mediated negotiation, the Chief Minister of Kerala had declared, 'Any agreement between Karnataka and Tamil Nadu on sharing of Cauvery river water will not be binding on his state' (*Deccan Herald* 1996). The over politicization of shared water issue in Kerala has restricted options for the ruling party to be flexible on this issue. The solution to this long-standing dispute over Cauvery water is nowhere in sight, rather it shows all the potential to explode sometime in the near future. In 1998 the Cauvery River Authority (CRA) was established after the Government of India stepped in. Although the establishment of the river authority has decreased some of the tensions, its limited power and politicized setup has stopped it from developing the resources of the basin (Naqvi 2006; Iyer 2002).

Dispute in the Krishna Basin

The River Krishna is the second largest of the east flowing rivers of Peninsular India after Godavari. Its basin includes the states of Maharashtra, Karnataka and Andhra Pradesh. In 1951, in an inter-state conference, the Krishna water was allocated to the then states of Bombay, Hyderabad, Mysore and Madras for 25 years. The reorganization of the states on a linguistic basis in the 1950s brought territorial changes and limited the Krishna basin to the three riparian states. In view of these changes, demands to scrap the 1951 sharing agreement and reallocate the Krishna water were opposed by the Andhra Pradesh state. As the riparian states could not reach any agreement, the Centre appointed the Gulhati Commission to assess the availability of water supplies in the Krishna and Godavari rivers. Because of the lack of adequate data on river flow, the Commission could not positively estimate the available water supplies. To avoid the impasse, the Centre intervened and made certain a tentative allocation of Krishna water to the riparian states till the expiry of the 1951 Agreement. In addition, 15 tmc of Krishna water were kept aside for the Madras City of Tamil Nadu to provide drinking water (Jain, Jacob, and Jain 1971). In spite of this interim allocation, the difference among the riparian states persisted.

In 1976, seven years after its formation, the Krishna Dispute Tribunal headed by Justice Bachawat finally presented an allocation plan. It allocated 700 tmc of Krishna water to Karnataka, 800 to Andhra Pradesh and 560 to Maharashtra. This 2060 tmc of water was calculated as the total yield of the Krishna Basin with a 75 per cent rate of dependability. The states were asked to utilize their allocations before the year 2000, after this the awards will be reviewed to decide the sharing of excess water available in Krishna at a 100 per cent rate of dependability. In their effort to show maximum utilization of Krishna waters, all the riparian states are in a hurry to build large reservoirs (Down to Earth 1996). One of these projects, Almatti dam, has recently raised a bitter political fight between Andhra Pradesh and Karnataka.

Karnataka plans to raise the height of the Almatti dam from its original 519 meters to 524.25 meters. Andhra Pradesh fears that its project, built downstream of the Almatti dam will be redundant once Karnataka goes ahead with its expansion plan. The collection of excess waters by Karnataka would harm the interests in the command area under Nagarjunsagar and Srisailam projects in Andhra Pradesh. Karnataka has rejected arguments by Andhra Pradesh and has determined to use its share of water. The embers of the on-going bilateral conflict over the dam height got rekindled with the disclosure of the Centre's allocation of 2 billion rupees in August 1996. Karnataka, being the home state of the then Prime Minister Deve Gowda further complicated the matter and this issue threatened the United Front Government at the Centre (Nagaraj 1996).

The Central Government, in order to get out of this political predicament, formed a committee of four chief ministers to decide the issue on the basis of the report by an expert panel. The 'neutral' experts came up with their findings in March 1997 and opined that the raising of the dam height by Karnataka is an unnecessary act. Karnataka refused to accept this report and instead an all-party resolution by the state assembly approved the go ahead of the Almatti dam expansion (*The Indian Express*, 22 March 1997). To counter this, Andhra Pradesh approached the Supreme Court. This issue inflamed passions in both Andhra Pradesh and Karnataka and turned to become politically suicidal for any state politician to offer any concession in order to reach an agreement.

Besides Almatti, Karnataka and Andhra Pradesh are also in dispute over the Hippargi Barrage (*Deccan Herald*, 18 September 1996) and Upper Tunga River

Project (Machaiah 1997) in the Karnataka side of the Krishna basin. While both Andhra Pradesh and Karnataka are fighting over their shares, they jointly oppose the projects undertaken by Maharashtra on the upstream of the River Krishna. Ignoring the opposition, Maharashtra has asserted its insistence on collecting its share of Krishna water by the turn of this century (*The Indian Express*, 30 May 1997). Out of its share of 594 tmc, till 1996 Maharashtra has been able to impound 447 tmc of Krishna water. To utilize the balance before the review of the award, Maharashtra has imposed a 55 per cent cut on government expenditures in order to transfer the resources to its ambitious Krishna Valley Development project (*Deccan Herald*, 12 July 1997).

In August 2003 the Centre Government formed a tribunal to discuss the Krishna water issue, but has been unable to solve the problem. In 2008, Karnataka filed a complaint to the Union Water Resource Ministry, alleging that large-scale projects undertaken by Andhra Pradesh and Maharashtra would endanger the interests of its farmers in the Krishna valley. The growing water scarcity in this part is certainly going to intensify the dispute over the sharing of Krishna water in the near future (Outlookindia.com, 27 September 2008).

Politics over Water

After India's independence, the policy makers had taken water availability for granted while planning the country's path towards development. Acute water scarcity has now posed the threat of constraining not only the development process but also to the survival of a large number of the population. A sizeable number of big dams have been built, but the overall efficiency of these dams is in the order of 35 to 40 per cent. In addition, the rate of silting in some of the major reservoirs has already been alarmingly high. Steady denudation of forest cover in catchment areas and animal grazing of the hill slopes has gradually contributed to the higher rate of silting. Hundreds of dams remain incomplete due to scarcity of funds. Popular protests against displacement and inadequate rehabilitation measures have also contributed to delay the execution of several dam projects (Swain 1997).

About 82 per cent of water is used to irrigate agricultural land in India, while industrial and domestic sectors consume the rest. The country now spends about 50 billion rupees annually for the development of new major and medium irrigation projects. The official view is that the annual runoff from the country's rivers can be best utilized through large-scale irrigation works. However, the irrigation systems are not self-sustaining because the price charged for water has been kept very low. During 1951 to 1990, more than 600 billion rupees (at 1988–89 prices) were spent to create a huge canal network, but the direct financial recovery from these schemes was less than 3 billion rupees (Gulati, Svendsen, and Choudhury 1994). This huge cost-benefit difference has reduced the performance of these irrigation systems. Due to inadequate maintenance, the country has failed to efficiently utilize the irrigation potential already created by the water projects. The highly subsidized irrigation water is also insufficient to achieve the targeted growth rate in the agricultural sector. Government statistics show that in the 1990s (1991–97), the agriculture sector expanded by an average of just 2.9 per cent a year, though the target of the Ninth Plan was 4.5 per cent. The agricultural growth rate has now substantially slowed compared to the 1980s, when the registered annual growth was 4.5 per cent. This has raised serious doubts about the sustainability of growth in food production and also the future of intensive irrigation based agriculture. The heavy emphasis on large expensive water projects has not only failed to meet the irrigation needs, but they have been the source of bitter disputes between various states.

Nearly 60,000 villages of India still remain without potable water, forcing the women and children of these villages to walk several miles in order to fetch water. This is true even for the state of Orissa, which has an annual rainfall of 1,500 millimetres and the highest ratio of river to land in the country. It is not just the villages that are facing the water shortages. In the summer seasons, many of the cities including the national capital New Delhi do not receive water supply for days together.[4] All these reflect the abject failure of the country's water management policy. Contributing further to India's vulnerability to water conflicts.

There is a serious apprehension among international experts and policy makers that 'water wars' may be inevitable between different nations due to increasing water scarcity in the face of growing demand (Swain 1996). There may be differences of opinion about the war inducing tendencies of the river water resources in the international scene, but it has certainly precipitated many serious conflicts inside of the Indian Union. The list of inter-state river disputes in India is a very long one: Karnataka and Maharashtra's conflict over the Bhima River, Gujarat, Maharashtra and Madhya Pradesh's over Narmada, Gujarat and Rajasthan's over Mahi, Bihar and Uttar Pradesh's over Sone, Karnataka and Goa's over Mahadayi, to mention a few. Most of these river disputes are protracted in nature, and besides souring bilateral relations they have slowed development activities. Due to projected future demand for water – for irrigation, hydropower, industry and urban consumption – many new conflicts over this resource are beginning to unfold. They could soon flare up with a vengeance (Bandyopadhyay 1994).

The quantity issue has been the most important rationale for inter-state disagreements over the sharing of common river resources. In order to address the quantity issue, many new projects are being undertaken for water resource

---

4 According to a national daily, there are scores of eligible bachelors in a cluster of villages in south-west Delhi. Nobody wants to marry them because their villages do not get drinking water (Joshi 1997).

exploitation to increase the water supply. These new projects are also a factor fuelling social conflicts by altering the landscape and livelihood of many non-state actors. In recent years, India has witnessed an upsurge in new grassroots organizations, which are primarily involved with water distribution and management. The emergence of these new actors, i.e. water users' associations, has also complicated the process of water sharing negotiations between states.

The water sharing issue is increasingly becoming politicized in India. In the 1996 general elections, water as an issue figured prominently in at least nine states (Thakkar 1996). To attain political benefits, the state elites are also using the river water sharing issue to stir up ethnic identification of their people vis-à-vis other states and even against the Centre. Indus Water is being used by Akali Dal to kindle Sikh identity in Punjab, while the dwindling runoff of the Cauvery has helped the state politicians to awaken the identities of Tamils and Kannadigas in Tamil Nadu and Karnataka. The increasing water scarcity may further exacerbate the problems of national integration of India, whose state structure is already weakened by strong ethnic identities.

Challenges of Growing Water Scarcity

There is an urgent need for a comprehensive national policy on river waters management to avoid inter-state disputes. There have been several attempts in this regard, but politicking is blocking the way of better utilizing river waters as an invaluable national asset. In India's federal structure, a national consensus is required to plan for a river basin as a whole. While the water shortage states are strongly in favour of declaring major rivers as national assets, others, who have to contribute, resist the idea. Till now, there does not exist even a single river basin authority in India. State identities have proved too strong to allow a central planning authority to take charge of river resource use that crosses state boundaries for more optimal use of the of the water basins (Iyer 1994).

While the country has not yet been able to manage and develop the rivers on a basin based perspective, the planners in Delhi have regularly demonstrated the fancy idea of large-scale inter-basin river water transfer. In September 1996, partly to pacify the warring South Indian states, the Centre set up a ten-member commission to plan for the inter-linking of the major rivers of the country (*Deccan Herald*, 18 September 1996). The formation of this commission is the culmination of decades of debate on linking the rivers to transfer surplus basins water to deficit basins. Dr K.L. Rao who was India's irrigation minister in the 1960s first put forward the proposal of inter-linking rivers of the north with the south. His idea to transfer Himalayan water to the southern peninsula was also followed by another ambitious scheme called 'Garland Canals' by Captain Dastoor. Though these schemes have a certain political appeal for the southerners, they are all outside the practical realm, technically as well as financially (Dhawan 1987). Realising this, water engineers now contemplate the national planning in two components: first, the Himalayan component, aiming at connecting the perennial Himalayan rivers such as the Ganges, Yamuna and Brahmaputra for the drought-prone areas in the north and the second; and the peninsular component, for linking up the east-flowing and west-flowing rivers in the south by two separate canals. Though this scheme is less ambitious than the earlier ones, its execution will not be smooth either.

Since 1982, India has been carrying out detailed studies for inter-linking its major rivers. In December 2002, the Indian government appointed a task force to complete the feasibility studies for the linking of rivers and implementation of the projects by the end of 2016. The idea is through about 260 links, to transfer water from river basins with 'excess' water to deficient river basins (Alagh, Pangare, and Gujja 2006). According to some Indian Press reports, the Indian plan contemplates to transfer some of the Brahmaputra water to the peninsular rivers, like Mahanadi in Orissa and Godavari and Krishna in Andhra Pradesh. India's insistence on working bilaterally with Nepal for the augmentation of the Ganges water is perceived by Bangladesh as India's desire to utilize the increased water supply to meet its growing demand in the highly populated northern states. Moreover, India also needs increased supply in the Ganges for its proposed Ganga-Cauvery link.[5] India's interest in the Ganges-Brahmaputra Link-Canal multiplies due to its potential as an excellent navigable connection between its troubled north-eastern states.

Besides adverse environmental effects, these inter-basin water transfer schemes will be politically unfathomable. A feasibility plan for linking east-flowing peninsular rivers recently prepared by the national experts has classified Mahanadi in Orissa and the Godavari in Andhra Pradesh as surplus rivers and Krishna in Andhra Pradesh and Cauvery in Tamil Nadu as deficit rivers (The Hindu, 28 August 1997). Any attempt to carry out the plan from surplus to deficit basins will not only infuriate the existing river sharing disputes in this part, it will also likely introduce many new conflicts between the new actors.

In general, inter-basin water transfer has always been a conflict inducing option. A number of large-scale water transfer schemes have been planned all over the world but most of them are not being implemented due to political-environmental reasons. Even in the United States, two major water diversion schemes are being

---

5   The Government of India has, for a long time, been contemplating a big water resources project, which is known as the Ganga-Cauvery link. The proposed 2,500 kilometres long canal would link the Ganges River in the north (from a point near Patna in the state of Bihar) with the Cauvery River (this river has been the cause of a serious conflict between two Indian states, Tamilnadu and Karnataka for some years) in the south.

kept under wraps, though its south-western part is facing severe water scarcity. These proposed transfer plans are: (1) Alaska to California by under-sea pipeline; (2) Alaska to Canada to USA to Mexico through rivers and canals. Before embarking upon any new inter-basin water transfer projects, the Indian water experts need to learn from their own experiences if they do not want to look outside. The political and environmental problems associated with long distance water transfer projects like Sutlej Yamuna Link, Indira Gandhi Canal and Telugu Ganga Project should be sufficient enough to deter them from carrying out any future projects of this nature. Moreover, when the individual states are becoming politically powerful at the cost of the Centre after the collapse of the 'Congress System', the inter-state water transfer at the behest of the Centre is not an easy task anymore.

To prevent water scarcity, large-scale water transfer projects may not provide the right answer. Water resource exploitation in an environmentally unsustainable manner will never be able to meet increasing demand; rather it will bring further human and political crises. There is a need for basin based river management and adjustment of irrigation and crops keeping in mind the water availability of that region. Instead of diverting rivers, emphasis may be given to the transfer of 'virtual water' – water intensive agricultural products can be produced in water surplus areas and the water deficit regions may import those products.[6] This form of water transfer may not lead to political and environmental problems. There also is a need for an overall better irrigation management to increase food production with the limited availability of water.

Water is not as plentiful as is commonly believed. It is a scarce resource and its use should be restricted. It should not be treated as a free commodity either. The pricing of water, which could ensure the efficient and reduced use of this scarce resource, is not being implemented properly due to political considerations. Water pricing needs to be adjusted on the basis of economics rather than politics. Most of the Indian states lack institutional mechanisms to manage the distribution of water and collection of water revenues. Institutions, particularly the ones that deal with water resources have been slow to transform in the face of new changes, usually lagging behind the need for appropriate policies. State institutions also need to be strengthened to meet the challenges of the water scarcity. Unless the water scarcity issue is handled by an ingenious national water management policy, river water conflicts may soon create serious dangers for the development as well as unity of the country in the near future.

---

6   Professor Tony Allan of the School of Oriental and African Studies (SOAS), London has coined the term 'virtual water'.

Movements against Big Dams

Immediately after independence, India faced the food scarcity due to division of the country and subsequent huge population displacement. In the First Five Year Plan (1951–1955), 'young' India emphasized the increasing of agricultural production, and 29 per cent of the total budget was allocated to irrigation (Hansen 1966). After achieving growth in agricultural production, Professor P.C. Mahalanobis's development blueprint[7] was adopted in the Second Five-Year Plan, which established a 'mixed' economy structure. This strategy produced a dominant public sector in India that operated the industrial infrastructure and laid the ultimate emphasis on heavy industries. The energy requirement for the rapid industrialization and the need of water supply to achieve agricultural growth was increasing. This led the central government to give priority in building multi-purpose large dam projects. In the post independent period, Nehru launched these surface water development projects on a massive scale and in the very first year of his Prime Ministership, the construction of 160 large-dams was being considered, investigated or executed. Since then, the Government of India has indulged in a dam building spree as the panacea for shortages of irrigation water and electricity.

Beside the goal of achieving agricultural and industrial growth, Nehru's priority in building large-scale dams can also be attributed to other reasons. In the early years of independence, the mission of his leadership was to keep the country united, so the agenda for integration had a high priority at that time. For Nehru, national unity or national integration was the *sine qua non* of national independence (Parekh 1991). By allocating these centrally planned huge projects, which had become a 'symbol of prestige with local pressure groups' (Sen 1962: 17), the Indian leadership effectively brought various local political elites and the regions they represented to the national mainstream. No doubt, big dam projects helped the Central leadership to buy the loyalty of the local elites; it also helped the local elites to strengthen their own positions. The local elites used these projects to provide irrigation and electricity to buy the support of their constituency at the time of elections.

The massive dam projects taken up in the immediate post-independence period were the Bhakra Nangal Project on the Sutlej River in the North, Damodar River Valley Project and Hirakud Dam on the Mahanadi in the east and the Nagarjunasagar Project on the Krishna in the south. These projects, even today, continue to be some of the largest and highest in the world. The Hirakud Dam is still the longest dam in the world, whereas the Nagarjunasagar is the largest

---

7   The blueprint for Indian economic development was outlined on Nehru's invitation, by the distinguished statistician and planner Professor P.C. Mahalanobis and it is described by India's well-known economist Sukhamoy Chakravarty as 'still probably the single most significant document on Indian planning' (Chakravarty 1987: 3).

masonry dam and the Bhakra dam has one of the highest concrete gravity dams (Shah 1993). When Jawaharlal Nehru proclaimed that the big dams were the temples of modern India, he failed to realize the basic historical truth. Any huge monument of yester years had left behind a large section of the people who paid the price for its construction without getting any benefits. But, these 'modern temples', in addition, displaced massive populations and brought adverse changes to their living condition (Fernandes 1993).

The large river valley projects submerged vast areas of forest and agricultural land. The displacement of huge population by the projects of 1950s was not able to evoke any serious popular protest. The atmosphere of the early post-independence period was one of intense excitement and pride in the valour of the vision. The economic stagnation and financial timidity of the days of the empire were being replaced by a semblance of passion for speedy social progress, which was to be achieved through a trailblazing combination of the most advanced modern technology and massive popular mobilization. The celebration of the idea of modern development received little resistance from any front. The implementation of large development projects was carried out on a notion of the 'national interest', so that every local interest was morally compelled to make sacrifices. This is the attitude with which each community made way for big dams in post-independence India (Shiva 1994). The few voices of dissent were too weak to be seriously considered and they were dismissed as obstructionists to the path of progress. Even a democrat like Nehru arrogantly dismissed the powerful criticism posed by the Socialist leader Dr Ram Manohar Lohia against large dams and river-valley schemes. As Harsh Sethi described in early 1990s, 'Lohia's essays on these themes find a far more receptive audience today, more than two decades after his death, than they ever did while he was alive' (Sethi 1993: 124).

Besides a litany of environmental problems, the construction of large dams resulted in massive population displacement. Among the displaced population were often a sizable number of tribal people. There is a lack of reliable data on the exact number of these displaced people. While Vijay Paranjpye estimates the total number of people displaced by dam related construction since 1951 to 1985 are 21 million (Paranjpye 1990), Walter Fernades calculated this figure to a minimum of 14 million till 1990 (Fernandes 1993). The official figures also vary from one document to another. However, the number of displaced people in each and every estimate is quite high. Moreover, the rehabilitation of the displaced population has been extremely limited and unsuccessful (see Baboo 1991; Dalua 1993; Maloney 1990–1991; Singh 1985; Thukral 1992). In most cases, cash compensation was paid and it became subjected to corruption and exploitation. When the land was given, it was often inferior and unproductive. The landless people received nothing for their displacement. All these experiences led the rural population to believe that the large dams were mainly built to satisfy vested interest groups who intend to reap most of the benefits from these projects. Hence, the very people whose wealth and welfare the projects were supposed to enhance have ended up worse off economically and demoralized socially.[8] This led to their reluctance to make sacrifices for the projects of 'national interest'.

From the late 1970s, a new trend seems to have emerged. The opposition to the dam projects is steadily increasing. People in many areas, who are being adversely affected by the river-valley projects, are organizing. The mobilization is taking place from the grass roots level and in several cases, gradually spreading to the other areas. Not only directly displaced people, but also others in that river basin region are also increasingly participating in these protest movements on the grounds of environmental considerations. As Rajni Kothari describes the phenomenon, 'A revolution of right is on the upswing and becoming central to the democratic enterprise ... the rights of millions of people displaced, unemployed, and ravaged by 'development projects' (Kothari 1989a: 58). Besides the displacement of the population, issues like deforestation, water logging, down-stream water shortages, siltation and salinization are surprisingly key issues in the agendas of these protests. In some areas, voluntary groups coming from outside the affected areas are taking active roles in mobilizing and organizing these popular actions. These external groups or individuals are generally independent and non-professionals without having any political party or institutional affiliation. They are primarily motivated to arouse a conscious collective action against exploitation and oppression at a local level.

For a long time, popular opposition has developed against the Tehri dam project on the Bhagirathi River in the Himalayan region. With the active support and leadership of respected *Chipko* leader Sunderlal Bahuguna, the *Tehri Baandh Virodhi Sangarshan Samiti* (Committee for the Struggle Against the Tehri Dam) has been successful in blocking the building of the dam. This Russian-aided mammoth dam project has received widespread non-violent resistance from the local people. The other well-known *Chipko* leader, Chandi Prasad Bhatta, is leading another movement against the Vishnuprayag Dam on the Alakananda River in the same region. The tribal people in the Jharkhand region, who successfully resisted the government's effort of commercial plantation in the forestlands, have now taken up campaigns against the Koel-Karo dams in Bihar under the banner of *Jharkhand Visthapith Mukti Sangh*. The farmers and agricultural labourers from the regions of Ramanjeri and Thirukkandalm in Tamil Nadu are also campaigning against the state government's proposal to build two storage dams for storing excess water that the Poondi Dam cannot hold.

---

8   This argument is based on the views expressed by Dr George Mathew, Director, Institute of Social Science in a workshop at Delhi University (Chandhoke and Ghosh 1995).

One of the very few complete success stories among the 'dam protests' is the one against 'silent Valley Hydroelectric Project' in the state of Kerala. When it became clear that the dam would inflict considerable harm to the tropical rain forest, *Kerala Sastra Sahitya Parishad* (KSSP) became interested in the issue. KSSP is a local organization dedicated to the popular science education among common people. It is an association of school and college teachers, which has a widespread network among the villagers and its membership includes people at all levels of society. In spite of the opposition from the state government and political parties, KSSP organized several mass signature campaigns and public discussion forums in rural and urban areas. This helped to start a debate among intellectuals and policy planners in the state. KSSP also conducted classes on the 'silent Valley' Dam issue, which brought the common population to the debate. Its network all over the state helped to mobilize the people in Kerala opposing the dam. Besides KSSP, a large number of other local and national organizations also participated in the 'save the Silent Valley' movement. This well-organized popular protest successfully changed the government's decision and the project was cancelled in 1984.[9] Another successful protest movement, which is rarely reported, was against the Bedthi project in Karnataka. Farmers in northern Karnataka organized seminars and discussions and conducted impassioned lobbying which led the government to abandon the project in the early 1980s (Sharma and Sharma 1981).

Undoubtedly, India's most high profile dam protest movement is over the building of dams on the Narmada River. The Narmada is India's largest west-flowing river. It originates in eastern Madhya Pradesh, then skirts MP, Maharashtra, and Gujarat and finally runs through Gujarat and empties into the Gulf of Khambhat. First designed in the 1950s as part of Jawaharlal Nehru's vision, the plan is to harness the Narmada River in western India by building series of dams and canal in its basin. In many respects, the movement in the Narmada valley represents a significant proportion of those who will be affected by the Sardar Sarovar Dam Project (SSP), the terminal dam of this whole huge project. SSP will be the second largest concrete gravity dam in the world and form a reservoir that will submerge a total of 34,996 hectares in MP, Maharashtra, and Gujarat, including 248 villages with a population of 66,593 (Wood 1993). There are claims that when the total Narmada Project gets fully completed, it may displace over two million people (Kothari and Parajuli 993).

The affected people are both tribal and non-tribal population in three states, Gujarat, Madhya Pradesh and Maharashtra in the western part of India. After receiving conditional clearance in 1987 from the central government, the work of the SSP commenced. The protest for better compensation to the oustees was started from the village levels of non-tribal areas in Gujarat in the beginning of

---

9   For a detailed account of KSSP's organizational structure and its contribution to the 'save the 'silent Valley' movement (Zachariah and Sooryamoorthy 1994).

the 1980s. The rate of literacy is significantly higher among the non-tribal and they are more informed about the effects of the dam (Multiple Action Research Group 1990). Their village based social organizations played an important part in the inception of the protest and the demand of the protesters was better resettlement. One of the earliest groups in Gujarat was the Chhatra Yuva Sangharsh Vahini (student-youth struggle force); formed to demand for the people from nineteen Gujarati villages to be submerged by the SSP. Gujarat government was forced to accept these demands for better compensation by this group through a series of non-violent protests and legal proceedings. This group also directly participated in the resettlement processes initiated by the government. The protest for the better compensation in Gujarat, started from the grass-root level and later on, became coordinated by an umbrella organization, named 'Arch-Bahini'. The grass-root involvement, early mobilization, and awareness of positive as well as negative effects of the project have led to success of this protest movement, which has been able to achieve its objective in giving adequate compensation to the affected population. According to many, in the Gujarat side, the resettlement programme has become a relatively successful story. Due to government support and help, people who were previously leading a hand-to-mouth existence are living in relative comfort and have hand pumps, biogas plants, and street lights.

However, the story of an affected tribal population living in the forests of Madhya Pradesh and Maharashtra is different. They had no access to the information about the project like their non-tribal counterparts in Gujarat. In 1985, after several years of protest by the no-tribal population in Gujarat, the outside voluntary action groups and human rights and environmental activists mainly from the nearby big cities, Bombay and Delhi mobilized the tribes to protest. They formed the Narmada Ghati Navnirman Samiti (Narmada Valley new awakening committee) in MP and the Narmada Ghati Dharangrastha Samiti (Narmada Valley committee for the dam affected) in Maharashtra. Later, these groups merged to form the Narmada Bachao Andolan (Save the Narmada movement).[10] The protests in the tribal areas have been more radical and an outsider, the charismatic Medha Patkar, has led them. In 1989, the famous social activist Baba Amte and his supporters joined their ranks also. The selective information is provided to the tribal population by their organizers (Multiple Action Research Group 1990). Medha Patkar and Baba Amte are also using the novel form of protest 'jal samparan' (drowning in the water) after over exhausting their usual form of challenging through 'fasting'. The opposition of the tribal population to the dam only picked up when the reservoir water reached their household and they started demanding the cancellation of the project. Though, this protest has been able to change the mind of external donors, i.e., World Bank and Japan, and has received tremendous attention of both the national and

---

10   An impressive study on this protest movement has been written by Amita Bayiskar (Baviskar 1995).

international media, the project work is still going on. It is true that the protest movement of the tribal population started after few years of construction of the dam and the affected people could not be properly informed about the effects of the dam construction. They have been unsuccessful in their late demand to cancel the project altogether. It was unlikely that the Narmada projects would have been terminated at that late stage of the work. The issues for the protesters could have been to achieve the best possible protection and compensation, and to ensure that the least possible damage would be inflicted on the environment. However, due to occasional violent nature of the protest movement and non-cooperation from the affected population, the rehabilitation schemes have been also a failure in comparison to the Gujarat side.

The success in the Silent Valley and the high profile movements against the Narmada and Tehri Projects have set the stage for an intense questioning of these development schemes. Nearly one hundred groups from across the country have already formed the National Campaign Against Big Dams, which has helped to generate a debate around the policy. This network has brought together various organizations and movements from different parts of the country and has given them a unified voice. The environmental movements starting with locally based opposition to individual dam projects has moved to a critique of the states path towards development and asked for 'alternative' development of the country (Omvedt 1994).

The model of development adopted by the newly independent India diminished the rural poor people's power and ability to control and use natural resources. Every development project was presented as beneficial for the masses and the rural poor were often asked to make all the sacrifices. But now that they suspect the benefits go to the privileged few they are pressuring the government to redesign the pattern and extent of natural resources utilization to ensure social equality and environmental sustainability (Bandyopadhyay and Shiva 1988). In the context of a limited natural resource base and unlimited 'biased' development planning, the environmental movements have brought together the poor and marginalized people from various parts of India in order to struggle to protect their interest and survival.

Growing Number of Protests in Indian Democracy

Protests against population displacement and environmental destruction in India now pose a serious challenge to the dominant ideology of meaning and patterns of development. While doing so, they are not being bound or guided by any particular philosophy. One protest movement differs from another in its way of expressing demands, organizing the struggle and also in its perceptions about the development. Activists like Bahuguna are against any cutting of natural forests while Chandi Prasad Bhatt is not averse to the idea of some cutting to provide employment to the local population. In the protests against dams, some groups are against any big dam, some are willing to tolerate dams if they do not cause much harm to the environment, and others are not worried about dams or the environment but are concerned about proper rehabilitation of the displaced population. These movements represent a wide spectrum of groups and activities, which cut across specific regions and issues. They mobilize large masses of people, organize popular resistances that cut across political and social barriers, and create new socio-political actors in the country. The movement represents a wide range of collectives that fall outside the existing institutionalized groups of society (Augustine and Sharma 1995).

Guha in his effort to distinguish between the 'private' and 'public' face of Indian environmentalism identifies three ideological strands: Crusading Gandhian, Appropriate Technology, and Ecological Marxists (Guha 1988). *Crusading Gandhians*, while rejecting the modern way of life, uphold the traditional village community life as the protector of environmental and social harmony. Influenced by western socialism, *Appropriate Technology* strives to combine agriculture and industry, large and small units of production and modern and traditional technology. And, the *Ecological Marxists* have arrived at environmentalism after their protracted engagement with Marxism. In another study, Peritore also finds three types of environmental opinions among Indians: Greens, Eco-developers and Managers (Peritore 1993). *Greens,* by rejecting the western developmental model, favour the empowerment of people. *Eco-developers,* advocate changing India's developmental model to small-scale, environmentally friendly, intensive development. For the *Managers,* rational management of economic growth is desirable to incorporate environmental concerns. This ideological plurality in Indian environmentalism has helped to widen the sphere of the protest movements and sharpen the terms of the debate. Moreover, it has also facilitated the formation and collaboration of a varied number of protest organizations in Indian society.

In recent years, voluntary organizations have increasingly been viewed as an integral part of the process of development of the country (Mukherjee 1994). Hundreds of these organizations are now working at the micro-level to deal with developmental problems (Agarwal 1994). As part of these volunteer organizations' agenda of environmental concerns are relatively new but an overwhelming prevalent phenomenon. From the beginning of the last decade, almost all them have been working with environmental issues (Pandey 1991). India has witnessed in recent years an upsurge of new grassroots organizations, which are primarily involved with development and environmental issues. Community groups and non-governmental organizations (NGOs) constitute the major part of this grassroots movement. Community organizations have emerged due to local initiatives and also in some cases as a part of the social tradition to protect their rights and environment. NGOs, on the other hand are the local or external interveners who are creating and supporting such community groups in their efforts. In the present, more than 2,342 NGOs are involved in environmental issues alone in India (WWF India 2008). There has also been the resurgence of social action groups in the country (Paul 1989; Sharma 1992). Such groups are operating among the weaker sections of society and mobilizing them to fight in order to protect their interest and environment.

The National Alliance of People's Movement has brought together most of these organizations from a mixture of ideological traditions, but their rallying slogan is 'Vinash Nahin, Vikas Chahiye' (Development, not Destruction) (Bakshi 1996). With the new slogan, they have formed a popular network, which defies the regional boundaries and unifies the people from various streams. This effort is representative of the recent trends of non-party political activism in India today. Protest organizations are fighting the battle on a social plane rather than on a political one (Khator 1988). They have contributed to a new development that attracts a conventionally apolitical populace into expressing and fighting for their basic rights to participate in the decision-making process of the country in order to protect their interests. The 'civil society' function of the protest organizations includes both the 'supply side' approach, concentrating on the delivery of the development projects and the 'demand side' approach, helping people to articulate their concerns and participate in the development process. This participatory process restrains the power of the state and also helps to bring it under the control of society. Like its many other counterparts in India's civil society, protest organizations are working as a unifying force, while acting as a vital instrument for checking the potential abuses and violations of the law by the government, and subjecting them to public scrutiny.

Chapter 3
Kerala: The State of Successful Protest Mobilization

India can learn a lot from the experiences of other countries, which have done, in different ways, better than we have. More on that presently, but we must also note the fact that India has much to learn from India itself. We live in most diverse country, and in many spheres our records are extremely disparate. The average levels of literacy, life expectancy, infant mortality, etc., in India are enormously adverse compared with China, and yet in all these respects Kerala does significantly better than China (Sen 1997: 7).

As it has been discussed in the last chapter, India has managed to maintain its democratic structure for more than six decades with having a deeply divided society. Indian politics went through a period of serious uncertainties in the 1980s and 1990s (Bardhan 1984; Kohli 1990; Kothari 1989a; Kothari 1989b; Rudolph and Rudolph 1987). The last two decades of the 20th Century were quite difficult for India as it faced violent secessionist movements in many of its key states like Kashmir, Punjab, Assam and few other North Eastern states. Moreover, its secular political system was severely challenged by the assassinations of Indira Gandhi and Rajeev Gandhi, pogrom against Sikhs in 1984, demolition of the controversial Babri Mosque in 1992 and the following massive religious riots between Hindus and Muslims. India has managed to sustain and develop its secular democratic fabric in spite of all these challenges and has entered into the 21st century with having a much secure political health. However, the country is still not only maintains diversity in culture and tradition, there is also huge difference in political and socio-economic development between different regions of the country.

Kerala is one of the smaller states in India and lies in the southwest coast of the Indian peninsula. Its area of 38,863 square kilometres represents approximately one per cent of the total land area of India. The state was created by the 1956 States Reorganization Act, which reshaped the federal state structure of the Indian subcontinent along language lines. The state of Kerala was formed in 1956 by the merger of former princely states of Travancore and Cochin, and the Malabar District of Madras province and the Kasaragod District of the erstwhile princely state of Mysore. Malayalam is the principal language in Kerala and 96 per cent of the 36.8 million people speak this language (Government of India – Ministry of Home Affairs 2001).

In spite of its recent official creation, the state possesses a long-standing societal history, including many myths and traditions that shaped the social and cultural attitudes of its people over the years. Kerala has a tradition of maintaining high degrees of social and gender equality as well as religious harmony. At the time of the Malayalam new-year celebrations, Kerala people remember the myth of Mahabali or Maveli, which claims that all the people were equal and there were neither lies nor hypocrisy (Zachariah and Sooryamoorthy 1994). Moreover, Kerala has a long tradition of various religions living together peacefully. With its long seacoast of 580 kilometres, the state has always attracted traders from outside of India. Thus the state was historically exposed to many western influences as well Islamic influences from the Middle East. In contrast to India's religious composition of 80 per cent Hindus, 13 per cent Muslims and 2 per cent Christians, the balance is significantly different in Kerala. About 56 per cent of Kerala's population are Hindus, 24 per cent are Muslims and 19 per cent are Christians. So, the state houses a higher proportion of non-Hindus than any other major state in India, and still maintains itself as an example of peaceful religious coexistence.

The state is being regularly referred to as a success story in the developing world as it has managed to achieve significant progress in human development areas, in spite of its adverse social and demographic situation. Scholars described the cultural factors as one of the main sources for Kerala's outstanding social and human development. But notwithstanding its cultural progressiveness and its religious harmony, Kerala has not been able to achieve much in industrial output and agricultural production. In per capita income, Kerala still ranks below several other states in India. However, the statistic excludes the remittances of its expatriates, who are living and working in large numbers mainly in the Gulf countries.[1]

In recent years Kerala's economic development has taken an impressive leap and its income per capita is one of the highest in the country, at a level of USD 618.9 compared to the average per capita of USD 514.2 of the entire country in May 2004. Only 3.6 per cent of Kerala's population is below the poverty line as compared to the all-India percentage of 19.34. According to the Indian State Hunger Index from 2009 Kerala ranks second to all 17 Indian states. In a different way, this is reflected in other developmental statistics, e.g. Kerala has by far the lowest under-five mortality rate in India, standing at 1.6 per cent. The second lowest is Tamil Nadu with 3.5 per cent. These positive social development factors are the result of collective action, with which the state has implemented progressive social policies and could overcome its handicap of having a poor economy. Social movements, as will be discussed extensively in this chapter, have a very strong root in Kerala and the people of Kerala organize and mobilize to support or protest government policies more effectively than others in India.

---

1   K.P. Kannan's study has shown that in Kerala, the rate of rural poverty has declined since 1980s in spite of the slow rate of economic growth. That has been achieved, as Kannan argues, due to well-designed and implemented state intervention programmes and the social protection of the most vulnerable groups in the society (Kannan 1995).

The positive effect of these social policies is not just visible in poverty and hunger reduction, but is also apparent in other social indices. Kerala's performance compared to other states in India, in terms of literacy ratio, life expectancy, fertility rates, infant mortality and gender equality is therewith tremendous. In spite of having a developing economy, Kerala's social indices have registered a steady improvement to reach levels comparable to countries in the developed world. *The Atlantic Monthly* lists Kerala's success in social development (Kapur 1998):

– Life expectancy in Kerala is seventy-two years, which is closer to the American average of seventy-six than to the Indian average of sixty-one.

– The infant-mortality rate in Kerala is among the lowest in the developing world – roughly half that of China, and lower than that in far richer countries, such as Argentina and Bahrain.

– Population is just 1.7 births per women – lower even than Sweden's or America's.

– What is perhaps most impressive is that 90 per cent of Keralites are literate – a figure that puts the state in a league with Singapore and Spain.

From the point of view of education, literacy, health and advancement, Kerala performs extremely well compared to other Indian states. While Kerala's population growth rate is the lowest, its Human Development Index rating is the highest in India (Radhakrishna 2008).

Kerala reported the lowest population growth rate in the 2001 census with 9.4 per cent between 1991 and 2001, leading to a projected population for Kerala of 34,232,000 for 2008. The sex ratio of 1,058 women per 1,000 men is unmatched anywhere else in India, which has an average ratio of 0.93, a ratio that is remarkable for any developing country. Besides the positive development in its population, the state's health care system is also remarkable and moving ahead of other developing countries.

Kerala's literacy rate is estimated at 90.92 per cent (2001 census), compared to India's average rate of 65.38 per cent. The male and female literacy rates of Kerala are 94.2 and 87.6 per cent respectively. This may explain the high rates of newspaper and magazine subscriptions that Kerala maintains in the country. The fact that half of the state's population spends an average of about seven hours a week reading books, clearly reflects Kerala's first place standing in the Education Development Index (EDI) among 21 major states in India. The indicators of the Index are based on access to and infrastructure of education as well as teachers, and student performance. The performance of the political and bureaucratic

Table 3.1   Comparison of key developmental indicators between Kerala and the Indian average

	Kerala	India
Per capita net state domestic product (SDP) in Rs (2004–05)	27,048	23,222
No. of females per 1,000 males (2001 census)	1058	933
Female literacy rate (2001)	87.7	53.7
Percentage of women's employment to total employment (2003)	39.3	18.1
Percentage with regular exposure to media (TV, radio, newspaper at least once a week)	97	80
Total road length (km) per 100 sq km (2002)	386.8	74.7
Voting percentage (2004 elections)	71.45	58.1
Life expectancy at birth (1999–2003, Male/Female)	70.9/76	61.8/63.5
Number of infant deaths per 1,000 live births in the last five years	15	57
Vaccination coverage in per cent	75	44
Per capita expenditure on health in Rs (2001–2002)	1,858	997
Percentage of household have a television	67.7	44.2
Percentage of household have access to a toilet facility	96	44.5
Percentage of household use piped drinking water	24.6	42
Have electricity	91	67.9

Source: Outlook India, 16 July 2007.

system in Kerala is also worth mentioning. A survey by Transparency International conducted in 2005 ranked Kerala as the least corrupt state in India.

The outstanding social development of Kerala, which is not in the same way matched by its economic performance, produces a development paradox in Kerala (Mathew 1997).[2] In this context Kerala's spectacular achievements in the social

---

2   A pioneering study by the Centre for Development Studies (CDS) in 1975 raised academic interest in Kerala as a 'model'. This study challenged Dandekar and Rath's work on poverty in India and argued that due to the pattern of development policies pursued in Kerala, it has resulted in its higher degree of human development and quality of life in spite of low per capita income and consumption expenditure. However, due to the state's dismal record of economic growth, Amarty Sen refuges to accept the 'Kerala model' concept. According to him, a model is a frozen entity with an aura of perfection, so he prefers to call 'Kerala experience' instead (Sen 2000).

sector have been seen as something of a mystery. But Kerala's success in the social development sector can be traced to its history. In an attempt to unravel this mystery, Ramachandran argues,

> The achievements of the people of Kerala are the result of major social, economic, and political transformations. These changes have roots in Kerala's history, but they were also, in an important sense, achievements of public action in post-1957 Kerala (Ramachandran 1997).

The most important form of public action in Kerala has been mass movement against socio-economic oppression and anti-people government policies. Zachariah and Sooryamoorthy also argue in a similar way to describe the so-called Kerala model. They find, like Ramchandran, in Kerala's history, the tradition for formal education and also, the successful public action in the form of progressive social movements (Zachariah and Sooryamoorthy 1994). Since the 19th century, the princely states of Travancore and Cochin had adopted progressive policies in education and health. Way back in 1867, Britain acknowledged Travancore as a model native state for its modern administrative set up. The education system was then in vogue, which combined both traditional and modern ways, and was open to a wider section of the society. Native rulers also encouraged the activities of European missionaries, who also preferred to visit due to the presence of a sizeable community of Christians. Though native rulers and Christian missionaries started the process of social development, numerous progressive social movements carried it forward.

Protest Movements and the State of Kerala

The success of social movements in Kerala is quite remarkable. Social movements in the nineteenth century and early twentieth century were aimed at addressing caste-based discriminations. The famous 'breast-scarf controversy' came up in the first half of the 19th century when the lower *Shanar* caste women wanted to wear garments to cover their breasts like upper caste women (Jeffrey 1976). The mass actions in the *Izhava* Movement in the late nineteenth century and early twentieth century forced the rulers of Travancore to abolish the rules of restriction to the temple premises on the basis of the caste hierarchy (Heimsath 1978). Sri Narayan Guru, born in 1856 to an Ezhava family, rallied the reform movement on the slogan of 'one caste, one religion, one God for human-beings'. People belonging to lower castes replaced traditional Brahmin priests of the temples at many places. Like Izhavas, the lower caste Pulayas also organized movements for access to public roads, educational facilities and to end caste discrimination. The social reform movements were not only limited to the lower castes. Higher castes like Nayars, Nadars and Namboodris had also their own movements for better education, and against traditional rituals and practices. Even Christians in Kerala had their share of this social reform movement. These movements have broken up much of the rigid caste system, provided a conducive environment for the peaceful coexistence of various communities, and also helped to strengthen the position of women in society. Kerala is certainly less caste-ridden than any other area with a Hindu population.

Since the 1930s, Kerala also witnessed the rise of a strong socialist and trade union movement. The Malbar region witnessed an agrarian rebellion in the nineteenth century and in the beginning of the twentieth century. The political movement against British colonial rule also gained support from the struggle for agrarian change. This movement took the shape of a communist movement in the region. The communist party was established in Malbar in the late 1930s. And until today the communist and socialist parties continue to have a strong presence in Kerala.[3] The movement of peasant and working tenants resulted in a successful land reform in the state. The mass education provided by trade union movements have also helped the people to liberate themselves from dependence on landlords and made them conscious of their rights and privileges. There are some researchers, who argue that Kerala's progress in social development is due to 'the consistent struggle of the Left in general, both in the form of popular actions and radical state government interventions' (Tornquist and Tharakan 1996) (see also Franke and Chasin 1989). There is no doubt that the Left has played an important role in shaping the 'Kerala model', but giving it all the credit not only ignores the regions history but defies logic. Kerala is not the only state in India, which has a strong left movement. The communists have a powerful presence in states like West Bengal and Tripura. In West Bengal, the left has been in power since 1977 without any interruption. So, one might ask, why West Bengal has failed to emulate Kerala in many of its achievements? Or, why social movements are not as strong in West Bengal compared to Kerala? While recognizing the important role played by the Left in Kerala's long history of mobilization and its successful social development, it is also necessary to explore the strength of Kerala society, which makes it distinct from others in India.

A strong associational environment has enriched Kerala. The society is filled with associations of different types and sizes, and they existed long before the state or donor agencies gave incentives for these efforts. In the mid-1940s, Kerala saw the formation of the *Sahity Pravarthaka Sahakarana Sangham* (SPSS) and *Grantha Sala Sangham*. The aim of the SPSS, or the Literary Worker's Cooperative Society, was the publication of its members' works on a cooperative basis. This brought a revolution in terms of the availability of literature in their local language.

---

3 After its formation, Kerala became the first state or province within a federal system to democratically elect a communist government. Communist led front competes for power with the Congress Party and they usually rotate the government formation among themselves in each assembly election.

The *Grantha Sala Sangham* or the Library Movement came around the same time, which provided the people with a meeting place to read books and newspapers.

The *Sastra Sahitya Samiti* (SSS, Science Literary Forum) was inaugurated in 1957 with the objective to promote science writing and make science more accessible to the population. This necessitated and resulted in the translation of mainly English based academic discourses into Malayalam. The group started publishing scientific articles from multiple disciplines in the *Adhunika Sastram* (Modern Science), in 1958. The first edition of the publication would also be the last, however, the idea of bringing science to the people of Kerala lived on and became institutionalized in one of the most influential, successful and biggest movements which is still active in Kerala today (Zachariah and Sooryamoorthy 1994).

On the initiative of K.G. Adiyodi, 10 to 15 people came together in April 1962 in Kozhikode, driven by the goal to promote science in Kerala. As a result of the meeting, the *Kerala Sastra Sahitya Parishad* (KSSP, Kerala Science Literature Association) was established in September 1962 by this group of science writers in Malayalam. The forums objective was to popularize science among the people of Kerala in their mother tongue, Malayalam (Isac and Ekbal 1988). Encouraging interest and awareness in science was to be achieved through making science literature available in the local language, but also by organizing meetings and discussions, or movie presentations. The KSSP would also support other organizations with similar goals. Nevertheless, the organization in its early years was highly exclusive and membership was just granted to Kerala scientists or intellectuals. This changed over time as membership was expanded in 1965 and finally in 1966 opened to anybody. From approximately 50 members in 1966 the size of the organization grew to 120 members in 1967 when it was opened to the public, with several units inside of Kerala, but also outside in Bangalore and Calcutta (Zachariah and Sooryamoorthy 1994).

A major increase in the KSSP membership came in the mid-1970s. When Indira Gandhi declared a state of emergency in 1975 many of the proscribed political groups found their way into KSSP, which could act freely as it was non-political. Zachariah and Sooryamoorthy write that this had a significant effect, firstly on the number of its members, but secondly and especially on the political pronunciation of the movement. In fact the development of the movement in these years were seen as crucial for the KSSP. Many of the old leadership withdrew from the organization, not for political reasons, but because of its changing character from an elite scientist movement to a mass organization. The work of KSSP in these years changed towards the mass promotion of science through camps and classes, rather than through just publications and smaller discussions (Zachariah and Sooryamoorthy 1994).

In nearly five decades, KSSP has grown into a massive people's science movement, with a membership of about 60,000. All of its members work on a voluntary basis. Unemployed educated youth and teachers makeup the core constituency of the KSSP. Over these years, the KSSP has expanded its interests and activities. It is now broadly involved in three types of activities: agitative, educative and constructive, in areas like environment, health, education, energy, development, literacy, and micro planning. The KSSP enjoys a series of success stories. One of the most influential and nurturing for the movement is their universal literacy campaign. The success of this campaign is evident: In 1991 the state of Kerala claimed to be a completely literate state, as it met the norm of 95 per cent. Beyond this, Kerala has achieved a remarkable 100 per cent literacy from five to 60-year-olds.

By 1977 the KSSP had established total literacy of Kerala as one of their objectives. However, it took ten more years to find the appropriate way of achieving its goal. As a result KSSP declared the literacy plan at its annual meeting in the Ernakulam District in 1987 and the campaign was inaugurated in the least literate district, Malappuram. Building on this pilot project, the KSSP launched the Total Literacy Campaign in 1989, which would spread to the entire state. The KSSP, National Literacy Mission and the Kerala Association for Non-Formal Education and Development (KANFED) promoted and sponsored this popular movement. However, the KSSP remained in control of the educational curriculum for the campaign (Kumar 1993). A key element to the success of the campaign was due to the dedicated participation of scores of volunteers. They were organized through committees, representing political parties, trade unions, student associations and women's clubs (Zachariah 1997).

Nowadays KSSP has expanded its operation from spreading science and literacy to the practical use, combining research with practice. The KSSP claims on their webpage that their Research and Development Unit has developed a highly efficient wood-burning oven that saves up to 50 per cent of firewood. The movement states that already half a million households have installed the new oven, reducing energy needed in Kerala significantly. The movement also promotes other types of energy efficient techniques (KSSP 2009).

The success of these and other projects of KSSP received global attention and are seen as a role model for developmental movements. Consequently the movement was awarded the Right Livelihood Award 'for its major contribution to a model of development rooted in social justice and popular participation' in 1996 (Right Livelihood Award 1996).

People from various walks of life, academics and artists, provide support to the movement because the mass education of people in Kerala enabled artists and others to carry their messages to the people. This had significant influence on the liberation of people from dependencies and made them aware of their rights (Mahadevan and Sumangala 1987). The work of the movement also became a useful tool for policy introduction. The People's Campaign for Decentralized Planning, which was introduced in 1996 by the Communist Party, built successfully on the already established decentralized structures in Kerala. The campaigners received strategic support from the KSSP enabling social mobilization. However, although the KSSP and other movements in Kerala received goodwill and cooperated with leftist groups, the movements stayed impartial on the side of the issue and the people rather than on political ideology (Heller 2001).

Spreading Literacy to Opposing Dams

In the late 1970s, the KSSP was involved in opposing large-scale development projects that had adverse ecological effects. Its study of the harmful effects of the Kuttanad Development Project, a hydropower generation project, in 1978 was an eye opener for the KSSP. The Project had taken up the construction of dams and dikes at the southern side of the Lake Vembanad that had resulted in various adverse ecological effects. The experience of Kuttanad brought a shift in the KSSP's policy, which was formed to popularize science, now became involved in debates about technology and its best use in the context of Kerala's development (Isaac, Franke, and Parameswaran 1997). By the persuasion of Professor M.K. Prasad, a botanist, the KSSP's attention to the dam project shifted when his plea for a halt of the project was approved at the annual conference in 1978 (Zachariah and Sooryamoorthy 1994). Its decision to oppose the proposed Silent Valley Project brought the KSSP the most spectacular success in its environmental struggle campaign.

The Silent Valley is situated in the Palghat District of Kerala's Malbar region. It is one of the few tropical rainforest areas, which has escaped from human intervention. However, it also provides one of the most ideal sites for hydropower generation in the power deficient Malbar region. Though, this site was preliminarily identified in 1928 and the technical investigation was carried out in 1958, the project was sanctioned only in 1973. It took another three years for the Kerala State Electricity Board to start the preparation for the construction. It was only by then that some renowned scientists associated with Indian government raised objections on environmental grounds and advised against taking up the project. They pointed out that constructing a dam would lead to the destruction of the 'last vestige of natural climax vegetation of the region and one of the last remaining in the country' (D'Monte 1985). Scientists found that the biological and genetic pool, which the valley hosts, has an uninterrupted history of over 50 million years, making it not just a valuable reserve of biodiversity for India, but for the whole world (Kumar 2004). Interested in the issue, the KSSP conducted its own scientific assessments of the project leading the movement to oppose it in 1978, which also had the support of all the state's political parties. It reflected that the KSSP, though it mainly draws its support base from the Left, is not necessarily a front organization for the Left parties, but rather acts along its values.

In 1979, a five-member committee of KSSP experts published a pamphlet, in which they listed their arguments against the project (Prasad et al. 1979). The publication *the Silent Valley Hydroelectric Project* listed the arguments in favour and against the dam, maintaining that its conclusion against the dam was guided by reason and logic, which illustrated KSSP's commitment to its scientific roots, rather than a typical polemist and activist character (Zachariah and Sooryamoorthy 1994). This ensured KSSP's credibility in the process.

The KSSP joined hands with various other voluntary organizations in Kerala and began a prolonged and intense mass campaign against the Silent Valley project. Besides arranging meetings, lectures, seminars and writings in the mass media, KSSP also lobbied political leaders and took the help of the judiciary. For instance a petition by Joseph John, an environmental activist, could stop the construction of the dam for some weeks until the higher court overruled the ruling (Zachariah and Sooryamoorthy 1994).

The KSSP actively involved several activists and organization from India and abroad in this mass action. The facilitating and networking actions of KSSP were important pillars in the creation of the Save the Silent Valley movement. The involvement of the World Wildlife Fund (WWF) and the International Union of Conservation of Nature and Natural Resources (IUCN) gave further momentum to the environmentalist remonstration, and guaranteed resources and global attention.

In a last attempt to implement the project the Kerala authorities established a national park in Silent Valley in 1980, however, they planned to exclude the project sight from the park limit. In addition, Prime Minister Indira Gandhi appointed a committee to produce an impact evaluation of the dam project. Three years later the committee, led by Professor M.G.K. Menon, presented its final report speaking in favour of conservation and against the construction of the dam. As a result the central government of India withdrew its sanction of the project making the protest a success. Later, Silent Valley was declared a national park and in September 1985 the park, covering 89.52 square kilometres, officially opened.

Meanwhile, a new proposal was brought forth in 2004 aiming to build a new dam at the border of the Silent Valley Park. The new dam would be built 3.5 kilometres downstream from the old proposal site, thereby lying outside the boundaries of the national park. The new dam's specifications proposed a design 64.5 metres high and 275 metres long that would aim to generate 70 MW. Studies conducted in 2004 contradicted one another about the environmental impact of the project, which would affect 79 square kilometres of the Silent Valley National

Park (Kumar 2004). To date, the proposal has not been implemented. The Kerala government is waiting for the Union government to make a final decision (The Hindu, 7 June 2007). Despite the tremendous success for the KSSP, the Silent Valley protests also marked the first success for popular protests against large dam projects in India. This success pronounced the beginning of the new paradigm 'development without destruction' and opened a new chapter in the popular protest against large-scale development projects in India.

In the past two decades, India has witnessed a number of massive popular protests against the construction of big dams. Though technological prejudice and politics of hope still favour these large projects (Santhakumar, Rajagopalan, and Ambirajan 1995), the protest movements have forced the authorities to take into greater account their associated social and environmental cost. In 2001, of the 28 dam projects that were planned in Kerala only nine have been built while all other proposals are delayed or under investigation (*The Financial Express*, 24 August 2001).

One of the other major protest movements in Kerala is opposing a proposed project on the River Pooyamkutty, a tributary of the Periyar. The dam project would submerge around 2800 hectares of tropical forest and displace two tribal settlements, consisting of 115 families (Santhakumar and Sivanandan 1998; Santhakumar and Chakraborty 2003). Although the project enjoys the support of all the major political parties, various protest groups in the state are still successfully opposing it. They have formed an action council since 1994 in order to "save Pooyamkutty forest". This protest in Kerala also receives support from other social action groups in India.

Activists and NGOs successfully delayed the construction of the dam until 2001. By then a new smaller version of the first proposal was brought up. The state government has been insisting on the first phase of the Greater Pooyamkutty project that would eventually flood 2800 hectares of rainforest (The Financial Express, 24 August 2001). Many studies have concluded that the project would cause more destruction than benefit (Santhakumar and Chakraborty 2003; Mathew 2001). Until 2003 the project was again successfully delayed by protesters until a new ecological assessment concluded that a reduction of the mean sea level (MSL) height of the dam from 338 metres to 300 metres would decrease the environmental impact of the project by 50 per cent while equally just reducing the power generation of the dam by nine per cent (Pereira 2003). In October 2008, protesters and supporters of another dam project in Kerala clashed at the hearing over the Athirappilly hydroelectric power project. The project aims to build a 163 MW hydroelectric dam across the Chalakudy River. After the Ministry of Environment and Forest gave its approval for the project in the middle of 2007 it faced strong opposition by environmentalists. At the hearing, workers of the ruling Communist Party of India (Marxist) countered anti-dam activist protests (*The Hindu*, 23 October 2008).

Protest Movements Resisting Globalization – Fishery, Palmolein and Coca-Cola

Protests in Kerala are not only limited to large dam building projects. The state has also witnessed a successful movement by its traditional fishers community. Kerala has 10 per cent of India's coastline and contributes a very sizeable chunk to its total marine catch. In fact, it is the second largest fish provider in India. Although they have close to 10 per cent of coast line, Kerala's 190,000 fishers produce 20 per cent of India's total fish catch (Bauer 2006). Since 1962, there has been a steady induction of mechanized boats to the state's fish industry with both government and external support (Kurien 1978). The use of nylon nets in the mechanized fishing sector has led to increased setbacks for the local fishers by diminishing their total catch sizes.

While the mechanized industries thrived due to export, the traditional sector confined to a domestic market suffered due to declining catches. On the basis of this unequal competition a clear polarization took place between the industrialized and traditional fishers by the late 1970s and early 1980s. The domination of the mechanized sector by the non-fisher community[4] and its discriminate fishing led to the formation of fishers unions at the district level. The Roman Catholic Church was very much involved in the mobilization of the fisher community.[5] In 1977, the district unions of fishers joined together to form *Kerala Latheen Katholica Malsia Thozhilalee Federation*. The objective of the fish workers movement was social justice, fish workers rights, fishing communities' access to marine resources and the ecological sustainability of rapidly changing patterns or resource-use (Bauer 2006).

The name of the association brought some hindrance to the joining of the Hindu and Muslim fishers to the group, so in 1980, it changed its name to *Akhili Kerala Swatanthra Malsya Thozhilali Federation* (AKSMTF – All Kerala Independent Fishermen's Federation). Under the banner of AKSMTF, the traditional fisher community of Kerala rallied. They also joined with the traditional fishers groups of Tamil Nadu and Goa. The struggle took momentum and by 1984, it included most of the fishery villages in Kerala.

The AKSMTF organized a series of protests to place pressure on the Kerala Government to address their problems. Protests were organized in various parts

---

4   In 1980, out of Kerala's 2,630 registered trawlers, only 700 trawlers were owned by fishers or their cooperative societies (Menon 1988).

5   The involvement of clergymen in the struggle created a rift among the church establishment in Kerala. Unlike Latin America, the church in Kerala avoids being involved in agitations. The only previous exception was during the so-called 'liberation struggle' in 1959 against the Left Government, when the church only blessed the priest who were in the forefront of the movement.

of the state in the form of meetings, processions, demonstrations and even hunger strikes. In 1984, a spree of picketing started in several parts of the state to stop street and railway traffic. Gradually, the movement took up direct confrontations with the owners of mechanized boats and trawlers. Women were at the forefront of this struggle (Gulati 1984). Continuing protests by the fisher community forced the state government to appoint a number of committees in the 1980s to investigate the problem and provide policy recommendations. On the basis of some of these recommendations, the state government banned trawler fishing in coastal waters up to a 22 kilometres of limit in the monsoon season. By the late 1980s, the struggle of traditional fishers against mechanized trawlers, which had started in Kerala, took the form of a national level campaign. Thanks to this movement, the Indian government decided in December 1994 to freeze all the licenses of deep-sea trawlers and formed a committee under the chairpersonship of P. Murari. Following the recommendations of Maurari's Committee, the Central Government took several concrete steps in 1997 to conserve fish stocks and protect traditional fishers (Sundar 1999).

The adverse effects of globalization have also helped the Kerala farmers to organize themselves. Local farmers have been increasingly exposed to the falling prices of agricultural production. Since 2000, Kerala farmers have organized themselves to prevent the import of palm olein, which has been primarily responsible for the abysmal fall in prices of coconuts and coconut oil. People in Kerala generally use coconut oil for cooking, but the availability of imported palm olein at cheaper prices has affected the coconut growers in the state because more and more people and businesses use the cheaper oil. Within a half-year, in 2000, coconut oil prices had plummeted by about 20 per cent. That same year several rural *panchayats* protested by declaring the Kozhikode district palm olein-free. This campaign started spreading to the Kannur and Kasrgod districts in northern Kerala. The protests have been mainly peaceful, but occasionally they have resulted in violence. In October 2000, some of the farmer movements started seizing palm olein oil from depots to spill onto the road (*The Financial Express*, 22 October 2000; *Indian Express* 22 October 2000). The movement, which had nearly one hundred thousand members in the first half of 2001, has also received support from farmers groups in different parts of the country, particularly from Karnataka (*Deccan Herald*, 22 May 2001).

Because of WTO obligations, it is not easy for the Indian government to address the issue, which gives further strength to the movement. The movement succeeded in its efforts and forced the state government to request an increased custom duty on palm olein to protect the interests of Kerala's coconut farmers. The introduction of a duty on palm olein has led to a revaluation of palm olein prices increasing its price by about 44 per cent compared to 2000. However, in 2008 the Indian Farmers Association, INFAM, called for a boycott and ban on palm olein imports because there were 'vested interests exploiting loopholes in the law to cause distress to coconut growers by importing palm olein' (The Hindu, 6 January 2008, 18 December 2008). The movement is also actively discouraging the consumption of soft drinks marketed by multinationals and instead promoting the drinking of tender coconuts.

Like the fishers' movement, the farmers' movement receives support from a section of the Church.[6] A study by Mujeebur Rehiman claims that INFARM received particular support from the church: 'the Founding Trustees, itself reveals the fact that out of 34 members, 16 are priests from various regions and all the trustees except one trustee belongs to Christianity' (Rehiman 2003). Globalization in Kerala did not just impact other industries or production as in the case of the fisheries and palm olein. It even had a direct effect on the people living in Kerala. In Plachimada, the multinational corporation Coca-Cola built a plant to produce and bottle its product for the Indian market. The direct effect of the plant on local water resources has caused severe water shortages in the region, because the plant uses the ground water for the production of its drink. An estimated loss of 1.5 million litres of drinking water per day led to a decrease in the ground water levels from 150 to 500 feet (Drew 2008). One of the primary constituencies opposing the Coca-Cola plant is tribal women, who staged a sit-in in front of the gates of the plant. Support through other movements in the region made the women's protest possible (Drew 2008; Gupta and Gupta 2008). The protest against the Coca-Cola plant was not limited to the local area. In 2004 the Chief Minister of Kerala ordered the closure of the plant. And in 2005 the state government called upon the Supreme Court in an attempt to challenge Coca-Cola's right to use water in Kerala, as it would deprive the resource from villagers around the plant. Another reason behind the closure of the plant was that in the area around the plant high levels of lead were found. In response to the closure of the plant and the ban of Coca-Cola and Pepsi products in Kerala, the companies were forced to take up legal battles against the Kerala authorities (Sudworth 2006).

Protest Movements and Kerala Society

Kerala provides a fertile setting to study protest movement. As the Agora Survey of 1997–1998 points out,[7] people in Kerala participate in protest movements more

---

6   Father Anthony Kozhuvinal is the General Secretary of this Kozhikode based movement.

7   Agora research project of Uppsala University, Sweden was a collaborative effort between the Department of Peace and Conflict Research and Department of Government. To investigate social capital and its impact on democratic performance and protest mobilization in India and South Africa, with Swedish International Development Cooperation Agency's support, it worked together with political scientists from the Centre for Political Studies, Jawaharlal Nehru University, New Delhi, Department of Political Science, Utkal University,

frequently than their counterparts in other states of India. In 1997, more than 40 per cent of Kerala population confirms their participation in protest movements, while the figure is only 24 per cent in Orissa, 12 per cent in Uttar Pradesh, 14 per cent in West Bengal and seven per cent in Gujarat. Kerala has witnessed a large number of protest movements in recent years. To name a few of such protests: movement for the protection of Sasthamkotta Lake and Bharathappuzha river, movement against the pollution from Chavara titanium factory, agitation against Malabar asbestos, Chackosan chemicals, Galaxy chemicals, and Mothi chemicals and Nenmarara Carbide factory, movement against Gosree project for the protection of backwater, movement against Backel tourism resort and the movement against Peringom nuclear power project and Papinissery thermal power project. However, the list does not end there. There are several other protest movements for the protection of forest at Anakmpoyili, Waynad, Thirumenni, Kollam, Panthanamthitta, Kavilampara and Mookampetty; protests against industrial pollution at Chempottuvayal, Kuttipuram, Urakam, Waynad, Muchukunnu, Kannur, Thodupuzha, Urakam, Kayamkulam, Elappully, Marangattupuzha, Mulamkunnathukav, Chavara, Kottayam, Ernakulam and Mulamkunnathukavil.

Table 3.2   People that joined protest movements in their area

Joined	Per cent	Did not join	Per cent
138	40	197	57

Note: Missing percentage answered 'don't know'.

Kerala swarms with volunteer associations based on religion, culture, caste and class affiliation, political groups and so on. The number of these groups in Kerala is much higher than any other Indian state. According to the Agora Survey in 1997–1998, more than half of the Kerala population is a member of an association. Nearly 28 per cent have been part of village development associations, 33 per cent of youth associations, 20 per cent of caste-based associations and 25 per cent of professional associations (see Table 3.3). In the morning, teashops in Kerala become filled with villagers to eat a *dosa*, but more importantly, to read

Bhubaneswar, India and Department of Political Studies, University of Witwatersrand, Johannesburg, South Africa. The project had interviewed 3120 respondents in 31 areas in five (Kerala, Orissa, undivided Uttar Pradesh, West Bengal and Gujarat) of the 25 states in India in 1998 and 1999. This Agora Survey had used multi-stage cluster sampling with the ambition to render the sample representative of the areas and states. In Kerala, 700 respondents were interviewed in seven areas: Calicut city, Irikkur, Iritty, Muvattupuzha, Trivandrum rural, Trivandrum city and Nemom.

Table 3.3   Frequency and percentage of people that have taken part in associations

	Yes	Per cent	No	Per cent	Total
Village development association	189	28	491	72	680
Youth association	224	33	458	67	682
Caste organization	138	20	544	80	682
Women's organization	141	21	541	79	682
Farmer's associations	112	16	569	84	681
Trader's associations or business groups	82	12	593	88	675
Professional associations	167	25	512	75	679
Cultural or religious associations	245	36	439	64	684
Any other group (e.g. political party)	281	41	403	59	684

the Malayalam language newspapers that arrive on the first bus.[8] These teashops are one of the 'public spheres' in a Kerala village, where the villagers sit together and discuss among themselves. As it has been observed: 'In towns and villages, hanging from the tiled roofs of otherwise nondescript houses, one sees signs advertising soccer clubs, film clubs, and youth clubs – all providing occasions for the kind of interaction conducted in tea shops. Nearly every village has a public library, another hub of social life' (Kapur 1998).

The contribution of this vigorous civic associational life to the social development and collective action in Kerala is undisputable. The study of Mahadevan and Sumangala provides startling statistics to prove this point:

> In 1985, Kerala had 12,120 schools and 168 colleges. Most of these are run by private agencies. Of the total number of colleges, 132 are run by volunteer agencies; only 36 are in the public sector. There are 4,977 libraries functioning in Kerala. Most of them are run as cooperatives by the people (Mahadevan and Sumangala 1987: 33).

Each and every major village in Kerala has at least one public library. These libraries, though they receive a small grant from the Panchayat administration, are primarily maintained by the voluntary service of the people.

---

8   According to the National Readership Survey of India, Kerala has the highest newspaper readership of any other state in India.

The survey has shown that the effect of the high literacy rate combined with access to literature and newspaper resources affected the political awareness of people in Kerala. About 80 per cent of the interviewees had answered that they would have a good understanding of important issues that India is facing and 50 per cent were convinced that they would be able to change a wrongful decision by the government.[9] The political awareness in Kerala has shown a reformist attitude rather than a revolutionary one. Over 50 per cent of Kerala's population hold the belief that society must be gradually improved by reforms, and only 14 per cent had asked for radical change by revolutionary action.

According to the 1997–98 survey people are equally proud of their regional-sate identity (94 per cent) as well with their national-Indian identity (94 per cent). The survey clearly revealed that there is a strong societal solidarity among the communities. Most of the people decided to join a protest movement because of their own will and not because they were persuaded by political leaders. The progressive character of Kerala society goes beyond the mere facts of a high literacy rate or regional pride. 45 per cent of women in Kerala were found to be working or studying, while just 36 per cent are housewives. And more women than men are literate, with 77 per cent of women finishing at least high school. The childcare facilities, *Anganwadis*, are very common in Kerala's villages, supporting gender advances in society.[10] In most parts of Kerala, these *Anganwadis* have taken over the responsibility of looking after children in their pre-school period. This has of course helped mothers to take up jobs; simultaneously becoming a strong centre for social interaction in other formal organizations.

Mahilamandals or women's clubs are widespread in Kerala, as women have organized themselves to provide recreation, informal education and vocational training. The Agora survey shows healthy participation of women in women's organizations, which are primarily voluntary in their nature. The women's clubs receive some support from the village or bloc level administration, but their main source of income comes from local contributions. These women's clubs are active participants in the management of the *Anganwadis*.

The participation of women within the communities is in general very high, as indicated by the survey that 47 per cent of women participate in village meetings. In addition, 32 per cent of women participate in protest marches or demonstrations, and even 61 per cent discuss the problems with other people in the area (see Table 3.5).

---

9   The survey confirmed the political understanding by asking who the prime minister in their state is what 97 per cent answered correctly.

10   In 1972, *Anganwadi* programme was started in Kerala with UNICEF support. The support of the villages is provided to get the premise and also village level women associations are directly involved to manage its activities and provide help to the workers of the *Anganwadis* to run them efficiently.

Table 3.4   Gender wise participation in village meetings (percentage in brackets)

	Yes	No	Total
Male	166 (59)	117 (41)	283
Female	72 (47)	82 (53)	154
Total	238	199	

There is also a healthy competition that exists among different communities of Kerala to promote education and health services. As Patrick Heller writes: 'Keralites of all walks of life, it would seem, appear to have an irresistible inclination to combine, associate and organize, and to do so without the outbreaks of violent disorder Huntingtonians might have anticipated' (Heller 1995). Movements in Kerala are not only supported by the presence of religious or caste-based associations, they also thrive due to the presence of village committees.

Table 3.5   Women participating in social action in the last 5 years (percentage in brackets)

	Yes	No	Don't know	Total
Actively participated in an association	89 (38)	141 (61)	2	232
Actively participated in a campaign	63 (27)	160 (69)	9	232
Taken part in a protest march or demonstration	74 (32)	151 (65)	7	232
Taken part in a sit–in or disruption of government meetings or offices	57 (25)	167 (72)	8	232
Used force or violent methods	8 (3)	215 (93)	9	232
Spoken with other people in my area about the problems	141 (61)	86 (37)	5	232
Notifying a court about the problem	47 (20)	179 (77)	6	232

Kerala has a long tradition of village committees.[11] Village communities, the *gram sabhas*, regularly hold meetings, air complaints, identify their problems, and even plan projects. If necessary, they summon on a common cause, and combine their

---

11   Since the days of the Khilafat movement, there has been an emphasis on village-level organization in the Malbar region. Congress and then the Communists have encouraged and extended the village-level organizations to other parts of Kerala (Ramachandran 1997). Since 1997, these village committees have received a greater boost due to allocation of greater resource to them by the state. The village *panchayats* and ward councils are directly contributing to the state planning within their areas of responsibility (Isaac and Harilal 1997; Franke and Chasin 1997; Mathews 1999).

resources for the success of a movement. The organizational resources come in handy for the movement organizers to mobilize the popular and material support for their cause. The usefulness of the village level associations in sustaining and spreading the movement became very clear while talking to some of the organizers of the movement. K.K. Balakrishnana, one of the supporters of the protest against the proposed Carbide factory in Nenmara Panchayat of the Palakkad District, described the use of the village associations for the extension of the movement:[12] 'When the movement started, we had only the support of the people in our village ward. Then we contacted the committees of nearby wards and also the nearby *Panchayats*. We received support from them, which helped to spread the movement.'

K. Krishnan, who was in the forefront of a movement to protect the dying river Bharathappuzha, also reaffirmed the utility of the village associations or *panchayats* not only in spreading the movement, but also in sustaining it:[13] 'The movement has been going on for last 10 years. In each meeting, we have the presence of at least 100 people. Every *panchayat* through which river flows, has set up a unit for this movement and these units organize meetings regularly.'

The success of the movement's mobilization depends upon the synergy of the commitment of the group directly participating in the movement and the support it receives from the outside sympathizers. In Kerala, there is no dearth of this synergy. Our discussions with several leaders of different movements in Kerala confirmed the near total commitment of the protesting group, and also regular support provided by the various volunteer organizations. The affected people themselves have started all the movements. The survey results confirmed that 77 per cent of those people polled see the formation of a group to state their demands in public as the best form of responding to problems in their communities. They are the ones who have participated in the demonstrations and raised money from personal contributions. Towards this effort, there has been always support from outside non-governmental associations and groups. The protesting group has been able to successfully link itself with groups from other areas. A close look at the protest movement for the protection of the Jeerakappara forest in the early 1990s illustrates this successful cooperation. K. Sreedharan, a retired professor who was the leader of the movement to protect the local forest from the loggers, describes:[14]

---

12   Interview with K.K. Balakrishanan at Palakkad on 12 February 2000. Interview was conducted with the assistance from Shanavas Elachola.

13   Interview with K. Krishnan at Malappuram on 5 March 2000. Interview was conducted with the assistance from Shanavas Elachola.

14   Interview with K. Sreedharan, at Chevayoor on 16 March 2000. Interview was conducted with the assistance from Shanavas Elachola.

The movement had good participation from the people. People from every political party and religion participated. It is a Christian dominated area and the priests from the churches also played an active role in it …. Due to protest, the 'forest lobby' have not entered the forest yet. That is the success of this movement. Even though the government has handed over this land to them, they could not cut or take out any wood from the forest for the last eight years. This was a big movement. We organized a "human chain" across the forestland and about 2500 people participated in it. We also asked others to help us in this struggle. Not only, environmental but cultural activists from all over Kerala had participated in this demonstration.

P. Narayan Kutty was one of the participants of the protest movement against the extension plan of State owned Kerala Clays and Ceramic Product Limited at Madayippara, Kannur. The local people have protested against the fear of waste from the mines since its emergence in 1995. It has been able to stop this extension plan. Narayan Kutty also substantiates the success of linking the protesting group with outside supporters:[15] 'Nearly 500 families live in the valley and all of them were full time participants of this movement. Besides the local support, some other environmental groups like Public Health Forum of Payyanoor also participated in the movement. It also received the support from the local Hindu temple.'

It is not the case that in places where protests have emerged, in Kerala, that there were no divisions within society. There were various groups mobilizing in the protest locality on the basis of caste and religion. However, their group loyalty did not prohibit them from joining with other groups in the area to protest. In this sense, it can be argued that they do have close bonding ties within their own group, but at the same time, this tie was not exclusive in its character. The presence of a strong bond among the groups has also helped the mobilization process. P.P. Krishanan, who was one of the organizers of a protest movement against the proposed Naphtha fuel thermal power project at Papinissery in Kannur in the second half of the 1990s, describes the mobilization of the protesters:[16]

A minimum of 5,000 people participated in the movement. The movement received support not only from the local people, but also from all environmental groups of Kannur District and most of the environmentalists in Kerala. The area, which is going to be affected by the project, has a majority Muslim and Christian community and hence the people who participated in the movement mainly belonged to these two communities. It was easy to organise the movement and

---

15   Interview with P. Narayan Kutty, at Payayangadi on 20 February 2000. Interview was conducted with the assistance from Shanavas Elachola.

16   Interview with P.P. Krisnan, at Talap, Kannur on 20 February 2000. Interview was conducted with the assistance from Shanavas Elachola.

mobilise the people, because of the existing groups of the two communities. The groups and its leader facilitated the mobilisation of the local people.

As the Agora survey has confirmed, people in Kerala, have strong bonds within their community and at the same time, that bond does not restrict them to interact with the outside. More than 70 per cent of respondents consider their own relatives as generally trustworthy; while more than 60 per cent put their own caste members in that category. However, that strong bond to their own caste or clan has not prohibited them from interacting with groups outside their own. Nearly 80 per cent of respondents talk to others in the village about the public issues. More than two thirds of respondents usually go to ask for help outside of their respective caste in a time of need. Nearly 95 per cent of them are regularly invited to attend wedding parties of other caste groups in the village. The children of more than 90 per cent of respondents regularly play with kids of other groups. To cap it all, nearly 75 per cent of respondents spend time every day with people of different castes and 72 per cent with people of a different religious background outside their work. This shows that while a strong bond exists at the group level, it does not restrict the people of Kerala to be part of a larger network. Rather, the strong bond helps to recruit support for the movement at the micro-level, while bridging ties with other groups helps spread movements at the meso-level.

Society that Matters

As the Kerala study suggests, it is not only economics or politics that matters in protest mobilization, but also society. Protest movement organizations in Kerala are not in possession of greater economic resources compared to their counterparts in other parts of India, however they do achieve a much higher level of success. If Communist Party organizations would be the key to this successful movement as some have claimed, then other states like West Bengal and Tripura should not have fallen behind in this respect. Without greater and sustained popular support, the movement usually loses its punch. The disadvantage of a small group is generally overcome through its flexible coordination. The diffusion of a movement would be impossible in the absence of flexible and inclusive forms of networks within the broad framework of collective action (Swain 2000). In Kerala, flexible coordination has been achieved through networks of smaller groups and associations, which complement each other to achieve collective efficiency for popular action. Protests have been able to get larger support through coordination or connections between various groups and associations. The existing vigorous associational life in the state has contributed immensely to this group's coordination.

For enhanced participation, an extended group network is needed, rather than restricted participation within the group. Some recent works on the historical study of movements have tried to trace the pattern of ties guiding individual's judgements about their belongingness to the type of political groupings or collectives (Padgett and Ansell 1993; Bearman 1994; Gould 1998). The more local, social and cultural ties become mutually reinforcing, the more likely people are to engage in collective defiance (Eckstein 1989). A strong intra-group tie within the groups, which can be found in Kerala, helps the recruitment to the movement from within the group. And, at the same time, that group bonding is flexible enough to co-ordinate with other groups. Thus, the strong bond that exists within the various groups in Kerala does not restrict the movements to attract support from other groups; rather it helps to draw more support from its own group.

The movement, the 'network of networks', thrives in a society rich with strong associational life. However, density of associations is not the only indicator of a society which hosts successful movements. For greater support, there is a need for the coordination or networking among the associations or groups in society. And that becomes possible, when the social ties have both bonding and bridging traits and they mutually reinforce each other. The Kerala society has become a fine example of it.

Chapter 4

Protest Mobilization with Regional Variation: Case of Orissa

As it has been discussed in Chapter 2, since the 1980s, India has witnessed an increase in the number of protest movements. India experienced this phenomenon even before achieving post-industrial society status. As a part of this phenomenon, movements against displacement have increased both in frequency and intensity. These movements are more widespread and involve a larger number of people from different sections of society. This popular opposition is directed against some displacement inducing developmental policies adopted by the state and has been a primary hindrance to their implementation (Swain 1997).

However, the emergence of these types of protest movements in the state of Orissa, located in the south-eastern part of India, is a new development and establishes an interesting puzzle for research. The signs of such trends are becoming visible in Orissa despite its 'backwardness'. Notwithstanding Orissa's low literacy rate, the state's poverty, industrial backwardness, having the largest proportion of 'scheduled' groups in the country, and a very weak record of popular movements in the pre and post independence period, the number of protest movements has been gradually growing.

In 1950, Orissa became a state within the Indian Union. Oriya is spoken by about 84 per cent of its population of nearly 40 million, representing less than four per cent of India's total population (Census of India 2001). Orissa is primarily a Hindu state; while 94.4 per cent of its population are Hindu, only 2.4 and 2.1 per cent are Christian or Muslim respectively (Census of India 2001). The Freedom of Religion Act of 1967, which aimed to protect the population of Orissa from being converted by Christian missionaries (Mahmood 2006), might somehow explain this low percentage, particularly of the Christian population, compared to other Indian states. While religious coexistence in the state of Kerala is remarkable, this pattern does not translate to the case of Orissa. The state has witnessed a number of violent religious riots recently. In 2008, the state drew international attention due to prolonged violent activities against its Christian population in its inland region (BBC, 16 October 2008).

In spite of recent economic development, Orissa is still the second poorest state in India after Bihar. Between 2002 and 2007 the Gross state domestic product (GSDP) has grown at 8.5 per cent according to the World Bank. In previous

Table 4.1   Religions in Orissa

Religion	Total population in 2001	Men	Women	Relative frequency
All religious communities	36,804,660	18,660,570	18,144,090	1.000
Hindu	34,726,129	17,615,951	17,110,178	0.944
Muslim	761,985	391,234	370,751	0.021
Christian	897,861	443,245	454,616	0.024

years it was approximately 5.5 per cent or even less (World Bank 2009). In the 1990s, while the annual per capita income of the country was 2,853 rupees, for Orissa it was only 1,630 rupees (*The Indian Express*, 20 November 1997). The sate possesses huge mineral resources, having 33 per cent of country's iron ore deposits, 25 per cent of the coal, 60 per cent of aluminium ore, 98 per cent of chromium ore, 67 per cent of manganese ore and 30 per cent of mineral sands. In spite of the abundance of minerals, in the industrial scenario, Orissa still stands at a lower rank compared to the rest of the states (Vyasulu and Kumar 1997). Only 37.53 per cent of the total population in Orissa in 1991 were workers (Government of Orissa 2001, Radhakrishna 2008). In the state, the proportion of male workers to the male population is 52.5 per cent, and of female workers to the female population 24.7 per cent (UNDP 2009). Orissa also has one of the largest shares of the country's population living below the poverty line. In 2000, 47.15 per cent of Oriyas lived below the poverty line, which is almost five per cent behind the then second poorest state, Bihar.

Moreover, after undivided Madhya Pradesh (23 per cent) and other tiny North Eastern states, Orissa has the highest density of tribal population in the country. In seven of its district, the tribal population is more than 50 per cent of the total population. When Orissa's *dalit*[1] population (16 per cent) is included, the two categories constitute 38 per cent of the population and gives Orissa the largest proportion of scheduled groups in the country (1995). After examining the socio-economic indicators, the relatively poor performance of the state becomes quite visible. Orissa ranks 11th in the Human Development Indicators (HDI) with a life expectancy of 59.2 years (all India 63.9, Kerala 73.9), and has the second highest infant mortality rate per 1000 live births with a rank of 73 (all India 57, Kerala 15) (Economic Survey 2007–2008 2009).

---

1   The scheduled status is conferred to the most oppressed sections of the Indian society, tribals and untouchables, by the Indian constitution. In this book, scheduled tribes are mentioned as tribals and scheduled castes are the *dalits*.

Even after fifty years of independence, in 1997, nearly 11,000 villages in the state of Orissa did not have primary schools (*The Indian Express*, 20 November 1997). Only 63 per cent of the people above the age of seven in Orissa were literate in 2001. In recent years, Orissa has made some progress in the area of education. Nevertheless, Orissa remains below India's literacy average of 64.84 per cent (Economic Survey 2007–2008, 2009). The female literacy rate in Orissa is at 50.5 per cent (UNDP 2009).

Studies show that literacy as such is less responsible for the spread of social movements than is the increasing ownership of books, and readership of newspapers and pamphlets (Chartier 1991). Sidney Tarrow claims that for the organization of the movements, newspapers are more important than books, because a person can read about a great event on the same day as thousands of others (s)he does not know and becomes the part of the same invisible community of others (Tarrow 1998). In this context, the growth of Oriya newspapers after the late 1980s has been spectacular. In 1961, the ratio of Oriya newspaper circulation was three dailies per 1000 people, which was the lowest in India for a major language. Oriya newspapers remained in this statistical category until the 1980s, but after that things began to change. Between 1981 and 1991, Oriya newspaper readership increased from roughly 7 per 1000 to 22 per 1000. By 1992, Oriya newspaper circulation had gone from being the lowest of 12 major languages to being ranked eighth, ahead of Telugu, Kannada, and Punjabi (Jeffrey 1997). According to the Agroa Survey in 1997, almost 54 per cent of the people in Orissa read the newspaper at least once per week, while 42 per cent read the newspaper every day.

Participation in Protest Movements

As the 1997 Agora Survey result shows, the participation of Orissa people in protest movements is fairly high. Nearly 57 per cent of respondents had heard about protest movements in their area. And 32 per cent had directly taken part in the protest movements in Orissa. However, participation in these protest movements was very ad hoc in nature as the movements in most cases were of a short-term duration. Associational life in Orissa, according to the 1997 Agora Survey, was very weak compared to Kerala. Only 15 per cent of the people those who had taken part in the Survey had been associated with one or more associations. While 21 per cent of respondents had participated in village development associations; farmer, trade or business association participation rates were below 5 per cent. However, in caste and religious organizations, the participation rate reached almost 40 per cent.

There was also noticeable disparity between male and female participation in these associations. While only 1.5 per cent of women respondents participated in one or more associations, for men the figure was 13.6 per cent.

Table 4.2   Frequency and percentage of women and men that have taken part in associations

	Women		Men	
	Yes	Per cent	Yes	Per cent
Village development association	6	2	172	35
Youth association	7	3	142	29
Caste organization	14	6	92	19
Women's organization	21	9	5	1
Farmer's associations	–	–	34	7
Traders' associations or business groups	2	0.9	18	3
Professional associations	16	7	100	20
Cultural or religious associations	29	13	247	51
Any other group (e.g. political party)	3	1	49	10

Gender imbalance in the associations was also reflected in protest movement participation as well. While 62.35 per cent of the men participated in protest movements 72.73 per cent of the women did not participate in those movements. As it has been discussed before, the news media plays a crucial factor in the participation process of protest movements. The Agora Survey in Orissa has confirmed this hypothesis as well.[2] In Orissa, according to the Survey, there was a big difference between men and women and their access to the media. Accounting for the three common types of media (Newspaper, Radio and TV), 25 per cent of men had no access to the news, while nearly twice as much, 40 per cent of women; also had no access in Orissa. Of the 75 per cent of villages in Orissa that organize village meetings; only 53 per cent of respondents participated in those meetings. Drawing comparisons between states, village meeting attendance amongst women stood at 47 per cent in Kerala, in contrast to a meagre 15 per cent of women in Orissa.

Table 4.3   Gender wise participation (in per cent) in village meetings

	Yes	No
Male	69.17	30.83
Female	15.24	84.76
Total	53.62	46.38

---

2   In a simple linear regression model shows that the relationship is significant at 90 per cent and the correlation coefficient between the variables is confirming the positive relationship with 0.0877.

Table 4.4   Statistical overview of coastal and inland parts of Orissa

	Coastal Orissa	Inland Orissa
Share of State population	47.61%	52.39%
Dalit population	17.78%	15.56%
Tribal population	7.82%	35.82%
Scheduled population	25.62%	51.26%
Literacy rate	57.76%	39.26%
Irrigated area	597,000 Hect	417,000 Hect
Electrified villages	81.9%	64.6%
Big factories	815	656

Source: *Statistical Outline of Orissa 1995* (Bhubaneswar: Government of Orissa, Director of Economics and Statistics).

Besides gender disparity, the following section also reveals the regional difference between the coastal and inland parts of Orissa. This regional difference is not only limited to development, but also reflects the mobilization of the protest movement.

Regional Disparity – An Investigation into Inland and Coastal Orissa

In the post-independence period, the coastal region of Orissa has been politically and economically more powerful than the inland region.[3] This regional disparity has given rise to a separate state movement in the under-developed inland part. In addition to the regional development disparity, we also observe the difference in the number, structure and outcome of the protest movements in these two regions of Orissa. The inland part is rich in natural resources: minerals, timber and water. In the post-independence period, a large number of major development projects (big dams, large industries and mines) have been undertaken in the inland region. In particular, a number of large dams were built as a result of the Indian government's policy of prioritizing irrigation and power infrastructure.

---

3   For this study, the four undivided districts of Orissa (Balesore, Cuttack, Puri and Ganjam) constitute the coastal region while the rest nine undivided districts (Bolangir, Dhenkanal, Kalahandi, Keonjhar, Koraput, Mayurbhanj, Phulbani, Sambalpur, Sundergarh) form the inland part. In the early 1990s, Orissa has been divided into 30 districts: in the new administrative set up, coastal region's original four districts have been subdivided into 11 districts while the inland part now constitutes 19 new districts.

Contrary to expectations, these projects have not succeeded in bringing economic prosperity to this region, and at the same time the construction of these projects have resulted in displacing large numbers of the population. In some cases, the affected people had protested against the projects, but these movements were not effective enough to shift the site of the project or delay its implementation for a considerable period of time.[4] The coastal region on the other hand, has not experienced large-scale population displacement by the big projects for a long period. From the mid-1980s, very few projects with population displacement potential have been planned in this region, but the affected people have successfully resisted their implementation.[5]

Several large-scale hydroelectric projects have been constructed or are under construction in the inland part of Orissa. In the post-independence period, these projects were praised as temples of modern India and a harbinger of development and progress. That era saw the completion of several big projects, displacing more than 20,000 families.

The inter-State Machhkund Hydel Project is located in Koraput District and was constructed between 1948 and 1960. Nearly 3,000 families were displaced because of this dam project, out of which 51 per cent were tribal and 10.21 per cent were of the *dalit* population. In between 1948 and 1957, one of India's largest dams, the Hirakud Dam in Sambalpur District was built, displacing 15,000 families. Out of these, 11.4 per cent were tribal and 5.84 per cent were of the dalit population. The Salandi Hydro Project in the Keonjhar District aimed to build an irrigation system for about 225,000 acres land. With support from the World Bank, the project was completed between 1960–1976. This project displaced 589 families, out of which 93.23 per cent comprised the tribal population. Another large-scale irrigation system in this region is the Balimela Dam across the Sileru River. This project is in the Malkangiri District and was constructed between the periods of 1962/63–1977. Out of a total 2,000 families that were displaced 79.31 per cent were of tribal origin.

These mega-hydro projects forced a large number of people to leave their homes. But besides these dams, the huge steel plant at Rourkela (Sundergarh District) in the 1950s also displaced nearly 2,500 families (50 per cent tribals, 30 per cent *dalits*) (IseD 1996). These big industrial projects like the hydro projects

---

4   The only exception is 'Save Gandhamardan Movement' against BALCO mining project. This movement was not against displacement, but to protect forest and environment, which had a religious significance.

5   Ongoing or recent protest movements in the coastal districts: Baliapal National Test Range Movement, Save Chilika Movement, and Movement against Gopalpur Steel Plant.

witnessed very little protest.[6] This is particularly puzzling, as the large steel plant in combination with other industries and mining along the Bramhani River, the second largest river in Orissa, have had a devastating effect on the population and ecology living along this river (Khatua and Stanley 2006).

As it has been discussed before, people are no longer acquiescing to their displacement in the name of India's national development. People's perceptions of large development projects in general have changed. From the late 1970s, the opposition to these projects has steadily risen in India. In several regions, especially those that are adversely affected by large projects, protest movement participation has steeply increased. According to an estimation provided by Walter Fernades, nearly 5 million people have been displaced in Orissa, particularly in its inland part due to various projects in the last 20 years. However, the 'democratic enterprise' does not seem to have developed in the inland part of Orissa, until the end of 1990s. Several large projects have been undertaken in this region in the post independence period without being much affected by popular protests. Some popular movements were successful in receiving compensation rather than forcing the cancellation or shifting of the project site.

The river valley projects, which recently displaced a large population in this region, are the: Rengali Project;[7] Upper Kolab Project;[8] Upper Indravati Project;[9] and Subarnrekha Project.[10] Among the industrial projects, the National Aluminium Company (NALCO) in the Koraput District was responsible for displacing 610 families in the 1980s, of which 47.7 per cent are tribals (IseD 1996). All these projects precipitated protest movements in one way or another but they had not been sustained long enough to enable the cancellation of the project or bring significant delay to its implementation. However, these protest movements were not been completely unsuccessful either. Particularly, the movement against the Rengali Dam Project, which produced a legalized rehabilitation policy in Orissa

---

6   The protest against Hirakud project is the only popular movement worth mentioning. However, that protest movement was more of political nature and was aimed at the division of Orissa state rather than protection of the environment or struggle against displacement (Baboo 1993; Baboo 1992; Tripathy and Nanda 1987).

7   This project is in Dhenkanal (new Anugul) District; Construction period: 1973–92/93; 11,000 families have been displaced out of which 15.69 per cent *dalit* and 10.75 per cent tribal population.

8   This project is located in Koraput District; Construction period: 1976–91; 3179 families have been displaced out of them 13.9 per cent *dalit* and 44.7 per cent tribals.

9   This project covers Koraput and Kalahandi District; Construction period: 1978/79–1998; affected population is 50,000 out of which 41.94 per cent tribals and 15.02 per cent *dalit*.

10   This on-going interstate project of two dams and two barrages that Orissa shares with Bihar and West Bengal. The affected District in Orissa is Mayurbhanj, 13,000 families will be displaced of which the break-up statistics is not yet officially available.

in May 1978 for the 11,000 displaced people (Government of Orissa 1979). Artabandhu Mishra of Sambalpur University describes: 'During the first phase of dam building like that of Hirakud, Balimela and Salandi, the affected population had to remain satisfied with whatever compensation was available, but later on during the Rengali Dam Project rehabilitation was taken up more systematically providing the oustees mostly forest land to be cleared by them for conversion into arable land' (Mishra, undated). The credit for this increased compensation scheme mainly goes to the funding agencies of these projects, which have recently become sensitive to the environmental and displacement issues.

However, protests against these projects were not to receive better compensation but to resist displacement, which either meant a cancellation of the project or shift in the site of the project. Neither of these aims was achieved by any of these protest movements in the inland part of Orissa. A study by Nath and Agarwal of the movement against the Rengali Project clearly highlights the weakness in the popular opposition: highly hierarchical leadership, confusion among the protesters about the plan of action, and non-universal participation. The description of one incident can very well describe the weakness in this protest movement: 'On 12 June 1978, a large number of villagers arrived and tried to break the police cordon to go to the place of *Satyagrah*. The police then fired a teargas shell and mistaking it for a bomb the people fled. All leaders were then arrested and sent to jail. Frightened, the people fled in such a hurry that a large number of them were injured in this process.... There, ended the agitation.' (Nath and Agarwala, undated). The weakness of these protests can be found in the low participation, and lack of proper coordination. The local landlords and money lenders (*gauntias*) acted as the leaders and the common people were forced to protest in a *pali* (rotation) system.

A similar problem is reflected in two protest movements against two large dam projects undertaken in the 1980s and 1990s in the inland region of Orissa, the Upper Indravati Project (Orissa Krushak Mahasangh and Indravati Gana Sangharsha Parishad, undated; Amin, undated) and Subarnarekha Project. Both of these movements experienced an absence of proper organization and extended popular participation. Consistent popular action was missing in both cases. The movements were guided and led by upper caste leaders and who failed to involve the affected *dalits* and tribal population. The leaders of these movements also changed their demands during the course of the movement without taking into account the local lower caste people.

Under the leadership of the local higher caste people the Subarnarekha Project was opposed by *Ganatantrik Adhikar Surkshya Samiti* (GASS). These elite leaders of the GASS brought out a list of reasons for opposing the projects in April 1990. Out of the eight reasons, the first six were common environmental problems like global warming, while the last two dealt with displacement and rehabilitation of the affected people. This act of playing high politics might aim to attract outside attention, but clearly was not enough to motivate the local people in the affected area to continue the fight and spread their struggle. Consequently the protest failed and the project was completed in December 2008 (ProcessRegister – Manufacturers Database 2009).

Upper Indravati, a multipurpose dam project in Koraput District[11] was officially commissioned in 1978/79. However, the work of the project virtually started in the second half of 1980s. Initially some affected villagers who had legal ownership of the land accepted the compensation given by the Government officials and left their land and migrated to other areas (Sun Times, 31 March 1992). Some others, particularly from the tribal population, who lacked proper government records to prove ownership of the land remained, and occasionally resisted the construction of the project. The movement was able to galvanize momentum among the affected tribal population in the early 1990s, but by this time almost half of the project work was completed. Thus, this movement under the banner of *Indravati Gana Sangharsa Parishad* (IGSP) started demanding better compensation. To foil the movement, project officials accelerated the process of permitting the establishment of more and more Country Spirit Shops in the project area in order to divert the attention of the tribal oustees. IGSP continued the protest in a sporadic manner in the first half of the 1990s and managed to get some concessions from the government towards better rehabilitation measures (Sambad 1 December 1991). However, the project work continued and the Upper Indravati Dam Project was completed on the 30 June 1997 and the Upper Indravati Hydel Power Project in 2001 (ProcessRegister – Manufacturers Database 2009).

None of the protest movements in the inland part of Orissa till the end of 1990s had been successful in resisting the population displacement of these large projects. However, the story of environmental protest movement in the same time period was sweepingly different in the case of the coastal region. Though, the coastal plain of Orissa is much more economically developed, its topography does not allow the construction of large dam projects which have been the main cause of population displacement in the inland part. However, since the late 1980s, three large projects were planned for implementation along the coastal region. The first one was the National Test Range Facility at Baliapal in Balesore District. Nearly 50,000 people were going to be displaced by this defence facility. This prompted mass protest in that region against the project. The protest was well organized and had universal and sustained popular participation. People from all walks of life in the region joined in the protest. The leadership of the movement remained with

---

11 Koraput District in the inland part of Orissa has witnessed the construction of many large projects in the post-independence period (Stanley 1996; Babu and Pattnaik 1987). Also the study of Walter Fernades and S. Anthony Raj deals with number of cases from Koraput District on displacement and popular response.

the affected local people of the area, and it gathered support from all sections of society. Even women came to the forefront of the movement, blocking the entry of any government official to that area from 1987 to 1989. The Indian government was forced to back out from such a highly sensitive defence project in the face of sustained popular opposition and moved the test site to a group of uninhabited islands in the Bay of Bengal (Mohanty 1995).

Another popular protest movement was successful in resisting the construction of a large Steel Plant at Gopalpur in Ganjam District. This project came about between 1995–1996, and was expected to displace between 10,000 to 15,000 people. The protest movement against this proposed steel plant was led by locally affected people, cutting across party and caste affiliations under the banner of the *Gana Sangram Samiti* (Committee for People's Struggle). The argument of the movement was two fold: Industrialization would lead to direct displacement. Second, it would result in the loss of livelihood for the villagers who are traditional Kewra flower growers (Mangaraj 1997). This movement has also embraced the help of local scientists who support their argument about the loss of Kewra flower farming (*Sambad*, 17 December 1996). Women's participation was also critical to this movement, providing more strength and support to the protest. In this case popular opposition was able to spread its support base despite the lure of jobs from the industry. The movement was adamant about forcing the Tata Industrial House to shift the location of the project to another area in order to reduce the number of people displaced. The decision of the industry to reduce its plant operations area did not satisfy the local people (Patnaik 1997). At this time the Steel Plant project was being used as a political slogan by the state government, so the official machinery was using all its state power to garrotte the movement. But, it ultimately failed in its effort due to the strong unity of the local opposition (Steel Plant at Gopalpur: Why People Oppose It? 1996). This locally based and democratically managed popular movement had forced the authorities to finally cancel the project.[12] Another small Steel Plant project in Coastal Orissa, at Duburi in the Cuttack district, has also faced opposition from the displaced population, which has delayed its construction (*The Telegraph*, 20 November 1997).

The second movement, which has also been successful in the coastal region, is the protest against intensive prawn farming in the Chilika Lake. Following increased international demand for prawn, the traditional leasing system for fisher rights collapsed and the state of Orissa began to auction the leases to the highest bidder. Up until 1991 the leasing policy for shrimp farming was done illegally in

---

12   The people those were displaced by the initial land acquisition by the Tata Company demand their land back, because the company failed in establishing the project. The land that was acquired by the company and displaced around 1,500 families is highly fertile irrigated land. Out of the 3,088 acres of land the steel company uses only 10.2 acres while the rest of the land is lying unused (*The Hindu* 2008).

the Chilika Lake. This practice led to an increase in the number of fishers in the region from 8,060 in 1957 to 27,200 by 1986. However, with the new leasing policy farming became legal and further commercialized. The intensified shrimp farming caused an overall decline in the fish yield of the lake. These changes had severe economic and environmental consequences (Pattanaik 2007) leading to protests and demands for traditional fishers to gain legal property rights to the lake (Bedamatta 2007). This was the initial trigger for the first protests at the Chilika Lake in early 1991.

Moreover, Orissa's state government also made attempts to profit from the lucrative prawn farming. It gave the contract to Tata Company to establish the Tata Aquatic Farm project at the lake (Bedamatta 2007; Pattanaik 2007). The affected fishers at the lake responded by protesting against the project, because they feared the farm would pollute the lake water further reducing their catch yield (Pattanaik 2006). Starting from the grassroots level of the locally effected fishermen, the Chilika Bachao Andolan, or Save Chilika Movement, developed into a large-scale social movement after several years. The movement carried on the protest and successfully resisted the implementation of the Tata Farm project (Biswas 1993). As Bharat Dogra describes in his article in January 1993:

> With all its problems and controversies the Chilika Lake area during the last one-and-a-half years has also provided a fine example of a social movement in which the educated youth has joined hands with the weaker sections of society to protect the resource base without which there can be no future for the common people of this area.... Another admirable aspect of the movement is that the leading activists have made a deliberate effort to avoid becoming leaders and making others the followers (Dogra 1993: 20–21).

In the same article, Dogra describes:

> The movement was able to mobilize over 8000 people to gherao (siege) the state assembly in September 1991. It mobilized people again to demolish an embankment, which had been illegally constructed by the Tata Company despite the pressure of nearly 400 armed policemen. Soon after this when the activists tried to prevent the entry of bulldozers for the construction of an embankment, the police unleashed severe repression against them. Nearly 70 people were arrested. Some were beaten so savagely in police custody that they could not walk for several days, others were subjected to the worst humiliations (Dogra 1993: 20–21).

The movement in Chilika, like other movements in the coastal region, grew up from the affected area and was sustained by the local people. It received support from the different class and caste groups in society, helping it to grow and expand its support base. They were also successful in coordinating with groups outside of

Orissa, in order to lend more strength to the movement. It is remarkable to note that the movement not only opposed the projects at the lake, but rather 'provided an alternative model of sustainable development of the lake as against the dominant and destructive model of development by the state' (Pattanaik 2007: 298).

Withdrawal of the Tata Company from the project did not bring the issue to an end. After Tata left the site, it was 'politicians and their relatives, top bureaucrats and shrimp merchants and their agents' that used the lake for shrimp farming (Pattanaik 2007: 299–301). Initially the state government refused to listen to the protests of the fisher community against these new encroachers. Gradually, the protest picked up strength with enhanced participation, and the protesters set up road blockades and demolished shrimp gharries. In May 1999 the situation escalated when police were mobbed after arresting protest leaders, and in retaliation police shot at the mob causing four deaths (Bedamatta 2007). The protest took on the form of a 'Do or Die Movement'. The movement was successful in achieving a legal victory. It forced the government to pass a bill in the state Assembly in 2002, further protecting traditional rights of fisher communities, though implementation of the new policy is yet to be satisfactory (Pattanaik 2007; Panigrahi 2009).

Why Did Some Oriyas Protest Better Than Others?

Some researchers use the customary class analysis to illustrate the difference between peoples of coastal and inland regions regarding their protesting competence against unfair government policies. As Fernades and Raj describe: '...precisely because of their powerlessness the displaced population of Koraput and Keonjhar (inland part of Orissa) who agitated against the project had to ultimately accept the project and limit themselves to demanding better rehabilitation. In that sense, their situation was different from the powerful middle caste farmers of Baliapal in Orissa and others elsewhere who have succeeded in either stalling or even stopping the project completely' (Fernandes and Raj, undated).

If class factor is the key to success of a movement, then how were the landless dalit fishermen of the Chilika Lake able to successfully protest against the state power and financial strength of Tata Industrial House? The organization and success of the Chilika movement in the coastal part of Orissa displays the weakness in the class-based explanation about the success or failure of the movement. If the lack of formal land ownership has been the reason for non-universal participation in the protest movements in the inland region, then how could the fishermen in Chilika put up a united fight to protect a Common Property Resource (CPR)? Most of the Kewra flower plants in the Gopalpur Steel Plant area are also grown on government land and this has not adversely affected popular opposition against the project. CPR is extremely important for the livelihood of the tribal population in the inland region, which they stand to lose due to these development projects.

However, they were not able to protect it as successfully as the people along the coastal region.

In order to find some answers to this puzzle, the Agora Survey from 1997 can be of use. This Survey used a multi-stage cluster sampling; three hundred respondents were interviewed in the coastal region and another three hundreds in the inland part of Orissa. The survey was designed to discover the level of popular involvement in various protests and organized movements.

It can be argued that in the inland part of Orissa, there were many grievances against the government, but local people had not been able to fight for their cause as often and as effectively as people from the coastal region. The diffusion of the protest is necessary in order to keep it alive when its initial spark begins to sputter. Protest marches and demonstrations need to be translated into an organized popular movement. A successful movement needs to transcend the 'volcanic' stage of collective action. The spread of a movement also creates difficulties for authorities by limiting their ability to use force to enforce order (Tarrow 1993). Every movement develops a participation scheme. The patterns, levels and types of participation define to a certain extent the strength of its goals. For enhanced participation, an extended group network is needed. Very few protests are observed reaching the stage of being organized movements in the inland part of Orissa until the late 1990s. The Agora Survey finds that people in the inland part of Orissa have not only experienced fewer number of popular movements, but that their participation in such organized actions are also very limited.

Table 4.5   Participation in protest movement, the regional variation

	Coastal	Inland
Occasional Protests		
Yes	42.33%	9.36%
No	57.00%	80.27%
Organized Protests		
Yes	68.87%	28.30%
No	31.13%	71.70%

The transformation of an occasional protest into an organized movement would be impossible in the absence of a flexible and inclusive form of a network within the broad framework of collective action. The weakness of a minor group can be prevailed over with active coordination with other groups. Effective coordination can be possible through networks of smaller and minor groups, which support each other to achieve collective strength for popular action. The existence of weak ties in society can set the pace for networking among the groups and thus can help the movement to spread and sustain in order to achieve its aim and objective.

The more the local, social and cultural interactions are mutually reinforcing, the more likely people are to engage in collective defiance (Eckstein 1989). An intra-group strong tie creates high trust within the group but at the same time brings suspicion about the others. By bringing exclusiveness to the group, strong ties may hinder the group's initiative or participation in broader movements. Communal ties need to take the back seat, leaving room for secondary associations in society in order to strengthen the movement. Unlike strong ties, weak ties within and outside the group may bring inclusiveness (or at least not exclusiveness) and help to build, spread and sustain the movement successfully.

The people in the inland part of Orissa, with stronger ties to one another in their own caste group, had lesser interaction with outside groups. This we believe significantly impeded coordination and limited popular participation in the movement before the end of the 1990s. But, the situation was different in the coastal part of Orissa. The survey results clearly demonstrated the presence of strong and exclusive ties among the people in the inland part of Orissa compared to the coastal region.

Table 4.6   Ties to the community

	Coastal	Inland
How would their children identify?		
Indian or Oriya	61.46%	49.82%
Hindu	19.79%	16.49%
Caste group	15.62%	32.98%
Voting outside caste		
Almost never	17.00%	25.33%
Sometimes	26.67%	44.67%
Almost always	55.33%	27.00%
Inter-caste wedding invitation		
Always	16.03%	3.70%
Sometimes	43.90%	17.85%
Never	40.07%	78.45%
Discussing public issues with others		
Regularly	55.85%	50.68%
Occasionally	37.13%	14.18%
Never	6.69%	27.03%

Not only was there a difference in the type of ties and social relationship, but there was also a distinct difference in the existing associational life in the two regions of Orissa. There was a strong presence of active and inclusive associations in the coastal region, where people have successfully protested against the perceived unfair policies of the government. Nearly sixty fishermen cooperatives were operating in the Chilika Lake region at the time when the shrimp project was announced. These cooperatives coordinated to form the apex organization, The Matsyajibi Mahasangh (Fishermen Association) and managed the movement. Like Fishermen Cooperatives in Chilika, the Betel Leaves Grower Associations in Baliapal and the Kewra Pluckers Committees in Gopalpur have helped to coordinate among themselves in order to provide strength and support to the popular protests.

The Agora Survey in 1997 also establishes the difference in popular perception about the efficacy of the associations in the two regions of Orissa. In the inland part, fewer numbers of people consider associations an efficient tool to bring about change in society. This popular perception is also reflected in their lower participation rate in associational activities.

Table 4.7   Associational perception and participation

	Coastal	Inland
Is Association Efficient in Solving Problems?		
Greatly Efficient	78.93%	21.67%
Not so Efficient	12.37%	43.00%
Completely Inefficient	6.02%	11.67%
Personal Participation in any Association		
Yes	73.33%	27.67%
No	26.67%	71.33%

Moreover, the types of secondary associations, which provide weak ties with other groups, were also wanting in the inland region of Orissa. The survey showed in the late 1990s the presence of a distinct pattern of associational life in the two regions of Orissa. While the people in the coastal areas involved themselves more in forming developmental, professional, farmer, and cultural associations, the people in inland Orissa tended to opt for youth and women's associations. This pattern clearly demonstrates the difference. The associations in the coastal areas were more inclusive in character and did not restrict themselves to a particular group or community. Groupings on the basis of development, profession and cultural activities are more likely to develop inter-communal networks in society.

Table 4.8   Existence of inclusive associations

	Coastal	Inland
Village Development Association		
Exists	59.67%	48.33%
Does Not Exist	40.33%	51.67%
Professional Association		
Exists	48.33%	19.00%
Does Not Exist	51.17%	81.00%
Cultural/Religious Associations		
Exists	96.67%	55.00%
Does Not Exist	3.33%	45.00%
Farmers' Associations		
Exists	26.67%	22.67%
Does Not Exist	73.33%	77.33%

Table 4.8 shows that the percentage of village development, professional, farmer and cultural associations in coastal areas was much larger than in the inland part of Orissa. However, when it comes to the youth (Yuvak Sangh) or women's associations (Mahila Samiti), the inland part happens to be in a better position (Table 4.9). These two types of associations in Oriya villages usually draw their members from a single caste group. If a village has more than one caste population, it is common to find the existence of more than one of these associations. Moreover, the various social programmes of the government also support these two types of associations. They flourish primarily due to governmental patronage.

Table 4.9   Existence of exclusive associations

	Coastal	Inland
Youth Associations		
Exists	71.00%	87.00
Does not Exist	29.00%	13.00%
Women Associations		
Exists	23.33%	41.33%
Does not exist	76.67%	58.67%

The inland part in the late 1990s not only suffered from the absence of inclusive forms of associations, but also was also further entrenched by the growth of associations, which develop strong intra-communal bonds and restrict individuals to their own groups. The associational life in this region was based on protecting or promoting the interests of traditional groups, and did not facilitate cross community engagements.

Again Society is the Key

Even though every protest movement has its own history and perpetuity, the timing of its collapse defines its quality. For broader and more successful movements, there is a need for larger and more sustained popular mobilization. This can be achieved in a segmented society mostly through coordination or networks of various sections or ties. In the inland part of Orissa, in spite of larger numbers of grievances against the government, people did not protest as often as their coastal counterparts. And even if they did protest, they were unable to expand and sustain it for a decisive result. The protest movements in the inland part primarily failed to gather momentum due to the failure of different groups to join together. Strong communal ties prevented the coming together for a common cause: it not only restricted associational life, but also curbed popular mobilization.

The study of Orissa in the 1990s shows that social network based on weak ties is crucial in order to facilitate the success of protest movements. It is particularly important in a highly segregated society. By just aggregating trust and associations, it is not possible to analyze the relationship between social network and social action. It is not just the number of associations but the quality of associations that help coordinate the effort in society. It is the quality of social ties that determine the type of associational life that influence popular mobilizations.

Chapter 5

Maoists and Missionaries: Changing Social Network Structure for Successful Protest Mobilization

As it has been explained in the previous chapter, the people in the inland part of Orissa did not protest as often as their counterparts in the coastal region, despite large-scale population displacement and environmental destruction due to big industries, extensive mining, and large hydro projects. Moreover, when they did take part in some protests, mobilization in the inland part was unable to sustain itself long enough or failed to gather the momentum needed to make an impact. This weak nature of protest mobilization was primarily due to the failure of the community to establish and encourage inter-communal ties. The limited associational life and small reservoir of weak ties in inland Orissa demonstrated its limited capacity to mobilize and sustain a protest movement. Overall, high bonding within the existing social network structure coupled with little bridging ties were significant reasons behind the failure of the movements.

In the last five years, the movement scenario in Orissa has gone through a noticeable change. The tribal population of the inland part has taken up coordinated and large-scale protest movements against various large development projects and policies. Several organized protests have challenged the proposed projects, which could potentially lead to population displacement. Even those who were displaced by development projects in the 1960s and 1970s have revived their protests in a more coordinated manner. There is a significant change being observed between the various tribal groups of Orissa, with enhanced cooperation and participation in protest movements. Widespread resistance by tribal people to projects causing displacement has forced the Orissa government to now plan a comprehensive relief and rehabilitation policy.

Opposition of tribal people to new industries because of displacement in the Kalinga Nagar area has resulted in the deaths of 12 protesters by police firing in January 2006. Under the banner of the Visthapan Virodhi Janmanch (People's Committee against Displacement), they have organized a series of programs to continue their protests. A main highway of the state had been blocked for traffic for more than one year since the firing incident. The movement has also spread to other parts of inland Orissa. Those who have already been displaced by various projects have started demanding better and further compensation.

Several projects, which are under construction or in the planning stage, are also being targeted to demand minimizing human displacement and providing a comprehensive compensation package. These movements are coordinating among themselves and are drawing strength from the support that is being extended by some civil society organizations and prominent citizens from different parts of the State and outside.

The inland region has in recent years been directly affected by the ultra-left Maoist movement. According to Orissa government's White Paper in 2009, 14 districts in the inland part have come under Maoist influence. Moreover, the region has also been recently exposed to the competing Christian and Hindu religious missionaries looking for new recruits. The growing involvement of these external actors and ideologies has brought significant changes to inter-community interaction and coordination. The changing character of social network has been helping the people in the region to protest more successfully. To analyze the link of social network and social action it is therefore important to assess the evolving character of interpersonal ties in protesting societies and its contribution to the strength of protest mobilization.

Thus a follow up survey was conducted in 2007 of 300 people in the inland part of Orissa to locate and evaluate the changing character of inter-personal ties. The 2007 survey was done in the same area (Koraput District) as it was in the 1997 Agora Survey. The same numbers of respondents, 300, were also selected using multi-stage cluster sampling. Results from the comparison of the two surveys reveals noticeable change in the inter-communal interactions and coordination, as well as societal perception of associational life and the effectiveness of the protest movements. The survey also tried to measure new external influences on the society since the post 1997 period, i.e. the influx of the Maoist movements as well as religious conversion.

Growing Political Radicalization in Inland Orissa

In the 1997 Agora Survey, 60.74 per cent of respondents in the inland Orissa saw reforms as the appropriate way to change society for the better. 7.38 per cent favoured revolutionary action, while 5.37 per cent considered society as good and worth defending. Comparing these results to the succeeding survey conducted in 2007, one finds interesting developments in these attitudes. The portion of the population in favour of reforms remains unchanged about 60.07 per cent. However, it is clearly visible that undecided people, answering with 'don't know', have made a shift towards a more radical path: in 2007, 18.09 per cent favoured defending society against subversive forces, an increase by 12.72 per cent; and more importantly, 17.06 per cent of the population, an increase by 9.68 per cent, favour radical change through revolutionary action. This development clearly

Table 5.1   Changing attitude towards societal change

	Survey 1997		Survey 2007	
	Freq.	%	Freq	%
The entire way our society is organized must be radically changed by revolutionary action	22	7.38	50	17.06
Our society must be gradually improved by reforms	181	60.74	176	60.07
Our society must be valiantly defended against all subversive forces	16	5.37	53	18.09
Don't know	79	26.51	13	4.44
	298	100	293	100

indicates the influence of external actors and ideology in recent years, which has caused undecided parts of the population to gravitate towards radical positions.

People in inland Orissa have not only changed their view about the way of achieving societal change, they have also gone through a perceptual change about various available means to reach that goal. These means range from taking part in elections as voters or political associations, to participating in protests or taking up arms.

The 2007 Survey shows a definite trend towards popular perceptions that they are capable of changing the problems of the country. Rebutting the Maoist philosophy, the survey reflects that people in the inland part of Orissa have greater faith in the election process now than before. In the 2007 survey, 58 per cent of the respondents believed that by voting in the elections they would be able to address the problems. In 1997 just 3 per cent saw elections as a way of solving the problems – an increase by a mammoth 55 per cent in 2007. Along with this, people's confidence in associational participation as a means to tackle problems within the country has increased by 46 per cent. Just 22 per cent regarded their active participation in associations as efficient or quite efficient in changing problems in 1997. In 2007 this number has shot up to 68 per cent. Participation in protest marches or demonstrations saw the same development and rose from 12 per cent to 56 per cent. The development has not been positive throughout. The popular belief in the efficiency of violence as a means to change society has also increased in 2007. 36 per cent of the surveyed population in 2007 regard the use of force or violent methods as an efficient or quite efficient means to change the problems of society – an increase of 34 per cent from 1997. There is no doubt that the inland part of the Orissa has recently become prone to greater violence, as it is not only witnessing armed rebellion by Maoists, but also experiencing inter-religious tensions. However, in general, the people have been quite decisive and

Table 5.2   Popular perceptions about ways to tackle the problems of the country

Do you think voting in the elections is capable of changing the problems in the country?

	Freq. 1997	Freq. 2007	% 1997	% 2007
1. Very much capable.	10	171	0.03	0.58
2. Mostly capable.	82	60	0.27	0.20
3. Capable	53	5	0.18	0.02
4. Mostly incapable.	62	13	0.21	0.04
5. Not capable.	27	20	0.09	0.07
8. I don't know	65	24	0.22	0.08

Do you think actively participating in an association is capable of changing the problems in the country?

	Freq. 1997	Freq. 2007	% 1997	% 2007
1. Very much capable.	6	43	0.02	0.15
2. Mostly capable.	59	156	0.20	0.53
3. Capable	47	20	0.16	0.07
4. Mostly incapable.	82	24	0.27	0.08
5. Not capable.	35	22	0.12	0.08
8. I don't know	70	28	0.23	0.10

Do you think taking part in a protest march or demonstration is capable of changing the problems in the country?

	Freq. 1997	Freq. 2007	% 1997	% 2007
1. Very much capable.	4	60	0.01	0.21
2. Mostly capable.	32	102	0.11	0.35
3. Capable	39	51	0.13	0.18
4. Mostly incapable.	83	26	0.28	0.09
5. Not capable.	61	19	0.20	0.07
8. I don't know	81	33	0.27	0.11

Do you think the use of force or violent methods are capable of changing the problems in the country?

	Freq. 1997	Freq. 2007	% 1997	% 2007
1. Very much capable.	0	58	0.00	0.20
2. Mostly capable.	7	48	0.02	0.16
3. Capable	11	12	0.04	0.04
4. Mostly incapable.	83	36	0.28	0.12
5. Not capable.	124	107	0.41	0.37
8. I don't know	75	30	0.25	0.10

Table 5.3   Inland Orissa population joining protest movements in their locality

	1997		2007	
	Freq.	Per cent	Freq.	Per cent
Yes	30	28.30	30	56.60
No	76	71.70	23	43.40
Total	106	100.00	53	100.00

Table 5.4   People influenced by the Maoist movement in inland Orissa in 2007

	Freq.	Per cent
Yes	128	42.67
No	153	51.00

Note: Missing to 100 per cent answered 'don't know' or answer not available.

clear about their views on these possible means of social change and the 'I don't know' answers have decreased approximately 10 per cent from 1997 to 2007.

These changes in attitudes and perceptions have also brought a noticeable change to protest mobilization in inland Orissa. As per the surveys, in 1997 a majority, 71.7 per cent, of the inland Orissa population did not join a protest movement in their area, this number declined in 2007 to 43.4 per cent. On the other hand, the number of people joining protest movements in 2007 has doubled, from 28.3 per cent to 56.6 per cent.

The new change in the process of protest mobilization in the inland region has no doubt come thanks to the recent entry of both the ultra-left and ultra-right groups to the arena and their impact on the network structure of the communities. The spectacular rise of the Maoist movement in the inland part in the last six years, has managed to break the traditional clan barrier among various groups to a large extent and create one tribal identity. In the past, the people in this region were clearly divided along their own clan identity and interaction among these sub-groups was limited, if there was any it was mainly hostile. The impact of the Maoist movement has helped to bring these sub-groups together and they now see themselves as tribes in their struggle against the 'oppressive' state and outsiders. As it is clear from the 2007 survey, a large portion of the population (42.67 per cent) in the inland region has been directly or indirectly influenced by the Maoist (Naxalite) movement's philosophy.

Table 5.5   **Religious missionaries approaching people for conversion in inland Orissa, 2007**

	Freq.	Per cent
Hindu religious activists	26	24.76
Christian Missionaries	72	68.57
Other Religion	1	0.95

Note: Missing to 100 per cent answered 'don't know' or answer not available.

Moreover, the conversion and re-conversion competition between Christian missionaries and Hindu radical organizations have also facilitated tribal groups' ability and possibility towards networking with each other as well as with the outside support groups. The tribal population in the inland region, which was keeping itself isolated from any interaction with outsiders before, thanks to the relentless endeavour of these religious activists, has gotten rid of that reluctance to a large extent.

The 2007 Survey shows that Christian missionaries have been very active in inland Orissa. 68.57 per cent of those surveyed in 2007 have been approached by one or more Christian missionaries to convert to Christianity. This intensified missionary engagement has been successful in changing many people's religion. While in 1997 none of the respondents in the inland region were Christian, by 2007 it had increased to 8.6 per cent, however, Christian missionaries are being increasingly challenged by Hindu religious activists. They are not only opposing the conversion plans of the Christian missionaries, but also actively working to reconvert some of the people back to Hinduism. As the 2007 Survey shows, a large number of Hindu religious activists are also engaged in the inland part of Orissa.

In the following section of this chapter, an attempt has been made to study and analyze the growing Maoist movement and the developing politics of religious conversion in inland Orissa. The aim is to measure their influence on changing social ties and the subsequent strength of protest mobilization capabilities in the region.

The Maoist Corridor and Protest Mobilization

The Maoist communist movement in India is commonly referred to as the Naxalite movement. The movement traces its roots to 1967, where a radical communist group in the neighbouring state of West Bengal led a violent uprising. Naxalbari, a small region in West Bengal's north, is the claimed birthplace of the movement and location of its first struggle. In 1967, a small group of people under the leadership of Charu Mazumdar and Kanu Sanyal broke away from the Communist

Party of India (Marxist) (CPI (M)) believing in the need of an armed revolution (Mehra 2000). This new movement's identification with the Maoist ideology and Marxism/Leninism brand of communism as well as the violent crush of the uprising resulted in ending the good relations between the CPI (M) and the Chinese Communist Party. This gave further momentum to the newly formed movement, which institutionalized itself in form of the Communist Party of India (Marxist-Leninist) (CPI (ML)) in April 1969. The new party was immediately recognized by the Chinese Communist Party (Dasgupta 1974).

After the government crushed the movement during the 1970s it fragmented into various factions. However, the main actors of the movement were arrested or killed during police operations in July and August of 1971. The leading figure Charu Mazumdar died shortly after having been arrested in prison in July 1972 (Dasgupta 1974). Although some of the Naxalite factions remained active in parts of Andhra Pradesh and Bihar, their influence was localized in nature. The three noteworthy factions, which stayed active in the time after the 1970s were the Maoist Communist Centre of India (MCC), the People's War Group (PWG), and a small remaining contingent of the Communist Party of India (Marxist-Leninist). The first was active in parts of Bihar and the latter two had their base in Andhra Pradesh.

With the economic liberalization and gradual withdrawal of the state from its commitment to welfare policies, the support for these radical groups has increased again in recent years. On the 21 September 2004 the Naxalite movement reappeared as a strong group when the MCC, PWG and CPI (ML) merged to form a new entity. The Communist Party of India-Maoist (CPI-Maoist) reaffirmed its commitment to the classical Maoist strategy of 'protracted armed struggle', which defines its objectives not in terms of the seizure of lands, crops, or other immediate goals, but the seizure of state authority. Within this perspective, participation in elections and engagement with the prevailing 'bourgeois democracy' are rejected, and all efforts and attention is firmly focused on 'revolutionary activities' to undermine the state and seize power. Estimates suggest that after the merger of the three groups, there are approximately 9,000 to 10,000 armed fighters. The movement is now affecting about 165 districts in 14 states, establishing a 'red corridor' through the Indian peninsula, from the northeast border with Nepal, where Naxalbari is located, down to Karnataka and Tamil Nadu (Singh 2007; *The Economist*, 17 August 2006).

The unity move by the Indian Maoists has provided the ultras a bigger base and greater strength. The rebels are forcefully and violently demanding for the creation of a communist state comprising tribal areas of the states of Andhra Pradesh, Maharashtra, Orissa, Bihar and Chhattisgarh. The purpose of their struggle is to improve the economic and social rights of the poor and of indigenous tribes in the region. However, according to Indian Government's Home Ministry's annual report of 2009, the Maoists insurgency has claimed more than 3,300 lives in the last five years.

In August 2006, the Indian prime minister, Manmohan Singh, linked the Maoist movement with terrorism and declared them the biggest threat to India's security (*The Economist*, 17 August 2006). However, the central government, particularly the Ministry of Home Affairs, was reluctant to use central paramilitary forces in a big way against Maoist groups for some time. This 'soft approach' was adopted by the then Home Minister, partly due to pressure from Left parties as the government was dependent upon their support for its survival. The election in 2009 gave larger parliamentary support for the Congress Party and the Left parties lost their bargaining power at the Centre. Though Prime Minister had labelled the Maoists as terrorists already in 2006, the Indian Government decided only in 2009 to proceed seriously against these groups in a 'long-haul strategy that will involve simultaneous, coordinated counter-operations in all Left-wing extremism-hit states' (*The Economic Times*, 6 February 2009).

Factions of the Maoist Movement started operating in Orissa from 1985 on, however not conducting any serious armed struggle till recently. In the last six years, most parts of inland Orissa have come under the influence of this radical left, i.e. becoming part of the Maoist corridor. Prior to their merger in 2004, the Peoples War Group (PWG) had a token presence in the southern districts of Orissa (Koraput, Malkangiri, Nabarangapur, Rayagada, Gajapati, and Ganjam); whereas the Maoist Communist Centre (MCC) had established its influence in the western region (Sundargarh, Mayurbhanj and Keonjhar). After the formation of the Communist Party of India (Maoist), the radical left movement has spread to the remaining parts of inland Orissa (Sambalpur, Kandhamal, Deogarh, Jharsuguda, Jajpur and Angul). The rapid upsurge of Maoists in inland Orissa has been possible due to a continuous process of underdevelopment in the region. Taking advantage of the acute poverty, rampant corruption and regional disparity in the inland parts of Orissa, Maoists have shown the tribal population the dream of a revolution. As Dash argues, the Maoist movement took advantage of the poor development situation in areas like Malkangiri. Among others, the high rate of poverty and its poor literacy rate further enabled the Maoist movement to attract the 'tribal youth to join their revolution' (Dash 2006: 37)

The socio-economic situation of the tribal population in the Maoist dominated districts of Orissa is extremely miserable. Hunger and malnourishment is very common and starvation death is a regular feature. The media regularly reports child sale by poor and hungry tribal parents in these areas. Various development schemes undertaken by state and central governments fail to improve the living standard due to massive corruption by government employees and other outside agencies. In India, corruption is rampant at all levels, however it hits the poor tribal people hardest. Thus, it is generally argued that Maoist leaders have found it easy to mobilize and organize the deprived and disillusioned tribal population to take up arms for their rights.

However, the surveys conducted in inland Orissa in 1997 and 2007 suggest that poverty and under-development are not the only reasons for the rising popularity of the Maoist movements. In the respective time period of ten years, from 1997 until 2007, education and other development indicators have improved in the region, despite the increased activity and participation/affiliation with the Maoist movement. More people than before are literate and have completed at least middle school. Also, the number of unemployed people has decreased by 3 per cent. This, however, should not hide the fact that inland Orissa still includes some of the poorest districts of India, but it does illustrate that the underdevelopment and grievance arguments do not merely explain why Maoists have been so successful in establishing their stronghold in the region.

Table 5.6   Educational levels, 1997 and 2007 surveys

	Freq. 1997	Freq. 2007	% 1997	% 2007
Illiterate	94	15	32	05
Literate, but no formal education	13	50	04	17
Primary	58	47	20	16
Middle School	27	54	09	18
High School	50	59	17	20
College	51	69	17	23

It is true that the state has seriously neglected its responsibilities towards the problems of the people, especially the tribal inland population in Orissa. The anger against the states' apathy has shifted the neglected people's support towards the Maoists. As Guha describes it in a very lucid manner:

> The Maoists are prepared to walk miles to hold village meetings, and listen sympathetically to tribal grievances. As a senior forest official was recently constrained to admit: "In the absence of any government support and the apathetic attitude of the forest management departments towards the livelihood of forest-dependent communities, the Naxalites have found fertile ground to proliferate..." (Guha 2007: 3309).

Whatever might be the reason for the spectacular growth of the Maoist movements, it has certainly brought a significant change in the people's ability to protest in order to protect their interests. The armed rebellion has been instrumental in bringing self-confidence to the tribal population and organizing them into a single group. Creating a common identity, which crosses community boundaries and overcomes local, single group vanity. They are gradually less inclined to be identified as 'Koya', 'Santhal', 'Parja' or Godava' or in any other of their own clan category, and more and more becoming part of a larger tribal identity. Thanks to this, the protest movement of tribal groups has not remained localized in nature. In any anti-government demonstration, there is also participation from groups who are not directly affected by the development or conservation projects.

Politics of Religion and Protest Mobilization

Besides the impact of the Maoist rebellion, the politics of religion has also brought changes to the inter-personal ties structure in the tribal society of inland Orissa, by encouraging interaction among various sub groups. Religious actors have been successfully converting and reconverting local populations, increasing distinguished religious identities and thus increasing new societal connections beyond traditional community borders. The new religion based worship centres bring together tribal groups who used to live and operate in seclusion to meet and interact. The religious preachers and activists, both from outside and local ones promote and support the inter-group interactions in a big way.

Christianity is not new to India as it was already present in some communities from the first century on. Since then various missionaries have contributed to the expansion of Christianity in the Indian peninsular. However, it was in the nineteenth and twenties century that India witnessed a substantial conversion to Christianity (Beaglehole 1967). As Clark argues, the religious conversion in India is not a phenomena, which has come purely from outside. India has witnessed large conversion of its Hindu population to other Indic religions, such as Buddhism, Jainism and Sikhism. There is no doubt of course that Muslim invasions and British Colonialism have played a significant role in bringing other religions into the country (Clarke 2007).

At the beginning of the twentieth century the Christian missionaries were particularly successful in their missions with tribal populations in India. Beaglehole argues that the focus on education was one of the most important strategies of the missionaries. Christian schools he writes: 'were almost the only agency for education among the Depressed Classes and tribes' (Beaglehole 1967: 61). This educational success was also visible in Orissa, where in the 1920s approximately 17 per cent of teenage Christian tribal members went to school, contrasted with 3 per cent of the non-Christian tribes. Besides education, as some argues Christianity also brought other advantages, as its practices aere not as intrusive and dominating as of Hinduism (Beaglehole 1967).

Despite the longstanding conversion activities of Christian missions in India in general and Orissa in particular, there was no record of violence between

Christians and Hindus in the country. Unlike Hindu Muslim riots, the violence between Christians and Hindus is a rather new phenomenon, as both groups lived alongside each other for a long period of time in relative harmony.

For many years now, the Christian missionary agencies have been active in the inland part of Orissa to support and promote the conversion of the tribal population to Christianity. Notwithstanding the successes of the missionaries in recent years (see Table 5.7), the Christian communities comprise approximately 2.3 per cent of the total Indian population (*The Economic Times*, 20 September 2008). In the inland Orissa, though the number of Christian population is increasing, but still very small in comparison to majority Hindu community.

Table 5.7   Changing religious preferences in inland Orissa

	Freq. 1997	Freq. 2007	% 1997	% 2007
Hindu	284	257	96	86
Muslim	0	15	00	05
Christian	0	26	00	09
Other	13	2	04	01

Although the Christian minorities do not pose any serious threat to the Hindu majority, the Hindu nationalists still worry about Christian conversion, not only culturally but also politically. Christianity with its progressive-looking social approach exposes caste systems and other social evils in Hinduism. Moreover, the educational and medical services of the Christian Missions gain the appreciation of the people and that creates some insecurity among the Hindu religious leaders (*The Economic Times*, 20 September 2008). The increasing number of Christians in some constituencies also creates additional political problems for Hindu political activists.

With the rise of Hindu nationalism in India in recent years, the clashes between religious communities have increased as well. The violence has not been limited to Muslims, but gradually increased against Christian minorities. Since the end of 2007, Christians in Orissa have been the target of violence, along with the destruction of their churches, homes and businesses (Bauman 2008). Violence also erupted in September 2008 in the state of Karnataka against the Christian community. Hindus as well as Catholic Christians alleged that the New Life Church was converting people in Karnataka. The dispute caused open violence, when Bajrnag Dal cadres, a Hindu fundamentalist outfit, attacked Christians in the region, irrespective of their membership in the Catholic Church or New Life Church (Satish 2008).

In 1967, the Government of Orissa had brought in the controversial Orissa Freedom of Religion Act, which prohibited 'the use of force or inducement or fraudulent means' to convert someone from one religion to another. Since then regular disputes have erupted around religious conversion. However, in recent years, the Christian missionaries are not only facing legal obstacles from the state, but also violent opposition from Hindu extremist organizations. According to Biswamoy Pati religious communalism and divisive politics have entered Orissa and have attained a high level of aggressiveness. Several Hindu fundamentalist groups have become active in the region. The competition between the two religious groups in recruiting support has also exposed the tribal population of inland Orissa to outside religious organizations and their mobilizing agents (Pati 2001).

After a new government came to power in Orissa's 2000 elections, the pro-Hindu party BJP became a major coalition member, intensifying anti-conversion actions. A "re-conversion" campaign has given rise to the active opposition to Christian missionary activities. Coleman writes: 'During the tenure of the BJP, anti-conversion legislation became a focal point for the resolution of the Indian 'national question', particularly the purposes of establishing a more resolute and extensive Hindu cultural identity' (Coleman 2008: 264).

Hindu fundamentalist groups in Orissa are regularly targeting the Christian community and missionaries. After the assassination of a local Hindu religious leader in 2008, prolonged violence against Christians broke out in the Kandhamal area of Orissa. At that time, with the government of Orissa under the influence of the major coalition partner, BJP, directed police to take limited action against Hindu rioters. This mindless violence killed many poor people and displaced thousands. Though, in the 2009 election, the BJP lost its political power, but still remains a major political force in Orissa, actively engaged in mobilizing against missionaries in the inland part.

One of the results of the religious polarization in inland Orissa is a significant increase of inter-communal violence experienced by the surveyed people from 11 per cent in 1997 to 28.78 per cent in 2007. On the other hand there is evidence that the conversion and re-conversion moves have facilitated the tribal groups to interact with other clans and castes as well as the non-tribal population and organizations. As it is presently experienced in the inland part of Orissa, social network structure is not a stagnant one and the intervention of external factors and actors can have a significant contribution to its evolution and character. Ideology and religion have been able to create larger identities in the society, in the process overriding the strong and exclusive bonding within smaller groups. This process has been facilitated by a large number of political and religious entrepreneurs. Weak and bridging ties developed through ideological and religious mobilizations have led to efficient sharing of information and concern cutting across social and geographical clusters, and in the process creating a strong network capital.

Table 5.8   Discussing common issues outside immediate family

	Freq 1997	Freq 2007	% 1997	% 2007	Change %
Every day	47	67	16	23	07
Once in a week/few times	103	67	35	23	-12
Once in a month/few times	35	94	12	32	20
Once in a Year/few times	7	33	03	12	09
Not at all/not frequently	80	19	27	06	-21
I don't know	24	13	08	04	-04

Table 5.9   Expression of own views in public discussions

	Freq 1997	Freq 2007	% 1997	% 2007	Change %
Many times	35	62	12	21	09
Most of time	63	66	22	23	01
Not always	27	113	09	39	29
Rarely	48	30	18	11	08
Not at all	89	14	31	05	-26
I don't know	29	7	10	02	-08

Outside actors are not exactly the same as 'movement entrepreneurs' (McAdam, Tarrow, and Tilly 2001) as they do not directly act as agents or brokers to help the process of moving a localized action to a coordinated and broader movement. The mobilization processes of the protests in the inland part have taken advantage of a changing social network structure, which has materialized primarily due to outside influences. However, these outside actors are involved in this social churning process and not with the express interest of helping the mobilization of these protests but because of their own selfish political and religious agendas.

Newly-created Ties Strengthen Protest Mobilization

External actors' contributions to manufacturing diffused and weak ties among the tribal population have led to their denser social network, helping them to identify within a larger social group structure. As result of this, local protests against large development projects, which were before limited in size and short in duration, have now been able to link with others to initiate coordinated actions. Broadening contacts have helped to mobilize larger and more sustained opposition against various projects in the inland part of Orissa. Several protest movements, like those demanding better compensation for the people who were displaced by the Hirakud Dam in 1960s, which met an untimely demise in the past, have been reborn to

Table 5.10   Time people spend outside of work with different social groups

You spend time with people whom you do not know well					
	Freq 1997	Freq 2007	% 1997	%2007	Change %
Daily	0	69	00	23	23
Some times in a week	9	42	03	14	11
Some times in a month	36	69	12	23	11
Some times in a year	79	57	30	20	-09
Not at all/ Not frequently	143	43	48	15	-33
I don't know	33	15	11	05	-06
You spend time with people having different lifestyle					
Daily	6	44	02	15	13
Some times in a week	33	57	11	19	08
Some times in a month.	63	32	21	11	-10
Some times in a year	66	97	25	34	10
Not at all/ Not frequently.	100	52	33	18	-16
I don't know	32	14	11	05	-06
You spend time with people of different castes					
Daily	60	164	20	55	35
Some times in a week	115	36	38	12	-26
Some times in a month	69	18	23	06	-17
Some times in a year	26	34	09	12	03
Not at all/ Not frequently.	20	29	07	10	03
I don't know	10	15	03	05	02
You spend time with people of different religion					
Daily	77	127	26	43	17
Some times in a week	85	42	28	14	-14
Some times in a month	64	12	21	04	-17
Some times in a year	31	61	11	22	11
Not at all/ Not frequently	27	41	09	14	05
I don't know	16	13	05	04	-01

place renewed pressure on government agencies to redress their lost rights and proper compensation.

A comparison of the 1997 and 2007 survey clearly demonstrates that in the last decade, the community in the inland part has been able to create a new set of inter communal ties, which were not present earlier. They have been politically active, discussing issues and expressing views with others. In the 2007 survey, the number of people not discussing common matters outside their family has dropped by 21 per cent compared to 1997.

It is not only that they discuss common issues; they are also more at ease to express their own views, and not only listen to others. That shows the ties are based on horizontal interactions rather than being vertical in nature. In 1997 about 31 per cent of the people in the community did not express their own view on common matters. This changed in 2007 by 26 per cent, where just 5 per cent of the people asked did not express their own position in a discussion.

The time people spend daily with unfamiliar people or people from other social, religious, or caste groups has also increased on average by 22 per cent. This becomes most obvious in the case of time spent with people from different castes. While in 1997, 20 per cent spent time across caste boundaries, it grew to 55 per cent in 2007 – a massive increase of 35 per cent.

Increasing inter-personal ties in inland society has also reflected growth in associational life. People in inland Orissa have come forward to participate and take up positions in various associations. Participation rates in various associations have increased in substantial numbers, particularly in Women Associations (increase by 27 per cent) and Professional Associations (increase by 31 per cent). It is not that people are participating more in the various associations, they are also willing to take further active role in managing these forums. Compared to 1997, in 2007 there were 39 per cent more people that took up organizational posts in Village Development Associations, 27 per cent in Women Associations, 23 per cent in Professional Associations, and 7 per cent in Cultural/Religious Associations.

A comparison between the two surveys confirms that the social network structure in inland Orissa has gone through a major transformation in a ten year period. People have not only become more aware and decisive about their social and political positions, they are also actively striving to achieve their goals. Moreover, and most importantly identity boundaries between the people have been submerging in order to take up a struggle against the state to protect their shared interests.

Chapter 6

Conclusion: Protests in Indian Democracy: Its Emerging Economy and Changing Social Structure

There is no clear consensus on the causal relationship between democracy and development. It is still a puzzle whether economic growth comes before democratization or democratization comes before development. Some argue that economic growth leads to democracy (Lipset 1959), while others suggest that a democratic system is more conducive to economic growth (Olson 1993). There are several examples of very poor and impoverished countries experiencing significant and rapid economic growth under undemocratic regimes. Some of the notable ones are: Chile, Singapore, Taiwan, Malaysia, Thailand, South Korea and current-day China and Russia. There are also many anti-development autocrats who have brought economic miseries to their peoples: the Congo under Mobutu, Zimbabwe under Mugabe, North Korea under Kim Jong II, and the Philippines under Marcos. Many rich countries are developed democracies, like US, Canada, UK and many other European countries. At the same time, there are a number of democratically elected regimes in the world, which have become restraining factors in their respective country's economic development. Some of the democracies, which have suffered from irresponsible macroeconomic policies, are: Columbia, Sri Lanka and Indonesia. Thus, it may be safe to argue that neither democracy nor dictatorship is a necessary condition for economic growth.

Comparing the Indian economy with the Chinese economy has become almost a pastime for many commentators. The economic surge of a non-democratic China's in post-1978 period had posed a stark contrast to near financial bankruptcy of Indian democracy in the early 1990s. Being branded as a 'dysfunctional democracy, India was cited as an example where traditional elites dominate the political parties and interest groups, and they subvert and compromise the institutions vital to the country's economic growth by adopting populist policies. Many started advocating that it is easier to achieve economic growth in a top-down command economy like China than a messy democratic system like India. However, India's extraordinary economic growth in the last decade has not only resulted in a transformation of the Indian economy, but also the tenor of the debate. China and India are taken in the same breath as two fast-growing giants, who are increasingly playing larger roles in the global markets and trying to acquire greater share of the global commons.

India and China are among the fastest growing economies in the world, and also the two most populous economies. India's current population is 1.16 billion, while China hosts nearly 200 million more; India is poised to overtake China by 2025, when each of them will respectively contribute approximately 18 per cent to the world's total population (*The New York Times*, 15 December 2009). While India's economic growth may be not as spectacular as China's, India's economic growth surpasses almost all other countries, hovering between 5 and 9 per cent since 1993. India's economy grew 9.2 per cent in 2007 and 9.6 per cent in 2006. Despite the global meltdown, Indian economy managed to grow around 7 per cent in 2008 and 2009. In the service and technology sectors, India's growth rate has been simply extraordinary. Democratic India's recent economic success, matched against authoritarian China may help at putting to rest the debate on the relationship between the form of government and economic development. Moreover, it will also help to convince the peoples and regimes in the South that democracy and popular protests do not necessarily impede economic growth in their part of the world. A democratic post-colonial state, without guarantee of long-run political stability, and also being home of thousands of protest movements, can provide a long-term safe environment for investment, innovation and entrepreneurship.

India and its Economic Growth

India became independent from British colonial rule in 1947. Annual economic growth of the country under colonial rule in 20th century (1901–1960) was less than one per cent, and because of population growth the per capita income remained stagnated. After independence, for three decades (till 1980), the economy grew with an annual average of 3.5 per cent and because of accelerated population growth the per capita income increase was around 1.6 per cent. These three decades of the 'license-permit-quota' based mixed economy model was primarily responsible for the so-called 'Hindu rate of growth'. From 1980, the growth rate of the Indian economy took an upward turn, with an average rate of around 6 per cent for the period 1980–2005. In the 2006–2007, economic growth had jumped to around 9 per cent on average. The global economic crisis in the 2008–2009 has brought down the growth rate to some extent, but the economy is fast recovering. In early 2010, Dr Kaushik Basu, Chief Economic Advisor in Indian Finance Ministry predicts that India's economic growth could reach ten per cent in the next couple of years and may even surpass that of China in the next four years (*The Hindu*, 5 January 2010).

There is some dispute about when and how this rise in growth rate took place. India for the first time experienced a spectacular economic growth of nine per cent in the year 1975/76. However, as that is the year associated with the declaration of the infamous internal emergency by Indira Gandhi, there is a reluctance to brand it as the path breaking time of an economic trend. It is also true that this trend did not last long and it was subjected to severe fluctuations, as 1979/80 became a worst one economically in the post-independent India witnessing a negative growth of 5.2 per cent. From 1980, India has witnessed a steady acceleration of its growth rate. In 1988/89, the growth rate touched the 10.5 mark. This year was followed by a severe financial crisis that took away the glamour from that year. The Indian economy has grown at 6 per cent a year from 1980 to 2002 and at nearly eight per cent a year from 2002 to 2007. There is a general perception that the Indian economy started performing impressively only after critical reforms were undertaken in the early 1990s in the aftermath of a serious financial crisis (Ahluwalia 2002). Some dispute this saying that as the 1980s witnessed a break with the growth rate trend, greater credit cannot be given to the economic reforms of the 1990s (Rodrik and Subramanian 2004). It is true that the Rajeev Gandhi's administration had embarked upon a modest reform in the mid-1980s, which helped to raise the growth rate, but these reforms were not sustainable in the long term as it was deficit based financing, mainly through borrowing from external sources (Srinivasan 2005). Some even blame those Rajeev Gandhi's reformist policies for bringing India to a point of serious financial crisis in the beginning of 1990s, which triggered a series of vital policy reforms in 1991 (Das 2006). It may be safe to argue that the rise in growth rates started in the 1980s, and that the reforms of the 1990s accelerated the process (Basu and Maertens 2007).

The architect of the second round of reforms in early 1990s was the then finance minister and present Prime Minister Dr Manmohan Singh. As newly-appointed finance minister, Dr Singh made an important speech in Indian Parliament in 1991, urging law makers to think big to help India to become a global economic power. To make his point he quoted Victor Hugo: 'No power on earth can stop an idea whose time has come' (McRae 2007). He embarked upon pursuing a comprehensive economic reform for five years as finance minister. Both the initial reforms and the critical ones in the early 1990s were put in motion by the Congress Party government. When the BJP government took power in the late 1990s it built on the reform plan. In 2004 the Congress party returned to power but has continued to pursue economic reform policies in spite of occasional roadblocks from his coalition colleagues.

India's then Finance Minister P. Chidambaram, in his speech at the Peterson Institute for International Economics in Washington DC on 27 September 2007, described India's economic success:

> The India story is now rather well known, but some aspects bear repetition. In the most recent four year period – 2003–04 to 2006–07 – India's GDP has grown at an average rate of 8.6 per cent a year. In particular, 2006–07 was a splendid year turning out a growth rate of 9.4 per cent. All the indicators are positive. Gross Domestic Capital Formation (GDFC) – that is investment – in relation to GDP is estimated at a little over 35 per cent. Inflation measured by the

wholesale price index (WPI) is 3.3 per cent. Foreign exchange reserves stand at over $230 billion US dollars. All sectors of the economy are contributing to the growth rate, although we are not entirely satisfied with the performance of the agriculture sector.

Most of the international financial organizations and markets also share this optimism. The Organization for Economic Cooperation and Development (OECD) in its first ever survey of India, published on 9 October 2007, has given much of the credit for the country's rapid economic expansion in recent years to the reforms undertaken in the early 1990s and predicts that India can accelerate its economic growth to 10 per cent if the country moves quickly to build infrastructure, reforms its labour market, and further opens up to foreign capital (OECD Economic Surveys 2007).

Is it Shining for All?

With economic growth, India has received consistently good press coverage in the West for the past five years. In the summer of 2006 alone, publications like *Time*, *Newsweek*, *Foreign Affairs*, and *The Economist* all produced special issues on India, highlighting its economic achievements. However, not all are enthusiastic about this 'success story'. The growth formula of open market and foreign investment is blamed for accelerating the divide between rich and poor. As Smitu Kothari describes:

> Only select sectors have experienced rapid growth and only a few have benefited. Most governments have failed to provide more equitable access to the processes and benefits of the market. So, you have a classic situation of widening expectations created by populist images of resurgent India and a reality of disenchantment (Kothari 2007).

Even the leadership has started acknowledging the seriousness of the problem. The reformer-in-chief, Prime Minister Dr Singh while addressing his nation on its annual Independence Day (15 August 2007) cautioned that 'India cannot become a nation with islands of high growth and vast areas untouched by development, where the benefits of growth accrue only to a few.' His finance minister also echoed the same line 'India must shine for all, not just a select few.' The general election of 2004, which brought unexpected defeat to BJP government has already shown that India has not shined for all and that a large number of the population has been left behind and not happy with the government's performance.

The recent OECD report on India claims that, between 1999 and 2004, the absolute number of people living under the national poverty line has fallen for the first time since Independence. The per capita income of Indians per month has increased from 280 rupees from 1951–52 to 3000 rupees in 2008–09. However, around 30 per cent of Indians, 10 million families, still live below the official poverty line. India is the home of nearly one-third of the world's income poor (poverty line of USD 1 per day). In spite of spectacular economic growth in recent years, India still has a long way to go in eradicating hunger, where it is ranked at 94th position well behind neighbouring China and Pakistan. According to the Global Hunger Index 2009 from the International Food Policy Research Institute (IFPRI), although India has improved its score of 23.90 on the index compared to 33.73 in 1990, with its 65th position it is lagging behind China and Pakistan ranked respectively at fifth and 58th positions, out of the total list of 118 countries (International Food Policy Research Institute 2007). The index is mainly based on proportion of undernourished in the population, prevalence of underweight and mortality rate in children below five years of age. Close to half of all the children in India under the age of three years are malnourished. In spite of a recent legal ban, an official estimate India has 12 million child labourers, while unofficially the figure is around 20 million. Only about three per cent of India's workforce is employed by the organized sector, which offers formal jobs with benefits. Is the country's macro economic growth leaving the poorer section of society behind? This is an important question not only for Indian democracy, but also for the overall global fight against absolute poverty.

Economists are divided over the impact of post-1990 growth on the poorest section of the Indian population. Some have argued that this impressive growth has led to more poverty reduction in 1990s than previous decades (Bhalla 2001), while others are sceptical of this claim (Sen 2001). According to Datt and Ravallion, India has probably maintained its 1980s rate of poverty reduction in the 1990s (Datt and Ravallion 2002). A recent study suggests that after 1999, there was greater decline in poverty than earlier years of the reform period (Dev and Ravi 2007). It is true that there has been a drop in the number of very poor people in rural areas, but the overall poverty reduction in the face of spectacular economic growth has been below expectation.

Free market enthusiasts argue that India's consumption driven model is people friendly and its economic growth does not increase inequality on the same scale that other developing countries do. With respect to income inequality, India is still behind China, Brazil, and the US but the current trend is moving in the other direction (World Bank 2006). With economic growth, India is not only expressing growing inequality, but also an increasing urban-rural gap and expanding regional disparities (Deaton and Dréze 2002). While some parts of Indian cities such as Delhi, Bangalore and Hyderabad resemble European city centres or American downtowns, many small-scale farmers commit suicide in rural India. There is also an increasing wage gap between skilled and semi-skilled workers and between service sector and manufacturing sector. Moreover, the agriculture sector, which employs more than 60 per cent of the country's population, has been left behind.

Several populous states in Hindi heartland are falling behind economically compare to states in the south and West. States with low human capital are primarily unable to take part in the economic growth. Economic reforms have been also adopted at different levels across states, and this has enhanced the inter-state variations in economic growth as well (Bhanumurthy and Mitra 2004). Economically high performing states are Gujarat, Maharashtra, Rajasthan, West Bengal, Punjab, Tamil Nadu, and Karnataka and they have less than 40 per cent country's total population (Sinha 2007). There has been very minor improvement in the economic performance of populous states like Bihar, Madhya Pradesh and Uttar Pradesh. It has brought larger disparity among the states in the Indian federation. As a recent International Monetary Fund paper points out:

> The gap in per capita income levels between the richer and poorer states has widened over the past three decades. Rich states have also grown over three times faster than poorer states so that by March 2004, the ratio of per capita income in the richest state (Punjab) to that in the poorest state (Bihar) had risen to 4.5 from 3.4 in 1970 (Purfield 2006: 5).

Unfortunately, the variation in economic growth and its impact on poverty reduction across Indian states does not seem to lead towards convergence in the long run (Sachs, Bajpai, and Ramiah 2002).

Minority Insecurity

Most analysts agree that critical to the survival of democracy in India has been the Indian states willingness to bargain and accommodate varying interests. This has been seen as key in maintaining the democratic system despite the deep ethnic and religious divisions in the society. The Indian political system has been primarily a rebuttal of the 'majoritarian electoral system', as Lijphart argues, where federal arrangements in which states and linguistic boundaries largely coincide, the rights of religious and linguistic minorities to have autonomous schools are protected, allowing for separate 'personal laws' for minorities (Lijphart 1996). Kanti Bajpai (Bajpai 1997), for example, argues that the Indian package to deal with minority issues has consisted of three main elements: (1) a political order marked by liberal constitutionalism, state backed secular nationalism, and state led social modernization and economic development (2) power sharing in terms of group rights and the devolution of authority to ethnic based lower levels of government, and, finally, (3) coercion and force if the first two fail.

India is currently facing several separatist violent conflicts from its various minority groups. A prime example is the widely reported Kashmir conflict, where a Muslim minority with direct support from neighbouring Pakistan has demanded secession for more than two decades. Other provinces in the Indian Union, which are experiencing acute minority challenges are Manipur, Nagaland and Assam. In prima facie, India seems to be a country where the "democratic peace proposition" for internal peace seems to have failed. However, using a judicious mixture of force and accommodation, Indian democracy has been able to bring an end to several minority challenges: Sikhs in Punjab, Tamils in India, and Gorkhas in West Bengal to name a few.

Besides numerous secessionist movements, India also regularly experiences religious tensions and riots mostly between the Hindu majority and Muslim minority. It often arises out of a complex assortment of specific historical, socio-economic and political circumstances generated over a period of time. Indian experience suggests that Hindu-Muslim tensions become problematic, and potentially explosive when a particular religious community is perceived to receive favourable treatment or when one of the religious communities persistently remains along the socio-economic and political margins of society. These tensions also get aggravated when religious identities are manipulated by political elites.

Coinciding with the growing economy, Indian democracy has also experienced the assertive presence of the right-wing Hindu nationalist party, the BJP. While the Congress party stands for secular nationalism, the BJP preaches Hindu nationalism (Mishra 2007). In 1992, this party led an illegal mob to demolish the sixteenth century mosque at Ayodhya, which led to major communal riots between Hindus and Muslims all over India. This Party was also directly involved in another communal riot in the state of Gujarat in 1992, in which over two thousand Muslims were killed. BJP, which was the leading ruling coalition from 1998 to 2004, is presently the main opposition party. BJP's main political agenda is to strive for a culturally homogeneous Hindu nation-state, provoking minority insecurity, particularly of the Muslim community.

Muslims represent nearly 13 per cent of India's total population and their numbers are more than the total population of Pakistan. This large Muslim minority seriously challenges BJP's narratives of social cohesion and homogeneity. BJP never misses any chance of spreading disinformation among Hindus in order to contribute to fantasies of national incompleteness, anger, and ultimately to a desire to purify the country of the Muslim minority. Muslims in India may be a minority in comparison to Hindus, however, there number is not that small and in some provinces and regions, they represent the majority. Moreover, as Appadurai aptly describes, thanks to globalization, the Muslim minority increasingly see themselves as sections of a strong global majority (Appadurai 2006). This fuels the sectarian tension further in the country.

Complicating the situation further, a majority of Muslims in India are poorer and less educated than their Hindu counterparts, and thus has less opportunity to take advantage of India's economic growth. A powerful panel headed by Justice

Rajinder Sachar that investigated the social, economic and educational status of Indian Muslims, submitted its report in 2006, which was subsequently presented to the Parliament. The report found that the Muslim community is 'lagging behind' other religious groups, particularly Hindus, in development indicators. It has come out with a series of findings, revealing that Muslims represent a mere 4.9 per cent of the total 8,844,669 Indian government employees, indicating that all is not well for the 150 million Muslims of the country. Similar situations prevail in the representation of minorities in government, police services, public sector enterprises, public sector banks, etc. Education disparities are also equally striking. In follow-up to this report, the Central government has agreed in principle to set up an Equal Opportunity Commission to look into grievances regarding discrimination against Muslims. In December 2009, Indian Government tabled the report of the National Commission for Religious and Linguistic Minorities in the Parliament, which has recommended practical measures for the welfare of the minorities, including job reservations. However, it is not an easy task to deliver the fruits of economic growth to the majority of Muslims who are at the bottom of the ladder. The growing inequality between majority Hindus and minority Muslims further provokes the minority community to mobilize and organize in order to demand for their share from the country's economic growth.

Maoist Rebellion

For the past six decades, India has been the world's largest democracy. It has regularly defied those who prophesized its imminent demise.[1] Worries that India will disintegrate or turn into dictatorship do not sell anymore (Rudolph and Rudolf 2002). India's then Prime Minister and the popular BJP leader, Atal Behari Vajpayee, in his famous New Year musing in 2001, wrote that:

> When I look back at free India's journey through the past five decades, I am filled with pride and disappointment in equal measure. Pride because we have been successful in preserving two ideals that are most precious to all of us: one, the unity of India, and two, our democratic system ... Nevertheless, I am as distressed as all my countrymen are at the wide gulf between India's indisputable potential and her actual performance (Vajpayee 2001).

His government and his party followed a free market policy, emphasizing deregulation in order to allow the country to achieve its potential. India in recent years achieved impressive economic growth, however not all in the society received the benefits.

---

1   As the country went to the polls for the second time in 1957, Selig Harrison, in an oft quoted remark, said, ' the odds are wholly against the survival of freedom ... in fact, the issue is whether any Indian state can survive at all,' (Harrison 1960).

One of the prominent losers of India's recent economic growth is its indigenous population, the *tribals*. These 80 million strong indigenous people are primarily landless and illiterate and they have been subjected to hopelessness and despair while the rest of the country is rejoicing about its economic achievement. This group mainly dominates larger parts of central and eastern India, particularly the states of Andhra Pradesh, Orissa, Jharkhand, Bihar and Chhattisgarh. A militant left movement, inspired by Maoist philosophy, has successfully spread to this region, thriving on the lush environment of alienation and disenfranchisement. The spectacular rise of the Maoist movement in the inland part in the last six years, has surprised many, and has even forced India's Prime Minister to describe it as the greatest internal security threat faced by India in its post independence period (*New York Times*, 15 March 2007). On 16 July 2009, India's Home Minister told Indian Parliament, 'For many years we did not properly assess the threat posed by Left-wing extremism. We underestimated the challenge and in the meanwhile they extended their influence. Today they pose a grave challenge. We are preparing to take on the challenge.' He refused to disclose the details of the plan but informed the Parliament that a special military advisor has been appointed to deal with the challenge and country's premier paramilitary force, the Central Reserve Police Force (CRPF) has been asked to assume the frontline role in the operation.

A radical communist group led a violent uprising in 1967 in the state of West Bengal. After the government crushed the movement, subsequently during the 1970s it fragmented into various factions. Some of these groups have remained active in parts of Andhra Pradesh and Bihar since then. However, with the economic liberalization and gradual withdrawal of the state from its commitment to welfare policies, the support for these radical groups has received a boost in recent years. The Maoist Communist Centre of India (MCC) which was active in parts of Bihar and the Communist Party of India (Marxist-Leninist) and the People's War (also known as the People's War Group or PWG) which had its base in Andhra Pradesh, merged to form a new entity, the Communist Party of India-Maoist (CPI-Maoist) on 21 September 2004. The new entity has reaffirmed its commitment to the classical Maoist strategy of 'protracted armed struggle', which defines its objectives not in terms of the seizure of lands, crops, or other immediate goals, but the seizure of power. Within this perspective, participation in elections and engagement with the prevailing 'bourgeois democracy' are rejected, and all efforts and attention is firmly focused on 'revolutionary activities' to undermine the state and seize power. The unity move of the Indian Maoists has provided them with a bigger base, increasing their influence and power. The rebels are violently demanding for the creation of a communist state, comprising the tribal areas of the states of Andhra Pradesh, Maharashtra, Orissa, Bihar and Chhattisgarh. Their struggle's demand is to improve the economic and social rights of the poor and indigenous tribes in the region.

The upsurge of Maoists in this part of India reveals a continuous process of underdevelopment, which largely designs today's explosive situation. Taking advantage of the persistence of acute poverty, growing inequality, rampant corruption and regional disparity in recent years, Maoists have shown the tribal population the dream of a revolution. This armed rebellion has been instrumental in bringing self-confidence to the tribal population and has organized them into a single group. Thanks to this, the violent opposition of any tribal group does not remain anymore localized in nature, and it has posed a serious security challenge to the Indian state.

India's economic growth has a strong group of beneficiaries. The Indian middle class is expanding and a significant group of the population has been able to take advantage of the new economic liberalization policies. However, a large section of the Indian population has been untouched by the fruits of India's impressive economic growth. In some cases, their socio-economic situation has deteriorated even further. However, most of the losers in this race, have decide to stay and shout within the system, and thanks to the presence of a democratic set up, they have been able to raise their voices and in some cases been successful in making the state agree to meet their demands.

Lamentably the radical left movement in the Central and Eastern parts of India has decided to move further, and it has already posed a serious challenge to the democratic system itself. They have taken up arms and refuse to take part in the electoral process. The current goal of these Maoists is to establish a 'Compact Revolutionary Zone', a zone of control that would extend from the Nepalese border to Andhra Pradesh in the south. They aim to convert the zone into an independent communist state. Indian government, in spite of initial reluctance is gradually pondering to suppress this challenge with brute force. However, it is difficult to imagine that sustainable peace in this part of the country can be achieved with the help of police and para-military forces only. It is important and urgent that Indian democracy restores the confidence of the growing anti-system advocates in the democratic system. To do this, the state needs to maintain a judicious balance between economic growth and supporting the creation of a fair and just society.

State of Public Institutions

With an improving economic situation, there are further demands from the people on public institutions for better public service, maintenance of law and order, and greater inclusion in the decision-making processes. Indian democracy has supported an open and vibrant society. With the help of the free media, public institutions are subject to greater public scrutiny. Civil society in India, as it has been discussed before, is vibrant and thriving and while it directly takes part in development activities, it also increasingly asserts stakeholder participation in policy as well as decision making processes. However, as of recent, Subramanian has pointed out that the quality of public institutions in India has not improved overtime (Subramanian 2007). It is not that all the public institutions in India have remained stagnated or weakened. In the last decades, particularly after the breakdown of the one-party domination at the centre, certain key institutions of the democratic structure, particularly the Presidency, the Supreme Court and the Election Commission have become effective and assertive (Rudolph and Rudolf 2002; Kapur and Mehta 2005). Some other federal institutions like the Union Public Service Commission and the Reserve Bank of India are also performing their duties in a credible manner. However, state institutions maintaining order, delivering justice, providing job, education and health care are in a very precarious situation. A closer look of the state of state run educational institutions can provide some idea about the other institutions assigned with the social sector.

The Indian constitution in 2002 made basic education a fundamental right. However, according to 'Global Education Digest 2007' published by the UNESCO Institute for Statistics (UIS), an Indian household on average pays for more than one-quarter, 28 per cent, of the cost to send their children to primary and secondary school. This presents a big barrier to the children of poor families who desire to obtain a primary education. But, at the same time, university education, which mostly helps the children of economically better off families, usually only, requires 12 per cent of the household's income.

While children of poor families go to state run schools, middle class families prefer private schools for their kids. The condition of government run schools is becoming perilous, as the education system is overly reliant on private contributions. Teacher absenteeism is much higher in state run schools and also suffers from a high student to teacher ratio. Private schools are generally manned with better-trained teachers and equipped with modern facilities, their students also perform better on examinations in comparison to government run schools (Subramanian 2007).

The state of higher education is not impressive either, which has prompted India's Human Resource Development Minister to publicly admit that it is the sick child of the education system (*The Hindu*, 11 October 2007). Nearly 75 per cent of all colleges and 56 per cent of all Indian universities have not been accredited on quality parameters by the National Assessment and Accreditation Council (NAAC) (*The Times of India*, 11 October 2007). There is an obvious need for serious restructuring of the higher education system, as not even 10 per cent of the graduates are employable in the formal sector. The allocation for education in the budget is still less than five per cent of the gross domestic product, and it seems like there is no immediate hurry to change this as upper middle class families tend to send their children to universities in North America, Europe or Australia.

It is not only the educational institutions. Other public institutions like the judiciary and law enforcement agencies have failed to evolve with the changing social and economic circumstances of the country. Like education, public health care has also deteriorated because the free market system has taken over basic functions of the state; and the rich and powerful have preferred to opt out of the public system in favour of the private sector.

Failure of public institutions to raise their standard to cope with the changing social and economic realities further complicates the issue of inequality in India and raises questions about the performance and quality of the government. Institutional performance determines popular feeling about elected leadership and overall satisfaction with democracy (Anderson 1998; Wagner and Schneider 2006). Citizens are likely to form expectations about institutional performance from an individual point of view of their own welfare. As recent election results in India indicate, there is large dissatisfaction with the performance of public institutions in spite of the country's impressive economic growth. Voters are consistently opting for a change in the regime particularly at the state level elections. However, the election system does not guarantee that the best and most efficient politicians will be elected; those who can seriously plan and act on reforming the countries police, judiciary, and overall social service system. It is true that the undertaking of efficient institutional reform is extremely difficult, however, Indian democracy cannot afford to postpone it for long. Constant and prolonged dissatisfaction with the institution's performance to deliver public goods get reflected in increased number of protest mobilization in different parts of the country.

Economic Development and Indian Democracy

As Shashi Tharoor describes India, 'the singular thing about India is that you can only speak of it in the plural' (Tharoor 2007). India is home to many ethnic groups, with distinct religious, language and cultural identities. This is land of bewildering diversity. The Indian system, with its federal and democratic character, has maintained this diversity and provided room for each group to compete. A policy in another direction, in neighbouring Pakistan, has resulted in division of that country since 1971. Democratic pluralism in India has given all social groups a place at the table, and with that most likely maintained the unity of the country. Many Indians, when they cast their vote, vote within their castes, but all these groups and their conflicts have been defused thanks to the presence of a democratic consensus in the country.

However, India's democratic political system cannot take credit for bringing this impressive economic growth in recent years. The Chinese success story in the neighbourhood dismisses any possibility of a claim in that direction. Similarly, the persistence of India's democratic structure is also not dependent upon the continuation of this trend of macro economic success. Indian democracy was not in serious danger before 1990 nor is it is now. For most of the population, it has become 'the only game in town'. However, as Ashutosh Varshney describes, 'India is attempting a transformation few nations in modern history have successfully managed: Liberalizing the economy within an established democratic order' (Varshney 2007: 93). India's growth has many winners but also plenty of losers. And, the number of those who are being left behind is not decreasing, but rather increasing. The gain of the economic growth is taking very long to filter down to the poorest and most deprived sections of the country's population. A majority of them do not reject economic reform, but they have started protesting forcefully because they have not benefited from it.

In 2004, Indian electorates overthrew the reformist BJP led government and returned the Congress led coalition to power. The Manmohan Singh led government has repeatedly pledged to follow a more inclusive reform program. The National Common Minimum Program of the ruling coalition had selected seven areas for attention: agriculture, water, education, healthcare, employment, urban renewal and infrastructure. Several government-sponsored schemes have been taken up, particularly for rural farmers, in an attempt to make growth more inclusive. There have been some increases in government spending on agriculture, health and education in the last couple of years. However, these attempts to restructure the reform policy have not been very successful, especially at withstanding pressures of a demanding democracy. The Congress Party has been able to come back to power at the centre in the 2009 election, but it still faces serious opposition in various important states.

Besides election worries, the Indian government is also worried about many violent protests, which have been precipitated by several industrial projects. Following the Chinese pattern, the Indian government came up with plans to set up a number of Special Economic Zones (SEZ) to provide a further boost to India's economic growth. These SEZs, offering tax incentives and good infrastructure facilities, aim to create investment enclaves. But, many of them are planned on prime agricultural land, which infuriate poor farmers and agricultural labourers. Strong opposition has forced the government to stop creating new SEZs. In India, democracy (applied in regular elections) forces the ruling elites to have one eye on public opinion and attitude before embarking upon any development policy. If not, the democracy also supports and strengthens numerous protest movements, which forces the government to not to ignore people in its development plan.

Changing Society and Increasing Protests

India is presently transiting through a phase of increased mobilization of various groups, while it is coping with the large alliance based governments as well as increased erosion of powers and capacities of political elites. The growing number of popular protests against various government policies has added to, what Kohli describes as the crisis of governability in Indian democracy (Kohli 1990). This emerging phenomenon contributes to bring democratic 'disorder' that creates apprehension among the students of Indian politics about the state's effectiveness as an agent of development. The blossoming of a democratic structure particularly in a developing country set-up is critically dependent upon the popular participation: not only participation in electing the government, but also in the formulation and execution of the development policies. Increasing number of protest movement in India manifest the desire of the common people to participate in important policy sectors. Conventional political theory generally looks at protest and participation as distinct and contradictory forms of action. But, they both can be complementary forms of action in a democracy, and like popular participation the protest movements may contribute to enhance the legitimacy of the democratic governance.[2]

Protest reflects the relationship between the rulers and the ruled (Andrain and Apter 1995). As a part of political participation, protest movements are organized to pressure the state authority to resolve the problems faced by the ruled. Protest generally arises from disagreement over limited issues, such as opposition to particular policies of a government (Gurr 1979). Country's political system directly influences the number and intensity of protests. Democracies are likely to experience larger number but less extremely violent protests than authoritarian states (Zimmermann 1980; Gurr 1993). The structure and ideals of a democratic system make it possible to respond to it challengers in conciliatory and accommodative manner, which strengthens the utility of protest over armed rebellion or total revolution (Gurr and Lichbach 1979).

A large number of protests in society originates and flourishes in the democratic system. Undoubtedly, multi-party democracy provides a fertile setting, which permits for a variety of protest movements to emerge and operate (Oommen 1990). Advocating the same line, Eckstein and Gurr write, 'the risk of chronic low-level conflicts is one of the prices democrats should expect to pay for freedom from regimentation by the state' (Eckstein and Gurr 1975). Democracy per se provides no immediate obstacles in mobilizing and organizing people on certain issues as liberty to do so is supposed to be guaranteed by law and tradition. Authorities in a democratic set up are institutionally handicapped from using the full strength of their coercive power against popular mobilization and group formation. Moreover, due to their dependence on popular support, the ruling elites more often respond favourably to the demands of various protest movements. Hence, there is greater probability for the occurrence of a higher number of protests and its positive outcomes in the democratic system in comparison to other ones.

---

2   A finding of this nature is seen in Subrat Kumar Mitra's work (Mitra 1991).

In this context, it can be argued that the growing number of protest movements, particularly movements against displacement in India is part of the democratic baggage, which the country has been carrying for more than 60 years. The Indian system is gradually becoming more competitive and more inclusive. The dominant Congress party system has collapsed paving the way for multi-party competition for power. The hierarchical social formation is also gradually paving the way for horizontal integration of people and groups. The political authority is learning to tolerate protest movements and becoming responsive to their demands. It is discovering ways to operate in a pluralistic democracy. The successful conception, evolution, and expansion of the protest movements reflect this effective diffusion of democracy in Indian society.

Indian people have learned to assert their rights and are trying to emerge as the chief actors through the participatory process. Using their options within a democratic framework, the people are working towards protecting their interests. Democratic developments have brought together the under-privileged sections of the country and given them a new spirit of questioning. This apparent 'chaos' works as a safety valve that strengthens democracy and the state rather than undermining them (Bhagwati 1995). The success of many protest movements may have hampered the implementation of government policies, but at the same time, it has helped to restore the faith of the people in the democratic institution. Popular protests enforce a learning process for the policy makers to be accountable. With the advent of these protest movements, Indian democracy might have become 'ungovernable' or 'disordered' or 'noisy' but one thing is certain, it has not weakened. Democracy is rather going through a process of consolidation by enticing aggrandized popular participation.

Protest movements in India primarily aim at protecting the interest of poor and powerless section of the society. These protests are not anymore confined to states like Kerala; they are spreading to the areas like interior part of Orissa, which had not experienced this phenomenon before. In some places, protest mobilizations have become more successful than other regions. But, in recent years, successful protest are not only limited to these areas. The regions, which had very poor record of protests before have started hosting successful mobilization against various state policies. As it has been discussed in the earlier chapters, existing and evolving social network structure provides reasons for the asymmetrical success of protest movements in India in the past.

Social network is the objective existence of social capital while ties of trust and norm of reciprocity represent its subjective part (Paxton 1999). Ostrom (1990) has argued that the network promotes norms of reciprocity and trust. The social network, both formal and informal ones, enhances a group's capacity to come together in collective action, to address common problems or to pressurize the authority to address these issues. For the successful mobilization, a protest movement depends primarily upon the existing social network, both formal and non-formal ones (Rose 1996).[3] It is quite surprising that the researchers studying the protest movements in South in general have almost overlooked the impact of social network on the mobilization process. In the relationship between social network and protest movement, the line of causation may run in others direction. Successful mobilization of a political movement helps to build trust among the protesters, leading to generating and strengthening social network (Foley and Edward 1996).[4] The newly acquired social network also helps to support the protest movements on other issues.

The disadvantage of smallness of a group can be overcome through flexible coordination. Flexible coordination can be achieved through network of smaller groups, complement each other to achieve collective efficiency for the popular action. Protest gets larger support through coordination or network of various groups of supporters. As we have noticed in Kerala and the coastal part of Orissa, for the enhanced participation, a democratic and extended group network is needed, not the pyramidal or restricted participation within the group. The more local, social and cultural interactions become mutually reinforcing and interact with external forces, the more likely people are going to engage in collective defiance.

However, societies and social ties are not static and they keep evolving as well with time. Putnam's 'Bowling alone' explanation argues the decline of social contacts and interactions in American society overtime (Putnam 2000). However, in the case of traditionally segmented Indian society, the trend has been reverse. Outside actors and events intentionally or not have acted as catalyst in this process of transformation. This changing social network structure greatly influences the societal ability to organize and mobilize protest movements. The tribal population in Indian state of Orissa has witnessed this phenomenon in their recent protest movement mobilization processes. The ongoing globalization process and new economic and political development in the country enlarge the possible influence of external actors and factors in transforming the social network structures of the Indian societies and that might transform the number and power of protest movements in many new areas.

Concluding Observation

The proper and effective implementation of development policies is difficult to achieve, if they are not understood, accepted, and supported by the populations

---

3   Emphasis should not be only on the number of formal associations and its membership, but also, research should include the importance of informal social networks.

4   Foley and Edwards points out the weakness in Putnam's works for not taking into account the role of social movements in fostering aspects of civic community.

that are directly and indirectly affected by them. Often development policies of the state fail to meet the needs and demands of poor population those traditionally survive on natural resources. Local demands for resource use in several cases conflict with development projects initiated by the state.

The experience from tribal dominated areas in India shows that a state may force through the implementation of development policies in disregard to the interest of the affected population. However, the changing social network structure may provide affected people possibilities in future to counter the non-consultative and non-inclusive policies of the state. Affected people and their supporters might be able to organize and mobilize large-scale opposition and highly motivated social actions even after the implementation of the policies. The suppressive and manipulative actions of a state may force reconciliation of the popular protest at the surface level, but it neither addresses the root of the problem nor helps to secure lasting benefits of the project.

Besides the policy value, this research here also shows a novel type of contribution of external agents, to the mobilization process of the protest movements. The left radicals and religious preachers, who have come into contacts recently with the affected tribal population in India for their own self-seeking interests, but inadvertently have helped them to strengthen their movements against development policies of the state. These outside actors have entered the region to motivate the tribes to join their political organization or religion. In the process, they have been able to trigger the interaction process among various sub-groups of the tribal population, and that has helped the tribes to create a larger social network, a greater identity, and successful mobilization against policies of the powerful state.

Bibliography

Agarwal, A. and S. Narain, eds. 1985. *The State of India's Environment 1984–85: The Second Citizen's Report*. New Delhi: Center for Science and Environment,.

Agarwal, Anil. 1994. An Environmentalist's Credo. In *Social Ecology*, edited by R. Guha. New Delhi: Oxford University Press.

Ahluwalia, M.S. 2002. Economic Reforms in India since 1991: Has Gradualism Worked? *Journal of Economic Perspectives* 16(3): 67–88.

Alagh, Yoginder K., Ganesh Pangare, and Biksham Gujja, eds. 2006. *Interlinking of Rivers in India: Overview and Ken-Betwa Link*. New Delhi: Academic Foundations.

Alcan't in India Solidarity Campaign. 2009 [cited 15 April]. Available from http://www.alcantinindia.org.

Alger, Chadwick F. 1997. Transnational Social Movements, World Politics, and Global Governance, in *Transnational Social Movements and Global Politics: Solidarity Beyond the State*, edited by J. Smith, C. Chatfield and R. Pagnucco. Syracuse, NY: Syracuse University Press, pp. 260–78.

Alley, Roderic. 2002. Ethnosecession in Papua New Guinea: The Bougainville Case, in *Ethnic Conflict and Secessionism in South and Southeast Asia: Causes, Dynamics, Solutions*, edited by R. Ganguly and I. Macduff. New Delhi: Saga Publications, pp. 225–56.

Amin, Md. Lower Indravati Area. Unpublished Manuscript.

Anderson, C.J. 1998. Parties, Party Systems, and Satisfaction with Democratic Performance in the New Europe. *Political Studies* 46: 572–88.

Andrain, Charles F., and David E. Apter. 1995. *Political Protest and Social Change: Analysing Politics*. London: Macmillan.

Appadurai, Arjun. 2006. *Fear of Small Numbers: An Essay on the Geography of Anger*: Durham: Duke University Press.

Arora, Dolly. 1994. From State Regulation to People's Participation: Case of Forest Management in India. *Economic and Political Weekly* 29(12): 691–698.

Asher, M. 2007. Striking while the iron is hot – A case study of the Pohang Steel Company's proposed project in Orissa, India. National Centre for Advocacy Studies.

Augustine, Clymes, and A.K. Sharma. 1995. Gandhi and the Contemporary Challenges: The Emergence of New Social Movements. *Gandhi Marg* 16(4): 437–51.

Baboo, Balgobind. 1992. *Technology and Social Transformation: The Case of the Hirakud Multi-Purpose Dam Project in Orissa*. New Delhi: Concept Pub. Co.

Baboo, Balgobinda. 1993. Hirakud Bandharu Sikshya (Lessons from Hirakud Dam). *Bikalpa Bichar* 1(4): 74–83.

Baboo, Balgovind. 1991. State Policies and People's Response: Lesson from Hirakud Dam. *Economic and Political Weekly* 26(41): 2372–79.

Babu, Ashok Kumar, and S.K. Pattnaik. 1987. Development, Displacement – A Case Study of Koraput District, Unpublished paper.

Bajpai, Kanti. 1997. Diversity, Democracy and Devolution in India, in *Government Policies and Ethnic Relations in Asia and the Pacific* edited by M.E. Brown and S. Ganguly. Cambridge: MIT Press, 33–81.

Bakshi, Rajni. 1996. Development, Not Destruction: Alternative Politics in the Making. *Economic and Political Weekly* 31(5): 255–57.

Bandyopadhyay, J., N.D. Jayal, U. Schoettli, and C. Singh, eds. 1985. *India's Environment: Crises and Responses*. Dehra Dun: Natraj Publishers.

Bandyopadhyay, Jayanta. 1994. South Asia at a Watershed. *Panscope* (39): 2–3.

Bandyopadhyay, Jayanta, and Vandana Shiva. 1988. Political Economy of Ecology Movements. *Economic and Political Weekly* 23(24): 1223–32.

Banyal, S.S. 1997. It's BJP vs BJP on Eradi Tribunal. *The Hindustan Times*, 7 November.

Bardhan, Pranab. 1984. *The Political Economy of Development in India*. Oxford: Basil Blackwell.

Barker, Jonathan. 1999. Power Shift: Global Change and Local Action, in *Street-Level Democracy: Political Settings at the Margins of Global Power*, edited by J. Barker. Toronto: Between the Lines, 8–26.

Basu, Kaushik, and Annemie Maertens. 2007. The Pattern and Causes of Economic Growth in India. *Oxford Review of Economic Policy* 23(2): 143–67.

Bauer, Joanne R. 2006. *Foreign Environmentalism: Justice, Livelihood, and Contested Environments*. Armonk: M.E. Sharpe.

Bauman, Chad. 2008. Postcolonial Anxiety and Anti-Conversion Sentiment in the Report of the Christian Missionary Activities Enquiry Committee. *International Journal of Hindu Studies* 12(2): 181–213.

Baviskar, Amita. 1995. *In the Belly of the River: Tribal Conflicts over Development in the Narmada Valley*. New Delhi: Oxford University Press.

BBC. 2008. Fear and fundamentalism in India. *BBC News*, 16 October.

BBC. 2007. UN chief warns on climate change. *BBC News*, 2 March.

Beaglehole, J.H. 1967. The Indian Christians? A Study of a Minority. *Modern Asian Studies* 1(1): 59–80.

Bearman, Peter S. 1994. *Relation into Rhetorics: Local Elite Social Structure in Norfolk, England, 1540–1640*. New Brunswick, NJ: Rutgers University Press.

Bedamatta, Satyasiba. 2007. Fishing in Troubled Water: Understanding Conflict in and around Chilika. *Kalinga Times*, 22 December.

Behar, Amitabh 2002. People's Social Movement: An Alternative Perspective on Forest Management in India. *Overseas Development Institute Draft Working Paper*, London.

Bhagwati, Jagdish. 1995. The New Thinking on Development. *Journal of Democracy* 6(4): 50–64.

Bhalla, S. 2003. Recounting the Poor: Poverty in India, 1983–1999. *Economic and Political Weekly* 38(4): 338–49.

Bhanumurthy, N.R., and Arup Mitra. 2004. Economic Growth, Poverty and Reforms in Indian States. In *Working Paper*. New Delhi: Institute of Economic Growth.

Biswas, Ranjita. 1993. Mother Chilika Fights off an Invasion of Prawns. *Panscope* 37.

Blomkvist, Hans, and Ashok Swain. 2001. Investigating Democracy and Social Capital in India. *Economic and Political Weekly* 36(8): 639–43.

Blumer, Herbert. 1969. Social Movements, in *Studies in Social Movements: A Social Psychological Perspective*, edited by B. McLaughlin. New York: Free Press, 8–29.

Borrie, W.T., S.F. McCool, and G.H. Stankey. 1998. Protected Area Planning Principles and Strategies, in *Ecotourism: A Guide for Planners and Managers*, edited by K. Lindberg, M.E. Wood and D. Engeldrum. North Bennington: The Ecotourism Society, 133–54.

Boudreau, Vincent. 1996. Northern Theory, Southern Protest: Opportunity Structure Analysis in a Cross-National Perspective. *Mobilization* 1: 175–89.

Bray, Francesca. 1994. Agriculture for the Developing Nations. *Scientific American* 271(1): 30–37.

Briet, Martien, Bert Klandermans, and Fredrik Kroon. 1987. How Women Become Involved in the Women's Movement of the Netherlands, in *The Women Movements of the United States and Western Europe: Consciousness, Political Opportunities and Public Policy*, edited by M.F. Katzenstein and C.M. Mueller. Philadelphia, PA: Temple University Press, 44–63.

Buechler, Steven M. 1993. Beyond Resource Mobilization? Emerging Trends in Social Movement Theory. *The Sociological Quarterly* 34(2): 217–35.

—— 1995. New Social Movement Theories. *The Sociological Quarterly* 36(3): 441–64.

Bush, R. 2008. Scrambling to the Bottom? Mining, Resources and Underdevelopment. *Review of African Political Economy* 35(117): 361–66.

Calderon, Fernando, Alejandro Piscitelli, and Jose Luis Reyna. 1992. Social Movements: Actors, Theories, Expectations, in *The Making of Social Movements in Latin America: Identity, Strategy, and Democracy* edited by A. Escobar and S.E. Alvarez. Boulder, CO: Westview Press, 19–36.

Canel, Edurado. 1997. New Social Movement Theory and Resource Mobilization Theory: The Need for Integration, in *Community Power and Grassroots Democracy* edited by M. Kaufman and H.D. Alfonso. London: Zed Books, 189–221.

Carlsson, I., S. Ramphal, A. Alatas, and H. Dahlgren. 1995. *Our Global Neighbourhood: The Report of the Commission on Global Governance*. Oxford: The Commission on Global Governance.

Castells, Manuel. 1983. *The City and the Grassroots: A Cross-Cultural Theory of Urban Social Movements*. London: Edward Arnold.

Census of India. 2001. Chapter 3 – Size, Growth Rate and Distribution of Population. In *Series 1, India, Paper 1 of 2001*. New Delhi: Census of India.

—— *Population by Religious Communities*. Census of India 2001. Available from http: //censusindia.gov.in/Census_Data_2001/Census_data_finder/C_Series/ Population_by_religious_communities.htm.

Centre for Development Studies. 1975. Poverty, Unemployment and Development Policy: A Case Study of Selected Issues with Reference to Kerala. New York: UN Department of Economic and Social Affairs.

Cernea, Michael, and Guggenheim, Scott, eds. 1993. *Anthropological Approaches to Resettlement: Policy, Practice and Theory*. Boulder, CO: Westview Press.

Chakravarty, Sukhamoy. 1987. *Development Planning: The Indian Experience*. New Delhi: Oxford University Press.

Chandhoke, Neera. 1995. *State and Civil Society*. New Delhi: Sage Publications.

Chandhoke, Neera, and Ashish Ghosh, eds. 1995. *Grassroots Movements and Social Change*. New Delhi: Developing Countries Research Center, University of Delhi.

Chartier, Roger. 1991. *The Cultural Origins of the French Revolution*. Durham, NC: Duke University Press.

Chaudhry, D.R. 1997. Punjab–Haryana Disputes–II: More of a Myth than Reality. *The Tribune*, 9 April.

Chhibber, Pradeep K. 1999. *Democracy without Associations: Transformation of the Party System and Social Cleavages in India*. Ann Arbor: University of Michigan Press.

Chitale, M.A. 1992. Development of India's River Basins'. *International Journal of Water Resources Development* 8(1): 30–44.

Christian Aid. 2001. *The Scorched Earth: Oil and War in Sudan*. London: Christian Aid.

—— 2007. *Human Tide: The Real Migration Crisis*. London: Christian Aid.

Clarke, Sathianathan. 2007. Transformation of Caste and Tribe, in *Religious Conversion in India. Modes, Motivations, and Meanings*, edited by R. Robinson and S. Clarke. New Delhi: Oxford University Press.

Cohen, J. 1985. Strategy or Identity: New Theoretical Paradigms and Contemporary Social Movements. *Social Research* 52(4): 663–716.

Cohen, Robin, and Shiin M. Rai. 2000. Global Social Movements: Towards a Cosmopolitan Politics, in *Global Social Movements*, edited by R. Cohen and S.M. Rai. London: The Athlone Press, 1–17.

Coleman, J. 2008. Authoring (in) Authenticity, Regulating Religious Tolerance: The Implications of Anti-Conversion Legislation for Indian Secularism. *Cultural Dynamics* 20(3): 245–77.

Coleman, James S. 1990. *Foundations of Social Theory*. Cambridge, MA: Harvard University Press.

Colson, E. 1971. *The Social Consequences of Resettlement*. Manchester: Manchester University Press.

Corell, Elisabeth, and Ashok Swain. 1995. India: The Domestic and International Politics of Water Scarcity, in *Hydropolitics: Conflicts over Water as a Development Constraint*, edited by L. Ohlsson. London: Zed Books, 123–48.

Couldrey, Marion, and Maurice Herson. 2008. Editorial: Climate change and displacement, *Forced Migration Review* (31): 2.

D'Anieri, Paul, Claire Ernst, and Elizabeth Kier. 1990. New Social Movements in Historical Perspective. *Comparative Politics* 22(4): 445–58.

D'Monte, Darryl. 1985. *Temples or Tombs? Industry versus Environment: three Controversies*. New Delhi: Centre for Science and Environment.

Dalton, Russel J., and Manfred Keuchler, eds. 1990. *Challenging the Political Order: New Social and Political Movements in Western Democracies*. New York: Oxford University Press.

Dalua, A.K. 1993. *Environmental Impact of Large Reservoir Projects on Human Settlement*. New Delhi: Ashish Publishing House.

Das, Gurcharan. 2006. The Indian Model. *Foreign Affairs* 85(4): 2–16.

Dasgupta, Biplab. 1974. The Naxalite Movement: An Indian Experiement in Maoist Revolution. *China Report* 10: 25–43.

Dash, Satya Prakash. 2006. *Naxal Movement and State Power*. New Delhi: Sarup & Sons.

Datt, Gaurav, and Martin Ravallion. 2002. Is India's Economic Growth Leaving Poor Behind? *Journal of Economic Perspectives* 16(3): 89–108.

Datta, Chandan. 1992. Yamuna River Turned Sewer. *Economic and Political Weekly* 27(49 and 50): 2633.

Deaton, A., and J. Dréze. 2002. Poverty and Inequality in India: A Re-examination. *Economic and Political Weekly* 37(36): 3729–48.

DeNardo, James. 1985. *Power in Numbers: The Political Strategy of Protest and Rebellion* Princeton, NJ: Princeton University Press.

Dev, S.M., and C. Ravi. 2007. Poverty and Inequality: All India and States, 1983–2005. *Economic and Political Weekly* 42(6): 509–21.

Dhagamwar, Vasudha, Subrata De, and Nikhil Verma. 2003. *Industrial Development and Displacement: The People of Korba*. New Delhi: Sage Publications.

Dhawan, B.D. 1987. Towards A New Water Policy. *Economic and Political Weekly* 22(44): 1850–1851.

—— 1988. Development and Management of Water Resources in North-Western India. *Economic and Political Weekly* 23(43): 2217.

—— 1993. Irrigation in Eighth Plan: A Critique. *Economic and Political Weekly* 28(26): A-38.

Diani, Mario. 1995. *Green Networks: A Structural Analysis of the Italian Environmental Movement*. Edinburgh: Edinburgh University Press.

Dogra, Bharat. 1993. Chilika Lake Controversy. *Economic and Political Weekly* 28(1 and 2): 20–21.

Doherty, Brian and Timothy Doyle. eds. 2008. *Beyond Borders: Environmental Movements and Transnational Politics*. London: Routledge.

Down to Earth. 1996. All About Almatti. *Down to Earth* 5(8): 13–14.

Downing, T.E. 2002. *Avoiding New Poverty: Mining-induced Displacement and Resettlement*. IIED and World Business Council for Sustainable Development.

Drew, Georgina. 2008. From the Groundwater Up: Asserting Water Rights in India. *Development* 51(1): 37–41.

Eckstein, H. and T.R. Gurr. 1975. *Patterns of Authority: A Structural Basis for Political Inquiry*. New York: John Wiley & Sons.

Eckstein, Susan. 1989. Power and Popular Protest in Latin America. In *Power and Popular Protest: Latin American Social Movements*, edited by S. Eckstein. Berkeley, CA: University of California Press.

Economic Survey 2007–2008, 2009. Government of India – Ministry of Finance.

Engelman, Robert, and Pamela LeRoy. 1993. *Sustaining Water: Population and the Future of Renewable Water Supplies*. Washington: Population Action International.

Envis Centre Punjab. 2009. *Shift in Cropping Pattern and Cropping Intensity in Punjab (Area in '000 ha)* 2005 [cited 15 April 2009]. Available from http://punenvis.nic.in/database_agri15.htm.

FAO. 2005. Global Forest Resources Assessment 2005: Progress towards sustainable forest management, in *FAO Forestry Paper 147*. Rome: Food and Agriculture Organization of the United Nations.

Fernandes, W. 1993. The Price of Development. *Seminar* 412: 19–24.

Fernandes, Walter, and S. Anthony Raj. 1992. *Development, Displacement and Rehabilitation in the Tribal Areas of Orissa*. New Delhi: Indian Social Institute.

Fernandes, Walter, and S. Anthony Raj. Displacement as a Process of Marginalization, Unpublished Manuscript.

Foley, Michael W., and Bob Edwards. 1996. The Paradox of Civil Society. *Journal of Democracy* 7(3): 38–52.

Francisco, R.A. 1995. The relationship between coercion and protest: An empirical evaluation in three coercive states. *Journal of Conflict Resolution* 39(2): 263–82.

Franke, Richard W., and Barbara Chasin. 1989. *Kerala: Development through Radical Reform*. San Francisco: Institute for Food and Development Policy.

Franke, Richard W., and Barbara H. Chasin. 1997. Power to the Malayalee People. *Economic and Political Weekly* 32(48): 3061–3068.

Frechet, Guy, and Barbara Worndl. 1993. The Ecological Movements in the Light of Social Movements' Development. *International Journal of Comparative Sociology* 34(1–2): 56–74.

Freeman, Jo. 1979. Resource Mobilization and Strategy: A Model for Analyzing Social Movement Organization Actions, in *The Dynamics of Social Movement*, edited by M.N. Zald and J.D. McCarthy. Cambridge: Winthrop Publishers, 167–89.

Gadgil, Madhav, and Ramchandra Guha. 1993. *This Fissured Land: An Ecological History of India*. New Delhi: Oxford University Press.

—— 1994. Ecological Conflict and the Environmental Movement in India. *Development and Change* 25(1): 101–36.

Gamson, William. 1998. Social Movements and Cultural Change, in *From Contention to Democracy*, edited by M. Giugni, D. McAdam, and C. Tilly. Lanham, MD: Rowman & Littlefield, 57–77.

Gamson, William A. 1975. *The Strategy of Social Protest*. Homewood, IL: Dorsey.

Ganatantrik Adhikar Suraksha Sangathan, and Orissa Environmental Policy. The Dam as the Disaster (Subarnarekha Multipurpose Irrigation Project), A Report to the Nation. Orissa.

Geisler, Charles C. 2002. Endangered Humans: How Global Land Conservation Efforts are Creating a Growing Class of Invisible Refugees. *Foreign Policy* 130: 80–81.

Gerlach, Luther P., and Virginia Hine. 1970. *People, Power, Change: Movements of Social Transformation*. Indianapolis: Bobbs-Merrill.

Ghimire, K.B., and M.P. Pimbert. 1997. *Social Change and Conservation: Environmental Politics and Impacts of National Parks and Protected Areas*. London: Earthscan.

Ghimire, K.B. 1994a. Parks and People: Livelihood Issues in National Parks Management in Thailand and Madagascar, in *Development and Environment: Sustaining People and Nature*, edited by D. Ghai. Oxford: Blackwell, 195–232.

Ghimire, K.B. 1994b. Parks and people: livelihood issues in national parks management in Thailand and Madagascar. *Development and Change* 25(1): 195–229.

Gittell, Ross, and Avis Vidal. 1998. *Community Organizing: Building Social Capital as a Development Strategy*. Thousand Oaks, CA.

Giugni, Marco. 1999. How Social Movements Matter: Past Research, Present Problems, Future Developments, in *How Social Movements Matter*, edited by M. Giugni, D. McAdam and C. Tilly. Minneapolis: University of Minnesota Press, xiii–xxxiii.

Global Future Foundation. *Deforestation: Causes and Implications* 2009 [cited 24 March 2009. Available from http://www.future500.org/articles/3/.

Goodwin, Jeff, and James M. Jasper. 2003. *The Social Movements Reader: Cases and Concepts*. Malden, MA: Blackwell Publishing.

Gordenker, L. 1988. The United Nations and Refugees, in *Politics in the United Nations System*, edited by L. Finkelstein. Durham: Duke University Press, 274–302.

—— 1989. Early Warning of Refugee Incidents, in *Refugees and International Relations*, edited by G. Loescher and L. Monahan: Oxford University Press, 355–71.

Gould, Roger V. 1991. Multiple Networks and Mobilization in the Paris Commune, 1871. *American Sociological Review* 56(6): 716–29.

—— 1993. Collective Action and Network Structure. *American Sociological Review* 58(2): 182–96.

—— 1998. Political Networks and the Local/National Boundary in the Whiskey Rebellion, in *Challenging Authority: The Historical Study of Contentious Politics*, edited by M.P. Hannagan, L.P. Moch and W.T. Brake. Minneapolis: University of Minnesota Press, 36–53.

Government of India – Ministry of Home Affairs. 2009. *Statement 3. Distribution of 10,000 persons by language – India, States and Union Territories – 1991* 2001 [cited 20 May 2009]. Available from http: //www.censusindia.gov.in/ Census_Data_2001/Census_Data_Online/Language/Statement3.htm.

Government of Orissa. 1979. Vide Resolution No. 13169. Irrigation and Power Department.

—— 2009. *POPULATION CENSUS, ORISSA – 2001* 2001 [cited 2 June 2009]. Available from http: //orissa.gov.in/census/cenmain.htm.

Granovetter, Mark. 1973. The Strength of Weak Ties. *American Journal of Sociology* 78(6): 1360–80.

Grindle, M.S. 1996. *Challenging the State: Crisis and Innovation in Latin America and Africa*. Cambridge: Cambridge University Press.

Guha, Ramachandra. 1988. Ideological Trends in Indian Environmentalism. *Economic and Political Weekly* 23(49): 2578–81.

—— 1991. *The Unquiet Woods: Ecological Change and Peasant Resistance in the Himalaya*. New Delhi: Oxford University Press.

—— 2007. Adivasis, Naxalites and Indian Democracy. *Economic and Political Weekly* 42(32): 3305–12.

Guhan, S. 1993. *The Cauvery River Dispute: Towards Conciliation*. Madras: Frontline Publication.

Guidry, John A., Michael D. Kennedy, and Mayer N. Zald, eds, 2000. *Globalization and Social Movements: Culture, Power, and the Transnational Public Sphere*. Ann Arbor: University of Michigan Press.

Gulati, Ashok, Mark Svendsen, and Nandini Roy Choudhury. 1994. Major and medium irrigation schemes: Towards better financial performance. *Economic and Political Weekly* 29(26): A-72.

Gulati, L. 1984. Fisherwomen in Kerala: The impact of new technology on their lives. *Manushi* (21): 33–9.

Gupta, Auna Das, and Ananda Das Gupta. 2008. Corporate social responsibility in India: towards a sane society? *Social Responsibility Journal* 4(1 and 2): 209–16.

Gupta, Dipankar. 1985. The Communalising of Punjab, 1980–1985. *Economic and Political Weekly* 20(28): 1185–90.

Gurr, Ted R. 1970. *Why Men Rebel*. Princeton, NJ: Princeton University Press.

Gurr, Ted R., and M.I. Lichbach. 1979. A Forecasting Model for Political Conflict within Nations, in *To Augur Well: Early Warning Indicators in World Politics*, edited by J.D. Singer and M.D. Wallace. Beverly Hills: Sage Publications, 153–94.

Gurr, Ted R. 1979. Political Protest and Rebellion in the 1960s: The United States in World Perspective, in *Violence in America: Historical and Comparative Perspectives,* edited by H.D. Graham and T.R. Gurr. Beverley Hills: Sage Publications, 49–76.

—— 1993. Why minorities rebel: A global analysis of communal mobilization and conflict since 1945. *International Political Science Review/Revue internationale de science politique* 14(2): 161–201.

Habermas, Jürgen. 1976. *Legitimation Crisis.* London: Heinemann.

—— 1984–1987. *The Theory of Communicative Action* (2 Volumes). Boston: Beacon Press.

Hannigan, John A. 1985. Alain Touraine, Manuel Castells and Social Movement Theory. *The Sociological Quarterly* 26(4): 435–54.

Hansen, A.H. 1966. *The Process of Planning: A Study of India's Five Year Plans 1950–1964.* Oxford: Oxford University Press.

Harrison, Selig. 1960. *India: The Most Dangerous Decades.* Princeton NJ: Princeton University Press.

Heggelund, G. 1993. China's Environmental Crisis: The Battle of Sanxia. In *NUPI Research Report.* Oslo: NUPI.

Heimsath, Charles 1978. The Functions of Hindu Social reformers – With Special Reference to Kerala. *Indian Economic and Social History Review* 15(1): 21–39.

Heller, Patrick. 1995. Social Capital as a Product of Class Mobilization and State Intervention: Industrial Workers in Kerala, India, Paper Presented in *Conference on Government Action, Social Capital Formation and Third World Development.* Cambridge.

—— 1996. Social Capital as a Product of Class Mobilization and State Intervention: Industrial Workers in Kerala, India. *World Development* 24(6): 1055–67.

—— 2001. Moving the State: The Politics of Democratic Decentralization in Keral, South Africa, and Porto Alegre. *Politics and Society* 29(1): 131–63.

Heller, Patrick, K.N. Harilal, and Shubham Chaudhuri. 2007. Building Local Democracy: Evaluating the Impact of Decentralization in Kerala, India. *World Development* 35(4): 626–48.

Hill, Douglas 2009. Boundaries, scale and power in South Asia, in *Water, Sovereignty and Borders in Asia and Oceania,* edited by D. Ghosh, H. Goodall, and S.H. Donald. London: Routledge, 87–103.

Hornborg, A. 2006. Footprints in the cotton fields: The Industrial Revolution as time-space appropriation and environmental load displacement. *Ecological Economics* 59(1): 74–81.

Human, Joe, and Manoj Pattanaik. 2000. *Community Forest Management: A Casebook from India.* London: Oxfam.

Ibarra, Pedro ed. 2003. *Social Movement and Democracy.* New York: Palgrave.

India Business Directory. *Maharashtra Special Economic Zones* 2009 [cited 15 April. Available from http: //business.mapsofindia.com/sez/india/maharashtra-special-economic.html.

India Water portal. 2009. Available from http: //www.indiawaterportal.org/ mapguide2008/MetDist/metstrut.do.

India: Social Development Report. 2006. New Delhi: Council for Social Development

Indian Express 2000. Kerala farmers unite to fight against import of palmolein. *Indian Express*, 20 October.

Indian Express 1997. Unshared Waters. *The Indian Express*, 18 July.

International Food Policy Research Institute. 2007. New Global Hunger Index Shows Most Countries Are Making Slow Progress. In *Press Release.* Washington DC.

Isaac, T., M. Thomas, and K.N. Harilal. 1997. Planning for Empowerment: People's Campaign for Decentralized Planning in Kerala. *Economic and Political Weekly* 32(1–2): 53–8.

Isaac, T.M. Thomas, Richard W. Franke, and M.P. Parameswaran. 1997. From Anti-Feudalism to Sustainable Development: The Kerala Peoples Science Movement. *Bulletin of Concerned Asian Scholars* 29(3): 34–43.

Isaac, T.M. Thomas, and B. Ekbal. 1988. Science for Social Revolution: Experience of the Kerala Sastra Sahitya Parishad. In *Peoples Science Congress.* Cannanore.

IseD. 1996. *Development, Displacement and Rehabilitation in Orissa 1950–1990.* Bhubaneswar: Institute for Social and Economic Development.

Iyer, Ramaswamy R. 1994. Federalism and Water Resources. *Economic and Political Weekly* 29(13): 733–36.

—— 2002. The Cauvery tangle – what's the way out? *Frontline,* 14–27 September.

Jain, S.N., Alice Jacob, and Subhash C. Jain. 1971. *Interstate Water Disputes in India.* Bombay: Tripathi Pvt. Ltd.

Jakesika, Jitu. 2009. Sacred fight of the Dongira. *The Guardian Weekly,* 21 October.

Jayal, Niraja Gopal 1999. *Democracy and the State: Welfare, Secularism and Development in Contemporary India.* New Delhi: Oxford University Press.

Jeffrey, Robin. 1976. *The Decline of Nayar Dominance.* New Delhi: Vikas.

—— 1997. Oriya: 'Identifying ... with Newspapers. *Economic and Political Weekly* 32(11): 511–14.

Jenkins, Craig J. 1983. Resource Mobilization Theory and Study of Social Movements. *Annual Review of Sociology* 9: 527–53.

Jenkins, J. Craig. 1995. Social Movements, Political Representation, and the State: An Agenda and Comparative Framework, in *The Politics of Social Protest: Comparative Perspectives on States and Social Movements,* edited by J.C. Jenkins and B. Klandermans. London: UCL Press, 14–35.

Jenkins, J.C., and C. Perrow. 1977. Insurgency of the Powerless. *American Sociological Review* 42(2): 249–68.

Jenkins, J. Craig, and Kurt Schock. 1992. Global Structures and Political Processes in the Study of Domestic Political Conflict. *Annual Review of Sociology* 18(1): 161–85.

Johnson, B.L.C. 1979. *India: Resources and Development*. London: Heinemann Educational Books.

Joshi, Poornima. 1997. Parched Villages Leave Bachelors High and Dry. *The Hindustan Times*, 12 April.

Kamrava, Mehran. 1993. *Politics and Society in the Developing World*. London: Routledge.

Kannan, K.P. 1995. Declining Incidence of Rural Poverty in Kerala. *Economic and Political Weekly* 30(41–2): 2651–62.

Kapur, Akash. 1998. Poor but Prosperous. *The Atlantic Monthly* 282(3): 40–45.

Kapur, Devesh, and Pratap B. Mehta, eds. 2005. *Public Institutions in India: Performance and Design*. New Delhi: Oxford University Press.

Karl, Terry. 1990. Dilemmas of Democratization in Latin America. *Comparative Politics* 23(1): 1–21.

Khator, Renu. 1988. Organizational Response to the Environmental Crisis in India. *The Indian Journal of Political Science* XLIX (1): 14–39.

Khatua, Sanjay, and William Stanley. 2006. Ecological Debt: A Case Study from Orissa, India, in *Ecological Debt: The Peoples of the South are the Creditors: Cases from Ecuador, Mozambique, Brazil and India*, edited by A.K. Peralta. Geneva: World Council of Churches, 125–68.

Klandermans, Bert, and Sidney Tarrow. 1988. Mobilization into Social Movements: Synthesizing European and American Approaches, in *International Social Movements Research: From Structure to Action – Comparing Social Movements Across Cultures, vol. 1* edited by H. Kriesi, S. Tarrow and B. Klandermans. London: JAI Press, 1–38

Kohli, Atul. 1990. *Democracy and Discontent: India's Growing Crisis of Governability*. New York: Cambridge University Press.

Kohli, Atul, and Vivienne Shue. 1994. State Power and Social Forces: On Political Contention and Accommodation in the Third World, in *State Power and Social Forces: Domination and Transformation in the Third World*, edited by J.S. Migdal, A. Kohli and V. Shue. Cambridge: Cambridge University Press, 293–326.

Kossinets, Gueorgi, and Duncan J. Watts. 2006. Empirical Analysis of an Evolving Social Network. *Science* 311(5757): 88–90.

Kothari, Rajni. 1989a. The Indian Enterprise Today. *Daedalus* 118(4): 50–67.

—— 1989b. *State Against Democracy: In Search of Human Governance*. New York: New Horizons Press.

Kothari, Smitu. 1995. Development displacement: Whose nation is it? PCD Forum Column.

Kothari, Smitu. 2007. Has Indian Democracy Failed? *Hard News*, August.

Kothari, Smitu, and Pramod Parajuli. 1993. No Nature Without Social Justice: A Plea For Cultural and Ecological Pluralism in India, in *Global Ecology: A New Arena of Political Conflict*, edited by W. Sachs. London: Zed Books, pp. 224–41.

Krishna, Anirudh. 2002. *Active Social Capital: Tracing the Roots of Development and Democracy*. New York: Columbia University Press.

KSSP. 2009. *Kerala Sasta Sahitya Parishath* 2009 [cited 4 May 2009]. Available from http: //www.kssp.in/.

Kumar, K.G. 2004. Silent Valley redux? *The Hindu Business Line*, 24 May.

Kumar, S. Mohana. 1993. Literacy Movement in Kerala: One Step Forward, Two Step Backwards. *Economic and Political Weekly* 28(41): 2187–91.

Kurien, John. 1978. Entry of Big Business into Fishing: Its Impact on Fish Economy. *Economic and Political Weekly* 13(6): 1557–65.

Langton, Nancy. 1987. Niche Theory and Social Movements: A Population Ecology Approach. *The Sociological Quarterly* 28(1): 51–70.

Levathes, L. 1993. Human Genes Give Clues to Ancient Migration. *International Herald Tribune*, 29 July 1993.

Levine, Daniel H. 1988. Paradigm Lost: Dependence to Democracy. *World Politics* 40(3): 377–94.

Lijphart, Arend. 1996. The Puzzle of Indian Democracy: A Consociational Interpretation. *The American Political Science Review* 90(2): 258–68.

Lipset, Seymour M. 1959. Some Social Requisites of Democracy. *The American Political Science Review* 53(1): 69–105.

Machaiah, M.G. 1997. Karnataka, AP now Clash over another Project. *The Times of India*, 21 May

Madsen, Stig Toft. 1995a. Recent Changes in India's Forest Policy. In *Conference on Rural and Urban Environment in South Asia*. Oslo: Nordic Association for South Asian Studies (NASA).

—— 1995b. Recent Changes in India's Forest Policy. In, *Fifth Annual Conference of the International Association for the Study of Common Property, "Reinventing the Commons"*. Bodoe, Norway.

Mahadevan, K., and M. Sumangala. 1987. *Social Development, Cultural Change and Fertility Decline: A Study of Fertility Change in Kerala*. New Delhi: Sage Publications.

Mahmood, Tahir. 2006. Religion, Law, and Judiciary in Modern India. *Brigham Young University Law Review*: 755–75.

Maloney, Clarence. 1990–1991. Environmental and Project Displacement of Population in India. In Field Staff Reports. Two parts (Asia) Nos 14 and 19. Sausalito: Universities Field Staff. International/Natural Heritage Institute.

Mangaraj, Pranab. 1997. Tisco at Gopalpur: Swords into Ploughshares? *Sun Times*, 8 February.

Martin, S.F. 1992. The Inhospitable Earth. *Refugees* 89: 12–15.

Marullo, San. 1998. Leadership and Membership in the Nuclear Freeze Movement: A Specification of Resource Mobilization Theory. *The Sociological Quarterly* 29(3): 407–27.

Marx, K. 1990. *Capital: A Critique of Political Economy*. Harmondsworth: Penguin Classics.

Mather, A.S. and K. Chapman. 1995. *Environmental Resources*. Harlow: Longman Scientific and Technical.

Mathew, E.T. 1997. *Employment and Unemployment in Kerala: Some Neglected Aspects* New Delhi: Sage Publications.

Mathew, Roy. 2001. Pooyamkutty project not viable. *The Hindu*, 6 August.

Mathews, George. 1999. Kerala's Success Story. *The Hindu*, 24 May.

McAdam, Doug. 1982. *Political Process and Development of Black Insurgency 1930–1970*. Chicago: University of Chicago Press.

—— 1986. Recruitment to High Risk Activism: The Case of Freedom Summer. *American Journal of Sociology* 92(1): 64–90.

McAdam, Doug, Sidney Tarrow, and Charles Tilly. 2001. *Dynamics of Contention*. Cambridge: Cambridge University Press.

McAdam, Doug, John D. McCarthy, and Mayer N. Zald, eds. 1996. *Comparative Perspectives on Social Movements: Political Opportunities, Mobilizing Structures and Cultural Framings*. Cambridge: Cambridge University Press.

McAdam, Doug, and Ronnelle Paulsen. 1993. Specifying the Relationship Between Social Ties and Activism. *American Journal of Sociology* 99(3): 640–67.

McAdam, Doug, and W. Richard Scott. 2005. Organizations and Movements, in *Social Movements and Organization Theory* edited by G.F. Davies, D. McAdam, W.R. Scott and M.N. Zald. Cambridge: Cambridge University Press, 4–40.

McCaffrey, Katherine T. 2002. *Military Power and Popular Protest: The U.S. Navy in Vieques, Puerto Rico*. New Brunswick: Rutgers University Press.

McCarthy, John D. 1997. The Globalization of Social Movement Theory, in *Transnational Social Movements and Global Politics: Solidarity Beyond the State*, edited by J. Smith, C. Chatfield and R. Pagnucco. Syracuse, NY: Syracuse University Press, 243–59.

McCarthy, John D., Jackie Smith, and Mayer Zald. 1996. Assessing Media, Electoral and Government Agendas, In *Comparative Perspectives on Social Movements: Political Opportunities, Mobilizing Structures, and Cultural Framings* edited by D. McAdam, J.D. McCarthy and M. Zald. New York: Cambridge University Press, 291–311.

McCarthy, John D., and Mayer N. Zald. 1973. *The Trends of Social Movement*. Morristown, NJ: General Learning.

—— 1977. Resource Mobilization and Social Movement: A Partial Theory. *American Journal of Sociology* 82(6): 1212–41.

McDowell, C. and G Morell. 2007. Development and Displacement: Institutionalizing responsibility. *Development* 50(4): 33–8.

McRae, Hamish. 2007. India's Democracy Will Make it a Winner. *The Independent*, 21 September.

Meadows, Donnela H. Dennis L. Meadows, Jorgen Randers, and William W. Behrens III. 1972. *The Limits to Growth: A Report for The Club of Rome*. New York: Universe Books.

Mehra, AK. 2000. Naxalism in India: Revolution or terror? *Terrorism and Political Violence* 12(2): 37–66.

Mehta, Ajay S. 1993. People's Participation. *Seminar* (406).

Melucci, Alberto. 1984. An End to Social Movements? Introductory Paper to Sessions on 'New' Movements and Change in Organizational Forms. *Social Science Information* 23: 819–35.

—— 1988. Getting Involved: Identity and Mobilization in Social Movements, in *International Social Movements Research: From Structure to Action – Comparing Social Movements Across Cultures, vol. 1*, edited by H. Kriesi, S. Tarrow and B. Klandermans. London: JAI Press, pp. 329–48.

—— 1989. *Nomads of the Present: Social Movements and Individual Needs in Contemporary Society*. Philadelphia, PA: Temple University Press.

Menon, Venu. 1988. Fishing for Trouble. *The Illustrated Weekly of India*, 4 September, 28–29.

Migdal, Joel S. 1994. The State in Society: An Approach to Struggles for Domination, in *State Power and Social Forces: Domination and Transformation in the Third World* edited by J.S. Migdal, A. Kohli and V. Shue. Cambridge: Cambridge University Press, 7–34.

Migdal, Joel S. 1988. *Strong Societies and Weak States: State–Society Relations and State Capabilities in the Third World*. Princeton: Princeton University Press.

Miller, K.R., W.V. Reid, and C.V. Barber. 1991. Deforestation and species loss: Responding to the crisis, in *Preserving the Global Environment: The Challenge of Shared Leadership* edited by Jessica Touchman Mathew. New York: W.W. Norton, pp. 78–111.

Mishra, Artabandhu. Displacement in Orissa: A Case. Unpublished Manuscript.

Mishra, Pankaj. 2007. Impasse in India. *The New York Review of Books* 54(11): 48–51.

Misra, Rabi N, ed. 2006. *Tribal Development: Post Globalization*. New Delhi: Discovery Publication.

Mitra, A., S.G. Warrier, and U. Shankar. 1993. The Cauvery Calamity. *Down to Earth* 2(7): 5–9.

Mitra, Subrat Kumar. 1991. Room to Manoeuvre in the Middle: Local Elites, Political Action, and the State in India. *World Politics* 43(3): 390–413.

Mohanty, Manoranjan. 1995. Anagrasaratar Rajniti (Politics of Underdevelopment). *Biklpa Bichar,* 3(3): 11–35.

Mueller, Carol M. 1994. Conflict Networks and the Origins Women's Liberation, in *New Social Movements: From Ideology to Identity*, edited by E. Larana, H.

Johnson and J.R. Gusfield. Philadephia, PA: Temple University Press, 234–63.

Mukherjee, K.K. 1994. Emerging Societal Changes and Voluntary Organisations: Challenges and Responses. *Gandhi Marg* 15(4): 389–414.

Multiple Action Research Group. 1990. *Sardar Sarovar oustees in Madhya Pradesh what do they know?* New Delhi: Multiple Action Research Group.

Naqvi, Syed. 2006. *Development and Growth in Northeast India: The Natural Resources, Water, and Environment Nexus.* Background Paper No. 9 – Brahmaputra–Barak River Basin Organization: Legal and Constitutional Issues.

Narayan, Deepa and Lant Pritchett. 1999. *Economic Development and Cultural Change* 47(4): 871–93.

Nath, G.B. and K.S. Agarwala. Politics of Agitation Against Rengali Dam Project: A Case Study. Unpublished Manuscript.

Nathan, Dev, and Govind Kelkar. 2001. Case for Local Forest Management: Environmental Services, Internalization of Costs and Markets. *Economic and Political Weekly* 36(30): 2835–45.

Neidhardt, F., and D. Rucht. 1991. The Analysis of Social Movements: The State of the Art and Some Perspectives for Further Research, in *Research on Social Movements* edited by D. Rucht. Frankfurt and Boulder: Campus and Westview Press, 421–64.

Nielsen, R. 2006. *The Little Green Handbook: Seven trends shaping the future of our planet.* New York: Picador.

OECD Economic Surveys. 2007. India, in *OECD Economic Surveys.* Paris: OECD Publishing.

Offe, Claus. 1985. New Social Movements: Challenging the Boundaries of Institutional Politics. *Social Research* 52(4): 817–68.

Olson, Mancur. 1965. *The Logic of Collective Action.* Cambridge, MA: Harvard University Press.

—— 1993. Dictatorship, Democracy, and Development. *American Political Science Review* 87(3): 567–76.

Omvedt, Gail. 1984. Ecology and Social Movement. *Economic and Political Weekly* 19(44): 1865–67.

—— 1989. India's Movements for Democracy: Peasants, 'Greens', Women and People's Power. *Race & Class* 31(2): 37–46.

—— 1994. Peasants, Dalits and Women: Democracy and India's New Social Movements. *Journal of Contemporary Asia* 24(1): 35–48.

Oommen, T.K. 1990. *Protest and Change: Studies in Social Movements.* New Delhi: Sage Publications.

Oommen, TK. 1991. Protest and change: studies in social movements. *China Report* 27(1): 86.

Orissa Krushak Mahasangh, and Indravati Gana Sangharsha Parishad. –. Collection of Documents in World Bank-funded Upper Indravati Project – Is it a Death Trap for the Poor? Undated.

Ostrom, Elinor. 1990. *Governing the Commons: The Evolution of Institutions for Collective Action*. New York: Cambridge University Press.

Outlookindia.com. 2008. Karna for new tribunal to adjudicate Krishna water sharing, 27 September

Owusu-Koranteng, D. 2008. Mining Investment and Community Struggles. *Review of African Political Economy* 35(3): 467–73.

Padgett, John F., and Christopher K. Ansell. 1993. Robust Action and the rise of the Medici, 1400–1434. *American Journal of Sociology* 98(6): 1259–1319.

Pandey, Shashi Ranjan. 1991. *Community Action for Social Justice: Grassroots Organisations in India*. New Delhi: Sage Publications.

Panigrahi, Debasis. 2009. Political Economy of Natural Resource Management: A Case Study of Chilka Lake, Department of Political Science, Utkal University, Bhubaneswar.

Paranjpye, Vijay. 1990. *High Dams on the Narmada: A Holistic Analysis of the River Valley Projects*. New Delhi: Indian National Trust for Art and Cultural Heritage.

Parekh, Bhikhu. 1991. Nehru and the National Philosophy of India. *Economic and Political Weekly* 26 (5–12 January): 35–47.

Pati, Biswamoy. 2001. Identity, Hegemony, Resistance: Conversions in Orissa 1800–2000. *Asia Research Centre Working Paper* 7. London.

Patnaik, Nageswar. 1997. Stonewalling Steel. *The Economic Times*, 28 March.

Pattanaik, Manoj. 2002. How Protected are the 'Protected Areas'? *Community Forest* 1(3 and 4): 4–9.

Pattanaik, Sarmistha. 2006. Commercialization of Shrimp Trade, Environment and Rural Poverty: A Socio-Ecological Exploration in Coastal Orissa. *IEG Working Paper Series No. E/274/2006*, Institute of Economic Growth, University of Dehli Enclave.

—— 2007. Conservation of Environment and Protection of Marginalized Fishing Communities of Lake Chilika in Orissa, India. *Journal of Human Ecology* 22(4): 291–302.

Paul, Samuel. 1989. Poverty Alleviation and Participation: The Case for Government – Grassroots Agency Collaboration *Economic and Political Weekly* 25(2): 100–106.

Paxton, Pamela. 1999. Is Social Capital Declining in the United States? A Multiple Indicator Assessment. *AJS* 105(1): 88–127.

Pearce, F. 1992. Tide of Opinion Turns Against Superdams. *Panscope* 33: 3.

Peet, Richard, and Michael Watts. 1996. Liberation Ecology: Development, Sustainability, and Environment in an Age of Market Triumphalism, in *Liberation Ecologies: Environment, Development, Social Movements*, edited by R. Peet and M. Watts. London: Routledge, pp. 1–45.

Pereira, Ignatius. 2003. Fresh proposal for Poyamkutty project. *The Hindu*, 7 December.

Peritore, N. Patrick. 1993. Environmental Attitudes of Indian Elites: Challenging Western Postmodernist Models. *Asian Survey* 33(8): 804–18.

Peterson, Abby. 2001. *Contemporary Political Protest: Essays on Political Protest.* Aldershot: Ashgate.

Pichardo, Nelson A. 1988. Resource Mobilization: An Analysis of Conflicting Theoretical Variations. *The Sociological Quarterly* 29(1): 97–110.

Piven, Frances Fox, and Richard A. Cloward. 1979. *Poor People's Movements: Why They Succeed, How They Fail.* New York: Vintage Books.

Prasad, M.K., M.P. Parameswaran, V.K. Damodaran, K.N. Syamsundaran Nair, and K.P. Kannan. 1979. *The Silent Valley Hydro-electric Project: A Techno-Economic and Social–Political Assessment.* Trivandrum: KSSP.

Press Release 1990. by the President of Ganatantrik Adhikar Suraksha Sangathan, Orissa in April 1990.

ProcessRegister – Manufacturers Database. 2009. *Industrial Projects.* ProcessRegister – Manufacturers Database 2009 [cited 9 June 2009]. Available from http: //www.processregister.com/projects/projects.asp.

Publication Division – Ministry of Information and Broadcasting – Government of India. 1996. India 1995: A Reference Annual. New Delhi.

Pugh, David. 2008. India's Combative Anti-Displacement Movement. *Monthly Review*, 16 October.

Purfield, Catriona. 2006. Mind the Gap – Is Economic Growth in India Leaving Some States Behind? In *IMF Working Paper No. WP/04/77.* Washington DC: IMF, Asia and Pacific Department.

Putnam, Robert D. 1993. *Making Democracy Work: Civic Traditions in Modern Italy.* Princeton, NJ: Princeton University Press.

—— 2000. *Bowling Alone: The Collapse and Revival of American Community.* New York: Simon & Schuster.

Radhakrishna, R, ed. 2008. *India Development Report 2008.* New Delhi: Indira Gandhi Institute of Development Research.

Ramachandran, Smriti Kak. 2007. Delhi has its way in water dispute. *The Hindu*, 5 September.

Ramachandran, V.K. 1997. On Kerala's Development Achievements, in *Indian Development: Selected Regional Perspectives*, edited by J. Dreze and A. Sen. New Delhi: Oxford University Press for the UNU/WIDER, pp. 205–356.

Ramana, M.V.V. 1992. *Inter-State River Disputes in India.* Hyderabad: Orient Longman.

Reddy, P.S. 1995. *Displaced Populations and Socio-cultural Change*: Commonwealth Publishers.

Refugees: Dynamics of Development, A Report for the Independent Commission on International Humanitarian Issues. 1986. London: Zed Books.

Rehiman, M.P. Mujeebu. 2003. INFARM: A Study of Emerging Farmers' Movement in Kerala Center for Development Studies Prasanthinagar, Ulloor Thiruvananthapuram

Right Livelihood Award. 2009. *Kerala Sastra Sahitya Parishad (KSSP) (India) (1996)* 1996 [cited 7 May 2009]. Available from http: //www.rightlivelihood.org/kerala.html.

Rochon, Thomas R. 1990. The West European Peace Movement and the Theory of New Social Movements, in *Challenging the Political Order: New Social and Political Movements in Western Democracies*, edited by R.J.D.M. Kuechler. Cambridge: Polity Press, pp. 105–21.

Rodger, J. 2000. *From a Welfare State to a Welfare Society*. Houndmills: Macmillan.

Rodrik, D., and A. Subramanian. 2004. From 'Hindu Growth' to Productive Surge: The Mystery of the Indian Growth Transition. *IMF Working Paper No. WP/04/77*.

Roper, J., and R.W. Roberts. 1999. Deforestation: tropical forest in decline. CIDA Forestry Advisers Network.

Rose, Richard. 1996. Social Capital: Definition, Measure, Implications. In *World Bank Workshop on Social Capital*. Washington DC.

Roy, B.K. 1991. Water Availability in India: An Analysis of Current Setting and Future Needs. *Water Resources Development* 7(2): 107–16.

Roy, Kartik C., and Clement A. Tisdell. 1992. Gandhi's Concept of Development and Nehru's Centralized Planning, in *Economic Development and Environment: A Case Study of India*, edited by K.C. Roy, C.A. Tisdell and R. Sen. Calcutta: Oxford University Press, pp. 1–16.

Rudolph, Lloyd I., and Susanne H. Rudolph. 1987. *In Pursuit of Lakshmi: The Political Economy of Indian State*. Chicago: University of Chicago Press.

Rudolph, Susanne. 2000. Civil Society and the Realm of Freedom. *Economic and Political Weekly*: 34(22): 1762–1769.

Rudolph, Susanne Hoeber, and Lloyd I. Rudolf. 2002. South Asia Faces the Future: New Dimensions of Indian Democracy. *Journal of Democracy* 13(1): 52–66.

Sachs, J.D, Nirupam Bajpai, and Ananthi Ramiah. 2002. Understanding regional economic growth in India. *CID Working Paper* (88).

Santhakumar, V., and Achin Chakraborty. 2003. Environmental costs and their impact on the net present value of a hydro-electric project in Kerala, India. *Environment and Development Economics* 8(02): 311–30.

Santhakumar, V., R. Rajagopalan, and S. Ambirajan. 1995. Planning Kerala's Irrigation Projects: Technological Prejudice and Politics of Hope, *Economic and Political Weekly* 30(12): A-30.

Santhakumar, V., and P. Sivanandan. 1998. *Social Impact of the Pooyamkutty Hydro-Electric Project, Kerala*. Thiruvannanthapuram: CDS.

Sardana, Sangeeta, Veena Sangwan, and Indu Grover. 1987. Population Explosion: A Mismatch of Resources. *Yojana* 31(3): 22.

Satish, D.P. 2009. *New Life Church under fire from Hindus and Catholics*, 8 September 2008 [cited 29 June 2009]. Available from http: //ibnlive.in.com/news/new-life-church-under-fire-from-hindus-and-catholics/73816-3.html.

Schock, Kurt. 1999. People Power and Political Opportunities: Social Movement Mobilization and Outcomes in the Philippines and Burma. *Social Problems* 46(3): 355–75.

Sen, Abhijit. 2001. Estimates of Consumer Expenditure and its Distribution: Statistical Priorities after the NSS 55th Round. *Economic and Political Weekly* 35: 4499–4518.

Sen, Amartya. 2000. Warm up to Globalisation: Amartya Sen to Kerala. *The Economic Times* 29 December.

Sen, Amartya. 1997. Radical Needs and Moderate Reforms, in *Indian Development: Selected Regional Perspectives*, edited by J. Dreze and A. Sen. New Delhi: Oxford University Press for the UNU/WIDER, 1–32.

Sen, S.R. 1962. *The Strategy for Agricultural Development and Other Essays on Economic Policy and Planning.* New York: Asia Publishing House.

Sethi, Harsh. 1993. Survival and Democracy: Ecological Struggles in India. In *New Social Movements in the South: Empowering the People*, edited by P. Wignaraja. London: Zed Books, pp. 122–48.

—— 2001. Movements and Mediators. *Economic and Political Weekly*, 27 January.

Shah, Ghanashyam. 1990. *New Social Movements in India: A Review of Literature.* New Delhi: Sage Publications.

Shah, R.B. 1993. Role of Major Dams in the India Economy. *Water Resources Development* 9(2): 319–36.

Sharma, L.T. and R. Sharma, eds. 1981. *Major Dams: A Second Look.* New Delhi: Gandhi Peace Foundation.

Sharma, Ravi. 2005. A dispute in the Krishna basin. *Frontline* 22(9): 31–6.

Sharma, S.L. 1992. Social Action Groups as Harbingers of Silent Revolution. *Economic and Political Weekly* 27(47): 2557–61.

Shefner, Jon. 1995. "Moving in the Wrong Direction in Social Movement Theory". *Theory and Society* 24(4): 595–612.

Shiva, Vandana. 1991. *Ecology and the Politics of Survival: Conflict over Natural Resources in India.* New Delhi: Sage Publications.

—— 1994. Conflicts of Global Ecology: Environmental Activism in a Period of Global Reach. *Alternatives* 19(2): 195–207.

Shiva, Vandana, and Jayant Bandyopadhyay. 1986. Environmental Conflicts and Public Interest Science. *Economic and Political Weekly* 21(2): 84–90.

Sikkink, Kathryn. 1993. Human Rights, Principled Issue-Networks, and Sovereignty in Latin America. *International Organization* 47(3): 411–41.

Simutanyi, N, and Institute for Security Studies. 2008. Copper Mining in Zambia: The Developmental Legacy of Privatisation. Cape Town: Institute for Security Studies Papers.

Singh, Damandeep. 1994. Farmers Learn to Make Political Waves. *Panscope* (40): 13.

Singh, Jagtar. 1997. Common Border, Shared Problems. *The Indian Express*, 27 March.

Singh, K.P. 1993. Supply and Demand of Water Resources – A Case Study of Punjab State, India, in *International Conference on Environmentally Sound Water Resources Utilization.* Bangkok, Thailand.

Singh, Prakash. 1995. *The Naxalite Movement in India*: Delhi: Rupa and Co.

Singh, Prakash. 2007. *The Naxalite Movement in India (2nd Edn)*. New Delhi: Rupa and Co.

Singh, Rajendra. 2001. *Social Movements, Old and New: A Post-modernist Critique*. New Delhi: Sage Publications.

Singh, Satyajit Kumar. 1985. From the Dam to the Ghettos: The Victims of the Rihand Dam. *Economic and Political Weekly* 20(39): 1643–44.

Sinha, Assema. 2007. India's Unlikely Democracy: Economic Growth and Political Accommodation. *Journal of Democracy* 18(2): 41–54.

Slater, David, ed. 1985. *New Social Movements and the State in Latin America*. Amsterdam: CEDLA.

Smith, Jackie, Ron Pagnucco, and Charles Chatfield. 1997. Social Movements and World Politics: A Theoretical Framework, in *Transnational Social Movements and Global Politics: Solidarity Beyond the State* edited by Ron Pagnucco, Charles Chatfield and Jackie Smith. Syracuse, NY: Syracuse University Press, pp. 243–75.

Smith, J. 2005. 'Building Bridges or Building Walls? Explaining Regionalization among Transnational Social Movement Organizations', *Mobilization* 10(2): 251–69.

Snow, David A., and Cynthia L. Philips. 1980. The Lofland–Stark Conversion Model: A Critical Reassessment. *Social Problems* 27(4): 430–47.

Snow, David A., Louis A. Zurcher, and Sheldon Ekland-Olson. 1980. Social Networks and Social Movements: A Microstructural Approach to Differential Recruitment. *American Sociological Review* 45(5): 787–801.

Somerville, Jennifer. 1997. Social Movement Theory, Women and the Question of Interest. *Sociology* 31(4): 673–95.

Srinivasan, T.N. 2005. Comments on "From 'Hindu Growth' to Productive Surge: The Mystery of the Indian Growth Transition. *IMF Staff Paper* 52(2).

Stanley, William. 1996. Machkund, Upper Kolab and NALCO Projects in Koraput District, Orissa. *Economic and Political Weekly* 31(24): 1533–38.

Steel Plant at Gopalpur: Why People Oppose It? 1996. *Voice Gopalpur* 1(1).

Subramanian, Arvind. 2007. The Evolution of Institutions in India and its Relationship with Economic Growth. *Oxford Review of Economic Policy* 23(2): 196–220.

Sudworth, John. 2006. Cola companies in Kerala battle. *BBC News*.

Sun Times. 1992. Rehabilitation of Indravati DPs: Myths and Realities, 31 March.

Sundar, Aparna. 1999. Sea Changes: Organizing around the Fishery in a South Indian Community, in *Street-Level Democracy: Political Settings at the Margins of Global Power*, edited by J. Barker et al. Toronto: Between the Lines, pp. 79–114.

Sunstein, Cass R. 2003. *Why Societies Need Dissent*. Cambridge, MA: Harvard University Press.

Swain, Ashok. 1996a. Displacing the Conflict: Environmental Destruction in Bangladesh and Ethnic Conflict in India. *Journal of Peace Research* 33(2): 189–204.

—— 1996b. Environmental Migration and Conflict Dynamics: Focus on Developing Regions. *Third World Quarterly* 17(5): 959–73.

—— 1996c. Water Scarcity: A Threat to Global Security. *Environment & Security* 1(1): 156–72.

—— 1997. Democratic Consolidation: Environmental Movements in India. *Asian Survey* 37(9): 818–32.

—— 1998. Fight for the Last Drop: Inter-state River Disputes in India. *Contemporary South Asia* 7(2): 167–80.

—— 2000a. Social Capital and Popular Mobilisation: Studying Environmental Protests in an Indian State. *Asian Journal of Political Science* 8(1): 33–46.

—— 2000b. Water Scarcity as a Source of Crisis, in *War and Displacement: The Origins of Humanitarian Emergencies*, edited by E.W. Nafziger, F. Stewart and R. Väyrynen. Oxford: Oxford University Press, pp. 179–205.

—— 2002. Social Network and Social Movement: Are Northern Tools Useful to Evaluate Southern Protests? *Uppsala Peace Research Paper, Department of Peace and Conflict Research, Uppsala University* 4.

—— 2004. Social Capita and Protest Movement: The Case of Kerala, in *Interrogating Social Capital: The Indian Experience*, edited by D. Bhattacharya, N.G. Jayal, B.N. Mohapatra and S. Pai. New Delhi: Sage Publications, pp. 296–322.

—— 2009. The Indus II and Siachen Peace Park: Pushing India–Pakistan Peace Process Forward. *The Round Table* 98(404): 569–82.

Swamy, P.M., and S. Rai. 1993. Jaya's Subtle Game: The Lady Exploits Tamil Insecurity. *India Today*, 15 August.

Tarrow, S. 1996. Social movements in contentious politics: A review article. *American Political Science Review* 90(4): 874–83.

Tarrow, Sidney. 1989. Struggle, Politics, and Reform: Collective Action, Social Movements, and Cycles of Protest. *Western Societies Program, Occasional Paper* 21.

—— 1993. Modular Collective Action and the Rise of the Social Movement: Why the French Revolution was not Enough. *Politics and Society* 21(1): 69–90.

—— 1998. *Power in Movement: Social Movements and Contentious Politics, 2nd Edn.* Cambridge: Cambridge University Press.

Tata Services. 1995. Statistical Outline of India 1995–96. Bombay: Tata Services.

Teitelbaum, M.S. 1992–93. The population threat. *Foreign Affairs* 71(5): 63–78.

Thakkar, Himanshu. 1996. Water of Contention. *Down to Earth* 5(3): 15.

Tharoor, Shashi. 2007. Indian Democracy at 60. *Khaleej Times*, 15 August.

The Economic Times. 2008. Christians: The Sangh Parivar's new target, 20 September.

—— 2009. Co-ordinated operations to flush out Naxalites soon. *The Economic Times*, 6 February.

The Economist. 2006. A spectre haunting India, 17 August.

The World Bank. 1998. Recent Experiences with Involuntary Settlement. Washington, DC: The World Bank, Operation Evaluations Department.

Thomas, Stephen R. 1996. What Are Social Movements Today? *International Journal of Politics, Culture and Society* 9(4): 579–85.

Thukral, Enakshi Ganguly, ed. 1992. *Big Dams, Displaced People: Rivers of Sorrow, Rivers of Change*. New Delhi: Sage Publications.

Tilly, Charles. 1978. *From Mobilization to Revolution*. Reading, MA: Addison-Wesley.

—— 1999. From Interactions to Outcomes in Social Movements, in *How Social Movements Matter*, edited by M. Giugni, D. McAdam and C. Tilly. Minneapolis: University of Minnesota Press, pp. 253–70.

Tir, J, and PF Diehl. 1998. Demographic Pressure and Interstate Conflict: Linking Population Growth and Density to Militarized Disputes and Wars, 1930–89. *Journal of Peace Research* 35(3): 319–39.

Todd, Malcolm J., and Gary Taylor. 2004. *Democracy and Participation: Popular Protest and New Social Movements* London: Merlin Press.

Tornquist, Olle, and P.K. Michael Tharakan. 1996. Democratization and Attempts to Renew the Radical Political Development Project: Case of Kerala. *Economic and Political Weekly* 31(28): 1851.

Touraine, Alain. 1971. *The Post-Industrial Society – Tomorrow's Social History: Classes, Conflicts and Culture in the Programmed Society*. New York: Random House.

Trexler, M.C. 1991. *Minding the Carbon Store: Weighing U.S. Forestry Strategies to Slow Global Warming*. Washington, DC World Resources Institute.

Tripathy, Prasanna K., and Sukadev Nanda. 1987. The Hirakud Rehabilitation and the Displaced People, in *Seminar on Development and Displacement*. Burla, Sambalpur: Institute for Study of Society and Culture.

U.S. Committee for Refugees. *Sudan: Nearly 2 million dead as a result of the world's longest running civil war* 2001. Available from http: //web.archive. org/web/20041210024759/http: //www.refugees.org/news/crisis/sudan.htm.

UNDP. 2009. United Nations Development Programme in India, 2009 [cited 2 June 2009]. Available from http: //www.undp.org.in/index.php?option=com_c ontent&view=article&id=351&Itemid=523.

Wagner, A., and F. Schneider. 2006. Satisfaction with Democracy and Environment in Western Europe – A Panel Analysis. *CESIFO Working Paper* 1660.

Vajpayee, Atal Behari. 2001. Call of the New Year: Clear Vision, Concerted Action. *The Hindu*, 3 January.

Wapner, Paul. 2001. Horizontal Politics: Transnational Environmental Activism and Global Cultural Change, in *International Studies Association Annual Meeting*. Chicago.

Varshney, Ashutosh. 2007. India's Democratic Challenge. *Foreign Affairs* 86(2): 93–106.

Vasquez, John. 1976. A Learning Theory of the American Anti-Vietnam War Movement. *Journal of Peace Research* 13(4): 299–314.

Weed, Frank J. 1989. The Impact of Support Resources on Local Chapter Operations in the AntiDrunk –Driving Movement. *The Sociological Quarterly* 30(1): 77–91.

Weiner, Myron. 1989. *The Indian Paradox*. New Delhi: Sage Publication.

Weitzer, Roland. 1991. Prostitutes' Rights in the United States: The Failure of a Movement. *The Sociological Quarterly* 32(1): 23–41.

Veltrop, J.A. 1993. Importance of Dams for Water Supply and Hydropower, in *Water for Sustainable Development in the Twenty-first Century*, edited by A.K. Biswas, et al. New Delhi: Oxford University Press, pp. 104–115.

Wignaraja, P. 1993. Rethinking development and democracy, in *New Social Movements in the South: Empowering the People*, edited by P. Wignaraja. London: Zed Books, pp. 4–35.

Wild Orissa. 2000. *Untamed Orissa: A Journey into the Wilds of Orissa*. Bhubaneswar: Wild Orissa.

Wiltfang, Gregory L., and Doug McAdam. 1991. The Costs and Risks of Social Activism: A Study of Sanctuary Movement Activism. *Social Forces* 69: 987–1010.

Wood, C.H. 1982. Equilibrium and historical–structural perspectives on migration. *International Migration Review* 16(2): 298–319.

Wood, John R. 1993. India's Narmada River Dams: Sardar Sarovar Under Siege. *Asian Survey* 33(10): 968–84.

World Bank. 1998. *Recent Experiences with Involuntary Settlement*. Washington, DC: The World Bank, Operation Evaluations Department.

—— 2006. *World Development Indicators* Washington DC: The World Bank.

World Bank of India. 2009. *Orissa 2009* [cited 2 June 2009]. Available from http: //go.worldbank.org/U3YA770CC0.

World Bank Sponsored Study in December 1989, Subarnarekha (Orissa) Irrigation Project, Resettlement and Rehabilitation.

World Commission on Dams. 2000. *Dams and Development: A New Framework for Decision-Making*. London: Earthscan.

World Commission on Environment Development. 1987. *Our Common Future*: Oxford University Press Oxford.

WWF India. 2008. *A Directory of Environmental NGOs in India 2008–9th Edition*. New Delhi.

—— 2009. *Forests* 2009 [cited 9 April 2009]. Available from http: //www. wwfindia.org/about_wwf/what_we_do/forests/.

Vyasulu, Vinod, and A.V. Arun Kumar. 1997. Industrialization in Orissa: Trends and Structure. *Economic and Political Weekly* 32(22): M46–M53.

Zachariah, K.C. 1997. Demographic Transition: A Response to Official Policies and Programmes, in *Kerala's Demographic Transition: Determinants and Consequences*, edited by K.C. Zachariah and S.I. Rajan. New Delhi: Sage Publications, 79–111.

Zachariah, Mathew, and R. Sooryamoorthy. 1994. *Science for Social Revolution? Achievements and Dilemmas of a Development Movement, The Kerala Sastra Sahitya Parishad.* New Delhi: Vistaar Publications.

Zald, Mayer, and John McCarthy, eds. 1987. *Social Movements in an Organizational Society.* New Brunswick, NJ: Transaction Publishers.

Zich, A. 1997. Before the Flood: China's Three Gorges. *National Geographic* 192(3): 2–33.

Zimmermann, E. 1980. Macro-comparative research on political protest, in *Handbook of Political Conflict: Theory and Research,* edited by T.R. Gurr. New York: Free Press, 167–237.

Zirakzadeh, Cyrus Ernesto. 1997. *Social Movements in Politics: A Comparative Study.* London: Longman.

Zuo, Jiping, and Robert D. Benford. 1995. Mobilization Processes and the 1989 Chinese Democracy Movement. *The Sociological Quarterly* 36(1): 131–56.

Index

www.ingramcontent.com/pod-product-compliance
Ingram Content Group UK Ltd.
Pitfield, Milton Keynes, MK11 3LW, UK
UKHW020351010325
455677UK00021B/391